## DATE DUE

# Healing
# Addictions

# Healing Addictions

## The Vulnerability Model of Recovery

BONNEY GULINO SCHAUB, MS, RN, CS
RICHARD SCHAUB, PhD

Delmar Publishers

*an International Thomson Publishing company* I(T)P®

Albany • Bonn • Boston • Cincinnati • Detroit • London • Madrid
Melbourne • Mexico City • New York • Pacific Grove • Paris • San Francisco
Singapore • Tokyo • Toronto • Washington

# NOTICE TO THE READER

Cover Design: Spiral Design
Cover Illustration: Kirsten Soderlind

**Delmar Staff**
Publisher: William Brottmiller
Assistant Editor: Hilary A. Everson-Schrauf
Senior Project Editor: Judith Boyd Nelson
Production Coordinator: Barbara A. Bullock
Art and Design Coordinator: Timothy J. Conners


COPYRIGHT © 1997
By Delmar Publishers
a division of International Thomson Publishing Inc.

The ITP logo is a trademark under license.

Printed in the United States of America

For more information, contact:

Delmar Publishers
3 Columbia Circle, Box 15015
Albany, New York 12212-5015

International Thomson Publishing Europe
Berkshire House 168-173
High Holborn
London, WC1V 7AA
England

Thomas Nelson Australia
102 Dodds Street
South Melbourne, 3205
Victoria, Australia

Nelson Canada
1120 Birchmont Road
Scarborough, Ontario
Canada, M1K 5G4

International Thomson Editores
Campos Eliseos 385, Piso 7
Col Polanco
11560 Mexico D F Mexico

International Thomson Publishing GmbH
Konigswinterer Strasse 418
53227 Bonn
Germany

International Thomson Publishing Asia
221 Henderson Road
#05-10 Henderson Building
Singapore 0315

International Thomson Publishing—Japan
Hirakawacho Kyowa Building, 3F
2-2-1 Hirakawacho
Chiyoda-ku, Tokyo 102
Japan

2   3   4   5   6   7   8   9   10   XXX   03   02   01   00   99   98   97

**Library of Congress Cataloging-in-Publication Data**

Schaub, Bonney Gulino.
    Healing addictions: the vulnerability model of recovery / Bonney Gulino Schaub, Richard Schaub.
        p.   cm. — (Nurse as healer series)
    Includes bibliographical references and index.
    ISBN 0-8273-7091-1
    1. Substance abuse—Nursing.   2. Psychosynthesis.   3. Recovering addicts.   I. Schaub, Richard, Ph.D.   II. Title.   III. Series.
    [DNLM:   1. Behavior, Addictive—nursing.   2. Nursing Care—methods.
    WY 150 S313h 1997]
RC564.S29   1997
616.86 —  dc21
DNLM/DLC
for Library of Congress                                                96-37002
                                                                              CIP

# INTRODUCTION TO NURSE AS HEALER SERIES

**LYNN KEEGAN, PhD, RN, Series Editor**

*Associate Professor, School of Nursing,*
*University of Texas Health Science Center at San Antonio*
*San Antonio, Texas*
*and Director of BodyMind Systems, Temple, Texas*

To nurse means to care for or to nurture with compassion. Most nurses begin their formal education with this ideal. Many nurses retain this orientation after graduation, and some manage their entire careers under this guiding principle of caring. Many of us, however, tend to forget this ideal in the hectic pace of our professional and personal lives. We may become discouraged and feel a sense of burnout.

Throughout the past decade I have spoken at many conferences with thousands of nurses. Their experience of frustration and failure is quite common. These nurses feel themselves spread as pawns across a health care system too large to control or understand. In part, this may be because they have forgotten their true roles as nurse-healers.

When individuals redirect their personal vision and empower themselves, an entire pattern may begin to change. And so it is now with the nursing profession. Most of us conceptualize nursing as much more than a vocation. We are greater than our individual roles as scientists, specialists, or care deliverers. We currently search for a name to put on our new conception of the empowered nurse. The recently introduced term *nurse-healer* aptly describes the qualities of an increasing number of clinicians, educators, administrators, and nurse practitioners. Today all nurses are awakening to the realization that they have the potential for healing.

It is my feeling that most nurses, when awakened and guided to develop their own healing potential, will function both as nurses and healers. Thus, the concept of nurse as healer is born. When nurses realize they have the ability to evoke others' healing, as well as care for them, a shift of consciousness begins to occur. As individual awareness and changes in skill building occur, a collective understanding of this new concept emerges. This knowledge, along with a shift in attitudes and new kinds of behavior, allows empowered nurses to renew themselves in an expanded role. The Nurse As Healer Series is born out of the belief that nurses are ready to embrace guidance that inspires them in their journeys of empowerment. Each book in the series may stand alone or be used in complementary fashion with other books. I hope and believe that information herein will strengthen you both personally and professionally, and provide you with the help and confidence to embark upon the path of nurse-healer.

*Titles in the Nurse As Healer Series:*

**The Nurse as Healer**

**Healing Touch: A Resource for Health Care Professionals**

**Healing Life's Crises: A Guide for Nurses**

**The Nurse's Meditative Journal**

**Healing Nutrition**

**Healing the Dying**

**Awareness in Healing**

**Creative Imagery in Nursing**

**Healing and the Grief Process**

**Healing Meditation**

**Healing Addictions: The Vulnerability Model of Recovery**

**Feminism in Nursing**

## *DEDICATION*

*To Kurt Andrew and Aisha Krista*

# C O N T E N T S

Exercises, xii
Preface, xiii
Acknowledgments, xvi
Introduction, xvii

**Part 1**  **THE NATURE OF ADDICTION AND RECOVERY, 1**

    *Chapter 1*    **The Cycle of Addiction, 3**
        The Early Stage of Addiction, 5
        The Turn toward Addiction, 7
        The Middle Stage of Addiction, 8
        The Late Stage of Addiction, 11
        Assessing Addiction, 12
        Summary, 13
        The Nurse-Healer Reflections, 13
        Reflections, 15
        References, 15
        Suggested Reading, 15

    *Chapter 2*    **Models of Addiction, 17**
        Addiction Theories, 20
        Summary, 26
        Reflections, 27
        References, 27
        Suggested Reading, 27

**Chapter 3**    ***Denial, 29***

Experiencing Denial, 30

Definitions of Denial, 31

The Power of Denial, 34

Recovery Is One Day at a Time, 40

Summary, 41

Reflections, 41

References, 41

Suggested Reading, 41

**Chapter 4**    ***The Cycle of Recovery, 43***

Hitting Bottom, 46

The Early Stage of Recovery —Detoxification and Abstinence, 47

Questioning and Planning, 49

Relapse, 54

Entering Middle Recovery, 56

Summary, 57

Reflections, 57

References, 57

Suggested Reading, 57

**Chapter 5**    ***The Vulnerability Model of Recovery, 59***

Vulnerability —The Key to Addiction and Recovery, 60

The Healing Potential of Vulnerability, 62

Vulnerability and Choice, 64

Summary, 69

Reflections, 70

References, 70

Suggested Reading, 70

**Part 2**    **THE CHOICES, 71**

**Chapter 6**    ***Willfulness, Will-lessness, and Willingness, 73***

"The Inner Tyrant," 73

The Need for a Second Recovery, 75

The Spectrum of Choices, 76

*The Universality of Willfulness and*
*Will-lessness, 79*
*Summary, 81*
*Reflections, 81*
*References, 81*
*Suggested Reading, 81*

**Chapter 7**   **Willfulness, 83**
*Mental Willfulness, 83*
*Emotional Willfulness, 86*
*Physical Willfulness, 88*
*Spiritual Willfulness, 91*
*Summary, 96*
*Reflections, 96*
*References, 96*
*Suggested Reading, 96*

**Chapter 8**   **Will-lessness, 97**
*Mental Will-lessness, 97*
*Emotional Will-lessness, 104*
*Physical Will-lessness, 106*
*Spiritual Will-lessness, 108*
*Obstacles to Spiritual Development, 112*
*Summary, 113*
*Reflections, 114*
*References, 114*
*Suggested Reading, 114*

**Chapter 9**   **Willingness, 115**
*Willingness as a Choice, 116*
*The Spectrum of Willingness, 118*
*The Three Actions of Willingness, 119*
*The Three Skills of Self-Care in Recovery, 123*
*Emotional Education, 131*
*Summary, 137*
*Reflections, 137*
*References, 137*
*Suggested Reading, 138*

**Part 3    INCREASING PEACE, 139**

**Chapter 10    The Spiritual Aspect of Recovery, 141**
Spirituality and Nursing Practice, 141
The Practicality of Spiritual Development, 143
The Spiritual Aspect of Human Nature, 144
The Higher Self, 147
Alcoholics Anonymous and Spirituality, 149
The Nurse and Spiritual Practices, 151
Health Practices and Spiritual Practices, 157
Spiritual Assessment, 158
Spirituality and Suffering, 158
The Good Ego, 164
Beyond the Ego, 166
Summary, 167
Reflections, 167
References, 168
Suggested Reading, 169

**Chapter 11    A Model of Consciousness, 171**
Assagioli's Model of Consciousness, 172
The Lower Unconscious, 175
The Middle Unconscious, 179
The Higher Unconscious, 180
The Field of Consciousness, 183
The Personal Self or "I," 184
The Transpersonal Self, 186
The Collective Unconscious, 191
Implications of Assagioli's Model of Consciousness, 192
Summary, 193
Reflections, 193
References, 193
Suggested Reading, 194

**Chapter 12   The Paths of Spiritual Development, 195**
Personalizing Spirituality, 195
The Paths, 197
Summary, 233
Reflections, 233
References, 233
Suggested Reading, 234

**Chapter 13   Obstacles to Spiritual Development, 235**
The Importance of Studying Obstacles on the
Spiritual Path, 236
Obstacles to Spiritual Development and the
Stages of Acceptance, 237
The First Assessment Tool: Obstacles to
Spiritual Development, 239
The Second Assessment Tool: The Stages of
Acceptance, 248
Summary, 263
Reflections, 264
References, 264
Suggested Reading, 265

**Appendix 1  Nursing Process: Assessment, 269**
**Appendix 2  Nursing Diagnoses Applicable to
Addictions, 271**
**Appendix 3  CAGEAID Questionnaire, 273**
**Appendix 4  The Vulnerability Model of Recovery, 275**
**Appendix 5  The Twelve Steps of Alcoholics
Anonymous, 277**

**Glossary, 279**
**Bibliography, 287**
**Index, 295**

# E X E R C I S E S

Chapter 1    Reflection on Middle Stage Addiction, 9

Chapter 2    Reflection on Addiction, 19

Chapter 5    The Lie Technique, 66

Chapter 6    Willfulness and Will-lessness, 79

Chapter 9    Willingness, 121
             Centering for Stress Reduction, 125
             Imagery for Stress Reduction, 125
             Centering for Sleep Difficulties, 126
             Progressive Muscle Relaxation, 127

Chapter 11   Images of Childhood Survey, 175
             The Party, 179
             The Higher Self, 181
             Mindfulness, 183
             Self-Identification, 185
             The Rose, 188
             Imagery from the Collective Unconscious, 191

Chapter 12   Reflection on Art, 200
             Reflection on Natural Object, 201
             Connecting with Life Energy, 206

# PREFACE

The addictions field is scattered among different models of addiction, different treatments, and different models of recovery. Some theories say addiction is just the surface problem of deeper emotional problems. Others argue addiction is completely biological. Still others argue family dysfunction or societal conditioning causes addiction.

Some treatments emphasize counseling and ignore the spirituality of the Twelve Steps of Alcoholics Anonymous. Others feel Alcoholics Anonymous is an absolutely necessary step for true recovery and are hostile to psychotherapy. Others argue for nutritional treatment or biochemical supplements and dismiss anything nonbiological as irrelevant. Others argue that researchers should find the right pharmaceutical treatment to cure addiction. (Heroin, incidentally, was recommended by the American Medical Association in 1906 as an effective way to avoid morphine addiction.)*

Some argue each addictive drug has its own peculiar characteristics and populations of users. Others argue that all addictions, including addictive behaviors such as compulsive gambling, compulsive sexual behaviors, compulsive eating, compulsive television viewing, compulsive shopping, and workaholism, are essentially one big category of the same disorder.

Some propose that there is definitely a distinctive addictive personality, while others say there is no such thing.

---

*McCoy, A. (1991). *The politics of heroin*. Brooklyn, NY: Lawrence Hill Books.

## A Unifying Model

In *Healing Addictions*, we offer a practical, unifying model of addiction and recovery. Since 1964, we have worked in every phase of healing addictions: detoxification units, inpatient rehabilitation centers, halfway houses, outpatient counseling, and ongoing psychotherapy with clients in long-term recovery. At present, 75 percent of our private practice clients are people in recovery who want to continue to grow both emotionally and spiritually.

Writing from this experience, we can see the essential features of healing addictions. We appreciate the various approaches and theories to alcohol and drug treatment, and we can see the central theme common to all of them. We have developed a synthesis model—The Vulnerability Model—which retains the essentials of all the other approaches. In one word, *vulnerability* is the key issue in recovery. As you will see in the book, the Vulnerability Model is sensitive to biological, emotional, social, and spiritual issues in the process of addiction and recovery. The vulnerability exists at all these levels. This bio-psycho-social-spiritual perspective is in complete congruence with nursing's holistic vision of the person.

In addition to nursing's vision, we are also grateful to another visionary: Roberto Assagioli and his conceptualization of psychosynthesis. We see his contribution as truly a unique and wise framework for understanding the interactions and dynamics of the human struggle. Attitudinally, this model permeates our clinical work and our education of professionals. This way of looking at the whole person reflects deep appreciation for the richness and potential of human consciousness as a source of wisdom and healing.

As educators and consultants, we teach both the personal and clinical value of this framework in our Higher Self Education and Clinical Imagery Training Program at the New York Psychosynthesis Institute.

We test our model out daily in our clinical work and in our international teaching and supervision of other professionals. We offer it to you to do the same.

*Healing Addictions* is a practical book. It places addiction within human emotion and common human experience. It shows you where the answers are. The answers to addiction are already available to us in the living examples of the people who have recovered from addiction.

Too often in treatment settings professionals become discouraged or cynical about the course of addiction. They see the same people return over and over again. What they do not see are those who have recovered and never return to the treatment facility, those who continue on their own attending Twelve-Step meetings and/or seeking out private therapy. We have worked with people who were hopelessly addicted to alcohol, heroin, cocaine, or other drugs, and who are now functioning well in the world. These people are our teachers. Whatever they have done that works, tells us what works. Whatever process they have gone through, tells us what process is necessary. Whatever learning they have done, tells us what learning we must do.

Beyond all theories, *Healing Addictions* bases its authority on thirty years of listening closely to people in recovery.

In Part 1, The Nature of Addiction and Recovery, we take you through the early aspects of recovery. In Part 2, The Choices, we offer a unified theory and treatment model that deepens recovery through emotional education and development. In Part 3, Increasing Peace, we provide you with specific maps and methods of spiritual development that help people in recovery restore themselves to a right relationship to their life.

In all of this information, remember this reality: In addiction work you can help someone completely change to a life of health and conscious development, to a life of sanity.

# ACKNOWLEDGMENTS

We gratefully acknowledge all of the help we have received in writing this book. Lynn Keegan, the series editor, gave us the first encouragement and allowed us to work in a creative environment. Our editor at Delmar, Hilary Schrauf, has guided us with clarity, good feelings, and patience all the way through the process. Our readers, Nellie Nelson and Agnelo Dias, took time out of their busy schedules to read the full manuscript and respond with encouragement and direction. Our colleague and friend, Deborah Wolf, has been kind enough to read every version of our early manuscripts and to respond with skilled advice.

We cannot of course name our clients, but we acknowledge the extraordinary privilege of being allowed to work with them. We hope we have done well in describing the truths they can offer others in recovery. We hope we have helped to pass it on.

# I N T R O D U C T I O N

When you work with someone in recovery, theories disappear. There is the person, right in front of you. No theory can capture the highly complex biological, psychological, social, and spiritual realities of this person's humanity and of your own. Instead of theory, we need an essential truth to begin with, to organize around, to stay close to, so that we can be truly helpful.

Through the years of listening to hundreds of people in recovery, we heard a truth emerging again and again: vulnerability. Above every other experience, it was vulnerability that led to addiction, and it was vulnerability that reappeared in recovery. It was vulnerability that had to be given attention, that had to be responded to in some new, life-affirming way.

This book offers a unifying model of recovery, a model that incorporates biological, psychological, familial, social, and spiritual factors. The book also includes many concepts, techniques, and exercises useful at various stages of recovery, with references to both traditional and holistic thinking on addiction treatment. It also provides a comprehensive guide to spiritual development— an important task as recovery progresses beyond concerns with substance abuse and toward living in peace.

But above all, our intention is for this book to give you confidence in working with people in recovery. You do not have to know exactly what to do or say. You do not have to apply exactly the right procedure. What you have to do is stay near the person's vulnerability. Listen for it, be curious about it, help the person to identify it, help the person learn new ways to respond to it. Vulnerability is the core of human struggle, and this truth will show itself to you over and over again as the drug use fades away and real feelings reappear. Stay close to this truth; we believe it will set your work free and keep it real.

Bonney and Richard Schaub
New York, August, 1996

# THE NATURE
# OF ADDICTION
# AND RECOVERY

# 1 | THE CYCLE OF ADDICTION

*Alcoholism is a mental obsession and a physical compulsion.*

"The Big Book" of Alcoholics Anonymous

## CASE STUDY | *Robert*

Robert grew up in a suburban, middle-class family. His father was an administrator at the local Navy base and his mother was a housewife. He had two older sisters. He remembers his childhood as "decent." His father was strict and everyone felt afraid of him, but he did not actually hit the children. His mother was basically good to him, though she did "control" everyone through guilt. School was all right, but Robert recalls always feeling "a little different" than the other children. He just never felt comfortable in his own skin. Something vague was bothering him, as if something bad was about to happen. This discomfort did not leave him for any long periods of time. He definitely recalls that, by age 10, he was seeking something to make the discomfort go away.

Robert started using alcohol at age 12. In junior high school, he began to hang out with older students and was introduced to other drug use. By the end of high school, he had experimented with cocaine, LSD, marijuana, Valium, barbiturates, and cough syrup and also continued drinking alcohol. By college, he had settled into daily use of alcohol and tranquilizers. He obtained the alcohol by figuring out which liquor stores would sell to underage customers. He obtained the tranquilizers "legally" by figuring out which doctors would give him drug prescriptions if he complained about nervousness. Despite his drug use, he did well in college, had friends, and after graduation worked in sales for a clothing business.

By age 30, he was fired from his third sales job because of lateness, emotional outbursts, and inattention to his work. His boss saw Robert as personable, intelligent, and with great potential— but completely unpredictable. By age 30, Robert had become not only unpredictable to his boss: he had become unpredictable to himself. His drug addiction had him cycling through periods of exhaustion, fear, disorientation, and panic attacks, with only brief episodes of relief. The relief would come immediately after drinking or taking pills. Unfortunately, the relief would wear off quickly, and he would be back to fear again.

### Observation

A basic cycle is present in all addictions. A basic cycle is also present in all recoveries. By recognizing these cycles, the stages of addiction and recovery can be identified. By understanding these cycles, you can see the specific kind of help someone like Robert needs at each step of the way.

# THE EARLY STAGE OF ADDICTION

The early stage of addiction is marked by acceptance of chemicals as a way to change feelings.
The early stage of the addictive cycle is:

1. unsafe feelings
2. mental focus on the feelings
3. a desire to get rid of the feelings
4. using chemicals to get rid of the feelings
5. nervous system disturbance because of the chemicals
6. unsafe feelings

## Unsafe Feelings

This is the onset of the cycle of addiction. Typical unsafe feelings include light-headedness, shakiness, heart palpitations, mental racing, confusion, extreme self-consciousness, feeling alien to your environment, and generalized anxiety. Robert would describe it as "not feeling comfortable in my own skin." This theme is frequently described by people in addiction:

"I feel like I don't have any skin."

"There's nothing protecting me from the world."

"I feel like I don't have a shield."

"Everything gets to me."

"Why does everything bother me?"

This unsafe feeling is always a form of human vulnerability. Vulnerability is a normal human emotion; everyone on earth can identify with vulnerability. Some people, however, feel it more intensely and more frequently than others. We can say they are more sensitive to vulnerability, or less able to tolerate it. In drug treatment settings, this pattern of feeling is often described as:

- low frustration tolerance
- inability to delay gratification
- low pain threshold

These phrases are attempts to put into words the kind of heightened sensitivity that is observable in the person involved in addiction.

## *Mental Focus on the Unsafe Feelings*

Many people now in recovery remember as early as elementary school the feeling that something was wrong with them. In Robert's case, these feelings included severe despair over any criticism, worrying something bad was about to happen, and sensing he was about to get into trouble. To cope with these feelings, Robert would try to avoid going to school by complaining of stomachaches to his mother or would get out of school early by going to the nurse's office for medical permission to go home. He became preoccupied with figuring out ways to stay away from situations that increased his vulnerability.

## *The Desire to Get Rid of the Feelings*

Robert could not tolerate his feelings. He experienced himself as much more sensitive than the other boys. At times, he was teased for being this way. He remembers that by age 10 he was very clearly "looking for something." Once the person finds a chemical (e.g., marijuana, alcohol, and so on) that gets rid of the feeling, he has found an answer. The person may think he is using chemicals because it makes him feel good, but in fact it is being used to stop feeling bad. This fact will become an important insight on the road of recovery. *Recovery* is taking the mental, physical, and spiritual actions that lead to living a conscious, sane life.

## *Using Chemicals to Get Rid of Feelings*

Robert was a vulnerable child. He spent years living with feelings of discomfort. At the age of 12, with a group of friends, he was introduced to alcohol. Suddenly, his feelings of discomfort disappeared. He felt right, good, at ease. Many people in recovery can look back and remember with great clarity that moment of relief through chemicals. Robert describes it as "the first time I felt like one of the guys." He remembers joking and feeling relaxed, as if all the years of sensitivity were gone. He felt more like a person. He felt more like he wanted to feel. In the face of this experience, Robert's search for something had ended. He had found what he was looking for. He had found a way to be comfortable in his skin.

### *Nervous System Disturbance Because of the Chemicals*

When Robert started drinking alcohol at age 12, he would be sick the next day. This disturbance to his nervous system produced a recurrence of unsafe feelings. His immediate thought was how he could get some alcohol. He convinced his friends to get some beer at lunch hour on school days. He had now come full cycle. He was once again experiencing unsafe feelings that could not be tolerated. We can clearly see that the feelings were in part nervous system disturbance from the depressant effects of alcohol. For Robert, the reason for the feelings did not matter. He only cared about getting rid of the feelings so that he could feel all right again. He now had learned that he could feel all right. Chemicals accomplished this for him.

## THE TURN TOWARD ADDICTION

Once the association between unsafe feelings and chemical use had been established, Robert's emotional and social development had taken a turn away from learning coping skills and toward addiction. *Coping skills* are healthy responses that help you through difficult situations.

Through chemical use, he now had a way to get rid of his vulnerability. He no longer had to learn to cope with it. The ability to cope with vulnerability, anxiety, stress, and other difficult emotions is an essential skill in living. These feelings are inevitable and entirely normal in our human situation. Robert had now stopped learning about these essential, worldly skills.

### *The End of Emotional Skill-Building*

Adolescence is a time of emotional turmoil. This is partly attributable to the fact that the adolescent is exploring his identity and sense of self. A part of this exploration involves his world away from his family—his peer group, his friends, his interactions with adults in the community. Learning how to negotiate the wide variety of reactions and feelings in these interactions is what engenders a sense of competence. This developing sense of competence is then carried forward throughout the person's life. When Robert stopped using drugs and alcohol at the age of 34, he had to begin to catch up on 22 years of emotional learning. Chemicals had replaced the development of any psychological resiliency and resourcefulness. At 34, he had to begin to live a sober life. *Sober* refers to a balanced attitude toward living without resorting to chemicals to alter difficult feelings.

## THE MIDDLE STAGE OF ADDICTION

The middle stage of addiction is marked by the immediate use of chemicals in response to difficult feelings.

The middle stage of the addictive cycle is:

1. unsafe feelings

2. using chemicals to get rid of the feelings

3. nervous system disturbance because of the chemicals

4. unsafe feelings

Before we discuss the middle stage, use this reflection to get a sense of what this stage is like for the person in addiction. We offer this reflection to help you see the trapped consciousness of the addictive process. By appreciating the obsessions and compulsions of addiction, you can better understand why it can take so long for the person in addiction to begin to break free of this behavior. *Obsessions* are demanding, repetitive urges and *compulsions* are demanding, repetitive actions. You may offer your professional skills to the addict and be ignored or rejected many times. This tells you that the addiction—the obsessions and compulsions—are still in command of the addict's life.

## *EXERCISE*

## *Reflection on Middle Stage Addiction*

After each suggestion, close your eyes, reflect on the suggestion, and then make some notes about what you experienced. Then go on to the next suggestion.

1. Imagine that as you are reading this book, images of smoking marijuana demand your attention. Imagine that you can smell it and taste it as you try to read.

2. Imagine promising yourself that you will keep reading, you will not give in to these urges.

3. Imagine putting this book down and going to get your marijuana supply.

4. Imagine it is four hours later. You are waking up from a heavy sleep caused by the marijuana. Imagine feeling groggy, drugged, and disconnected in your body and your mind.

5. Imagine thinking you should throw out your marijuana supply because you know you are smoking every day.

6. Imagine feeling fear at the thought of being without the drug.

7. Imagine deciding to keep the marijuana and feeling immediate relief at this decision.

8. Imagine it is Tuesday morning at work. You are at a case conference and you feel anxious. You are daydreaming about lunchtime when you can go to your car and smoke a joint. As you imagine this, you can actually taste the marijuana in your mouth. Really imagine this—you are at work, in a conference, tasting marijuana in your mouth. How do you feel?

9. Imagine it is Friday night. You have driven home from a party. You still feel high from the marijuana you smoked there. Suddenly, you realize you do not remember driving home!

10. Imagine thinking of stories of drunks who cause car accidents and do not even remember being there. Imagine a feeling of panic rising in you.

**11.** Imagine reassuring yourself that marijuana is different than alcohol and that you are in control. As a matter of fact, you believe that your reflexes are even better when you smoke.

**12.** Imagine that you smell something burning. Imagine seeing a pot, red hot, steaming on the stove, and then feeling fear because you do not remember putting it there.

### Discussion

This exercise gives you a sampling of typical incidences in marijuana addiction. You have thus far experienced only a middle stage of the addiction. It is likely this person will continue in the obsession (thoughts, urges) and compulsion (actions) for years. Perhaps she will be fired from her job or involved in a car accident. Maybe she will lose friends or suffer more severe memory impairments before the reality of the addiction is accepted.

---

### The Middle Stage of Addiction by Adolescence

In many profiles of addiction, this middle stage is already in place by early adolescence. Robert was using alcohol and pills daily by the time he was in high school. The middle stage is marked by the fact that an unsafe feeling and the answer to the unsafe feeling—chemicals—are tied together. The person does not think about the unsafe feeling. The unsafe feeling is not consciously experienced as a thought. It is only experienced as danger. The instinct is for immediate relief. He feels it and takes an action— he uses chemicals. This behavior has become a repetitive, maladaptive attempt to not feel bad. It has become an addiction.

### The Progression of Addiction

Inevitably, the middle stage gets worse. Addiction is a progressive process. It does not stabilize. It does not plateau. It does not settle down to a moderate, predictable level. The chemicals necessary to feel all right increase in amount and frequency. The cycle of chemical use and nervous system disturbance reinforce each other. This leads to the late stage of the addictive cycle.

# THE LATE STAGE OF ADDICTION

The late stage of addiction is marked by using chemicals to manage the disturbance caused by using chemicals.
The late stage of the addictive cycle is:

1. nervous system disturbance

2. using chemicals

3. nervous system disturbance

In the late stage, the unsafe feelings no longer start the addictive cycle. The human vulnerability that drove the cycle is completely replaced. The person is now fully suffering the consequences of chemicals disturbing the nervous system. Robert would get up in the morning to go to work with his nervous system trying to recover from late night drinking. He knew he could not go to work feeling so nervous. He would take several tranquilizers just to shave, shower, and get dressed. Then he would drink coffee to try to get some energy.

What he would actually get from coffee was stomach agitation, a generalized anxiety, and excessive sweating. He would then attribute this to being nervous about work. He would wonder if he should quit the job, and he would then feel a resentment about having to work at all.

When he was finally on his way to work, he was usually late. He typically forgot some work material or his wallet at home, but he always took his pills with him. His imagination would rehearse scenes about the boss criticizing him as he walked into the office. He would not make eye contact and would go immediately to his desk. He would sit there, sensing something bad was about to happen, just as he had felt as a child. In fact, in his late stage of addiction, he always felt like a child in a world of adults. He was now 33 years old.

## *The Culmination of the Cycle*

The addiction has become the beginning and the end. What started off as the answer to unsafe feelings has become the cause of unsafe feelings. The neurological damage is manifesting in constant instability, mental terrors and hallucinations, and inability to function at simple tasks. At this point, the person has probably lost her job, family, any non-drug-focused social contacts, and any real sense of control in her life. She has one thing left—the addiction. The chemicals she has chosen must meet the needs for relationships, for a sense of purpose, for a sense of self.

## ASSESSING ADDICTION

What are the warning signs of addiction? In *Nursing Care of Clients with Substance Abuse*, a nursing addictions theorist, Eleanor Sullivan (1995) cites the Michigan Alcoholism Screening Test (MAST) as a standard diagnostic instrument to screen for substance abuse. Though the questions are specific to alcohol, the same questions could be asked about any substance use. Let us look at the short version of MAST (figure 1.1), which the client can self-administer.

---

1. Do you feel you are a normal drinker? (By normal we mean you drink less than or as much as most other people.) (No)*

2. Does your wife, husband, a parent, or other near relative ever worry or complain about your drinking? (Yes)

3. Do you ever feel guilty about your drinking? (Yes)

4. Do friends or relatives think you are a normal drinker? (No)

5. Are you able to stop drinking when you want to? (No)

6. Have you ever attended a meeting of Alcoholics Anonymous? (Yes)

7. Has drinking ever created problems between you and your wife, husband, a parent, or other near relative? (Yes)

8. Have you ever gotten into trouble at work because of drinking? (Yes)

9. Have you ever neglected your obligations, your family, or your work for two or more days in a row because you were drinking? (Yes)

10. Have you ever gone to anyone for help about your drinking? (Yes)

11. Have you ever been in a hospital because of drinking? (Yes)

12. Have you ever been arrested for drunken driving, driving while intoxicated, or driving under the influence of alcoholic beverages? (Yes)

13. Have you ever been arrested, even for a few hours, because of other drunken behavior? (Yes)

*Alcoholism-indicating responses in parentheses.

---

**FIGURE 1.1    Short Michigan Alcoholism Screening Test (SMAST)**

Reprinted with permission from *Journal of Studies on Alcohol*, vol. 36, pp. 117–126, 1975. Copyright by Journal of Studies on Alcohol Inc., Rutgers Center of Alcohol Studies, Piscataway, NJ 08855.

## Comments on SMAST

Each SMAST question points to the classic indicators that alcohol use is out of control. The questions that ask for self-assessment, such as number 1, may be easily lied about. The person in addiction makes fine points about whether or not he is really an alcoholic. Such fine points are not necessary for the people around him at home or work or in the neighborhood. Other people can see the compulsive use of alcohol or other drugs and the damaging effects of such use. The SMAST asks the client to at least consider that other people see a problem.

A nursing assessment checklist and a nursing diagnoses checklist for addiction (Dossey, Keegan, Guzzetta, & Kolkmeier, 1995) are included in Appendix 1. In our clinical experience, a simple question to cut to the core of the issue is, "Are alcohol or drugs causing problems?" You may get a lie as an answer, but at least the question defines the problem at its most basic level.

# SUMMARY

Robert is a unique person. His story is the result of many complex factors. At the same time, his cycle of addiction is a completely predictable sequence of events that can be seen in the lives of most people in addiction. Robert's early answer to his unsafe feelings—chemicals—became the problem itself. The original reason for chemical use disappeared, and chemical use continued in order to end the disturbance caused by chemical use. Addiction is a process that advances into more and more illness until the chemical use ends. The observable cycles of the addictive process give you a beginning assessment guideline.

# THE NURSE-HEALER REFLECTIONS

Throughout this book, each chapter includes a section for your personal and professional reflections as a nurse-healer or helping professional. The nurse-healer concept is based on the principle that: "To become a truly effective nurse it is important to both build a scientific base and develop healing qualities" (Keegan, 1994, p. xii).

## Nurse-Healer Characteristics

Adapted from Dossey et al. (1995), the characteristics of the nurse-healer include:

- recognition that self-healing is an ongoing process
- openness to self-improvement and self-development
- willingness to identify creative and self-defeating personality patterns in self
- willingness to take responsibility for inner reactions to clients
- active efforts to expand personal and professional knowledge
- willingness to be a role model for self-care
- embodying the concepts that you are presenting— "Walking your talk"
- commitment to maintaining a sense of presence in your work
- respect and love for the humanness of your clients, regardless of who they are
- willingness to personally explore methods before teaching them to clients
- commitment to creativity and innovation
- trust in the potential of clients to find inner wisdom
- active listening
- paying attention fully to what is present in you and the client
- studying and integrating a bio-psycho-social-spiritual model of the person
- holding a goal of self-efficacy for your clients

# REFLECTIONS

How do I respond when I recognize vulnerability in someone else?

What do I identify as vulnerable moments in my own life?

Have I ever felt caught in a negative cycle of behavior?

What are my usual responses to experiencing vulnerability within myself?

What am I doing to support my healthy coping mechanisms?

## References

Alcoholics Anonymous. (1987). *Alcoholics anonymous* ("The Big Book"). New York: AA World Services.

Dossey, B., Keegan, L., Guzzetta, C., & Kolkmeier, L. (1995). *Holistic nursing: A handbook for practice* (2nd ed.). Gaithersburg, MD: Aspen Publishers.

Keegan, L. (1994). *The nurse as healer.* Albany, NY: Delmar Publishers.

Sullivan, E. (1995). *Nursing care of clients with substance abuse.* St. Louis: C.V. Mosby.

## Suggested Reading

Alcoholics Anonymous. (1987). *Alcoholics anonymous* ("The Big Book"). New York: AA World Services.

Keegan, L. (1994). *The nurse as healer.* Albany, NY: Delmar Publishers.

Yoder, B. (1990). *The recovery resource book.* New York: Simon & Schuster.

# 2 | MODELS OF ADDICTION

*The search for a single cause and/or cure (for addiction) is illusory and counterproductive.*

Dan Lettieri

## CASE STUDY | *Ellen*

Ellen, a thirty-five-year-old single woman, entered psychotherapy after seven years of sobriety and active participation in Alcoholics Anonymous and Overeaters Anonymous. She was successfully employed as an engineer and worked for a very demanding firm. She frequently worked fourteen-hour days and occasionally worked even longer hours.

Ellen was the younger of two siblings. She was introduced to marijuana and alcohol at ten years of age by her older sister. She was smoking and drinking on a daily basis by the time she was twelve years old. Ellen's childhood had been filled with brutality. Her mother, an extremely overweight woman, had beaten Ellen and her sister on a daily basis. Ellen described never knowing what might provoke her mother's rage, but remembered, as a child, trying to monitor her mother's "mood swings." Arriving home a few minutes late from school, spilling her milk at the dinner table, receiving a poor grade on her report card—any of these events could result in her being punched, kicked, or hit with a belt. Her father, who worked long hours and when home was absorbed in religious practices, never intervened during the beatings.

Meanwhile, Ellen, a very bright and resourceful girl, managed to maintain her grades. She also worked from the age of thirteen on, sometimes stealing money from her employers to buy drugs. She attended college, often attending classes or taking exams drunk.

After graduation, when living on her own, Ellen convinced her mother to attend an Overeaters Anonymous meeting. It was at this meeting that Ellen first confronted her own addictions. Her mother never returned to OA, but Ellen continued, realizing that she had addictive eating behaviors. Soon after joining OA, she joined AA and stopped all of her substance abuse. Ellen remained extremely concerned about her mother's weight and its impact on her health, often expressing deep fears about her mother dying.

Ellen described early on in her sobriety listening to a woman at an AA meeting speaking about being beaten as a child. Ellen was shocked to hear the group members' horror at the violent descriptions because they sounded totally familiar to her. Ellen said this was the first time it fully registered with her that not all children were beaten on a daily basis. It was not until years later that she realized that her mother's "mood swings" were actually the effects of her mother's addiction to diet pills and other prescription medications.

### Observation

Ellen's traumatic history points to the complexity of explaining addiction. There are so many possible causes of addiction in her story. We will refer back to her as we examine a spectrum of models of addiction.

## EXERCISE

### Reflection on Addiction

The purpose of this exercise is to discover and reflect on your beliefs and attitudes about addiction. After this reflection, you will be able to examine the spectrum of addiction theories with awareness of your own perspective.

1. Take a moment to reflect on the people in addiction you have encountered in your life, both personally and professionally. Select one that you feel comfortable focusing on.

2. Take a moment to close your eyes and imagine this person in front of you now.

3. What feelings does this person arouse in you? What is most striking about this person?

4. What are the beliefs, attitudes, and judgments you have in regard to this person?

5. Do you identify with this person in any way? Are there any addictive patterns in your life?

Make some notes on your thoughts and reactions to this reflection.

### Discussion

What are your speculations as to why this person is addicted? Do you think people are addicted because of any of the following reasons:

- withdrawal pains

- genetics

- behavior learned in the family

- too much anxiety or depression

- a poor sense of self

- lack of nurturing in infancy

- drug high feels so good

- drugs give instant gratification

- a character defect

- a desire to feel free of inhibitions

- a spiritual desire to expand consciousness

## ADDICTION THEORIES

There are at least eleven theoretical models of addiction. In reviewing these models, it will be clear there is not one addict personality, nor is there one overriding model of causation. Addiction is not a unidimensional problem. The quest for a definitive cause, while it would be convenient, will never come.

### The Medical Model

In this model, an addiction is the progression of (1) drug use leading to (2) body tolerance for the drug, leading in turn to (3) the need for greater and greater amounts of the drug to produce the desired effect, leading in turn to (4) physical craving for the drug if it is discontinued. This craving, this physiological withdrawal symptom, is then considered the proof of addiction. This physiological response, e.g., seizures, fever, chills, delerium tremens (DTs), is referred to as an abstinence syndrome. If it does not occur upon stopping the intake of the substance, then the patient is not considered addicted. Addiction and dependency are differentiated in this model, with addiction seen as a physical problem and dependency more a psychological problem.

Addiction occurs as a result of taking an addictive drug such as heroin or cocaine. Brain chemistry is altered with the ingestion of psychoactive drugs. If a person consumes a drug that releases excitatory chemicals into the brain, the brain decreases its natural production of excitatory neurotransmitters. It then becomes necessary to increase ingestion of the drug to experience the same effect (tolerance).

This attitude towards addiction is often implied in the media when references are made to a public figure such as an athlete or other celebrity going through a thirty-day rehabilitation program and then the person is referred to as having been "treated" for addiction. The use of the past tense implies that treatment is completed, as if there were some medical procedure that took place and now the addiction is cured.

**Ellen** If our case study, Ellen, were assessed from this model, she would not be considered an addict. Despite daily use of alcohol for many years, she never experienced any withdrawal symptoms when she stopped. Her cessation of use was abrupt and done on her own without any medication.

### *Genetic Disease Model*

This model has been applied primarily to alcoholism. It proposes that the vulnerability to alcohol is based on some inherent brain chemistry deficit or imbalance that is traceable to a genetic, hereditary predisposition. This disease is chronic and progressive if not rendered inactive by abstinence from alcohol. This would then explain the prevalence of alcoholism within families or cultures. This, along with the medical model, is the prevailing trend within the medical field.

Extensive research has been conducted on familial patterns in alcohol dependence. The risk factor for alcoholism is seen as three to four times higher in people who have close relatives who are alcoholic. The risk increases with closer genetic relationships to the alcoholics, with greater number of affected family members, and with greater severity of their alcohol-related problems. Twin studies show a greater risk to the monozygotic twin of an alcoholic as opposed to the dizygotic sibling. Additionally, adoption studies indicate the risk of developing alcoholism is three times greater in children of alcoholics, even if they have been raised in a non-alcoholic environment (American Psychiatric Association, 1994).

***Ellen***   In Ellen's case, while neither of her parents were alcoholic, her mother did abuse food and prescription drugs. Additionally, Ellen's sister was an active alcoholic.

### *Self-Medication Model*

This model assumes the addicted person possesses a preexisting psychopathology or brain chemistry deficit or imbalance that results in an incapacity to self-soothe. From this outlook the person is, in effect, self-prescribing medication to alleviate symptoms. This model comes from the clinical observation that addicts often experiment with a variety of substances before they find the right match. It is not unusual to hear a substance abuser say that the particular chemical they are using makes them feel "normal." It is clinically important, when working with patients, to get a clear picture of the desired effect they are seeking from their substance of choice. A drug like alcohol has strong antianxiety and disinhibiting effects for some people, while others may be seeking to alleviate depression. Heroin has potent antipsychotic effects, and marijuana is effective in counteracting boredom and feelings of emptiness. Cocaine and other stimulants produce feelings of power, aggressiveness, and self-confidence.

***Ellen***   We could view both Ellen and her mother as self-medicators.

### *Dysfunctional Family System Model*

This model looks at addictive behavior as a learned response. Certainly witnessing a parent respond to stress and conflict by pouring a drink or taking a pill day, after day, after day, has a profound effect. The message to rely on substances as a problem-solving strategy is deeply communicated to the child. The pattern of denial within the substance-abusing family system is usually powerfully developed. It is often not until the child within the family has reached adulthood, and possibly their own sobriety, that the full extent of the role of addiction within the family is recognized.

***Ellen*** Clearly, Ellen's family failed in teaching her any positive life skills. Her mother was out of control and, by example, taught her children that drugs or food were sources of comfort. Her father used his religious practices as a way of ignoring his family and avoiding conflict.

## *Psychoanalytic Psychosexual Model*

This model comes out of Freudian concepts of psychosexual stages of development. The earliest phase of this development is the oral phase. The infant who does not experience adequate nurturing and nourishment at this phase becomes fixated at this stage and continues to seek soothing and comfort through oral behaviors. Addictive behaviors such as bingeing and smoking, as well as the consuming of drugs and alcohol, become replacements for the infant's unmet oral needs.

Intravenous drug users often describe the full body sensation of warmth that follows the initial injection of their drug. At times, when heroin is not available, they will prepare some other substance such as sugar water or saline solution to inject. They do this to experience the intense bodily sensation that occurs as a result of sudden change in blood volume. The desire for this sensation could be understood as a fixation on the unmet need of the infant for the blissful physical contentment at the mother's breast.

***Ellen*** We can easily surmise that Ellen's infancy was marked by deprivation of basic needs.

## Ego Psychology Model

When the infant's environment does not provide a good enough source of nurturing and acknowledgment, the child grows into an adult with an impaired sense of self. Issues of inadequacy, borderline emptiness, narcissistic isolation, and other disorders of the sense of self make the person feel vulnerable and unsafe in the world. The addictive behaviors are self-soothing activities that attempt to ease the emptiness.

***Ellen***   This model is an elaboration of the Freudian psycho-sexual developmental model. Ellen's history certainly fits the description of insufficient nurturing and the resulting need for self-soothing to abate emptiness.

## Cultural Model

This model views our culture as one in which we are taught to look outside ourselves for quick fixes. Psychosocial stressors of epidemic proportions have led to a society of impulse-disordered people seeking instant gratification. We are told there is a pill for every ill, and we can feel great and be happy right now.

***Ellen***   Ellen and her mother both handled their stress through the instant gratification of drugs and food.

## Character Defect Model of Alcoholics Anonymous

In this model, alcoholics and other addicts are characterologically and morally different than nonaddicts. While this "moral" model is no longer taught in addiction treatment centers, its language still remains central in AA literature and is the cause of many negative reactions and confusion. It is an early reference, despite its language limitations, to some inherent vulnerability in the person who becomes addicted. A person in recovery influenced by AA may explain his difficulties in changing attitudes and behaviors as stemming from "my character defect."

***Ellen*** Ellen and her mother could be surmised to be suffering from a missing element that makes life too difficult to bear.

## Trance Model

This model emerges from hypnosis and learning theory. It posits that once a certain level of pleasure, via a substance, is experienced, it is never forgotten by the pleasure-seeking, pain-avoiding level of our brain. The memory of the experience then serves as a deeply planted suggestion to be mindlessly sought, regardless of consequences, over and over again. "The urge to repeat the experience of becoming 'high' is so strong that we will forsake . . . our responsibilities and values . . . our families, our jobs, our personal welfare, our respect and integrity . . . to satisfy the urge" (Hazelden Foundation, 1987, p. 2). Consuming the substance becomes an automatic behavior, like learning to ride a bike. Once you get the feel of riding, you do not forget it. This model strongly supports the need for lifelong abstinence.

***Ellen*** This model ignores the trauma in Ellen's history. However, in view of such suffering, the brief pleasure of drug use could account for her continued attachment to it.

## Transpersonal-Intoxication Model

Some highly sensitive people are acutely aware of the anxious, limited, time-bound sense of self and seek substances for consciousness expansion. *Consciousness expansion* is experiencing the self beyond the limits of ordinary personality awareness and includes mystical, spiritual, meditative, and religious states of awareness. This model points to the prevalence of drug and alcohol addiction amongst creative people as examples of seeking to break free of mental and emotional limitations. For example, a striking number of Nobel prize-winning American authors, e.g., Ernest Hemingway, F. Scott Fitzgerald, Eugene O'Neil, John Steinbeck, William Faulkner, and Sinclair Lewis, were all alcoholics (Keehn, 1989). This model also corresponds to the recent literature on drug use as part of a spiritual search.

***Ellen***    This seems to have little surface application to Ellen or her mother. The cause of Ellen's mother's struggle, however, is unknown and could possibly be found in this model.

### Transpersonal-Existential Model

This model starts from the premise that the human condition is inherently anxious. The human is considered anxious because she is conscious of her temporary existence, of her inevitable death. Human consciousness makes us aware of our condition without having any answer for us. In this model of addiction, it is posited that some people are more acutely aware of our time-bound, limited sense of self and must seek substances to reduce this anxiety. This is very close to the self-medication model. Both models point to the need for relief from a basic anxiety. In the self-medication model, however, the underlying cause of anxiety is a biochemical deficiency of naturally soothing opiates in the brain.

***Ellen***    Again, in trying to understand the need for self-soothing in both Ellen and her mother, this model offers a possible explanation.

## SUMMARY

Clearly, these descriptions are greatly simplified, but they do give you an introduction to the spectrum of addiction theories. Nine of these models indicate that the unsafe feelings of anxiety and vulnerability—whether caused by genetics, biochemistry, ego damage, family, or society—are central to addiction. Of the remaining two models, the Medical Model ignores the reasons for drug use and the Trance Model views organismic pleasure-seeking as central to drug use.

Theories are more than intellectual debates. Theories lead to funding, research, publicity, policies, and practices. For example, if addiction is seen as a biochemical deficiency, the apparent answer to addiction becomes correcting that biochemistry through biochemical medicines. If, on the other hand, addiction is seen as a dysfunctional attempt to cope with life, then new coping skills learned through counseling and teaching become the answer. For the authors, the theories are consistent enough to single out vulnerability as the problem. The healthy response to vulnerability then becomes the answer.

# REFLECTIONS

At the beginning of this chapter, we asked you to reflect on people in addiction that you have known personally and professionally. Now that you have read the models of addiction, have any of your thoughts and feelings changed?

Does the person in addiction still seem the same to you?

At this point, what is your own understanding of addiction?

## References

American Psychiatric Association. (1994). *Diagnostic and statistical manual of mental disorders* (4th ed.). Washington, DC: American Psychiatric Association.

Hazelden Foundation. (1987). *The twelve steps of alcoholics anonymous.* New York: Harper/Hazelden.

Keehn, D. (1989). Writers, alcohol, and creativity. *Addiction and Consciousness Journal, 4*(1), 9–15.

## Suggested Reading

*Journal of Psychoactive Drugs.* San Francisco: Haight-Ashbury Publications. An excellent, research-based publication with wide-ranging topics.

# 3 DENIAL

*When the inner Addict penetrates my mind, it begins to talk and use arguments to convince me to get high. These arguments are extremely clever, but they all contain flaws. It exaggerates the positive and minimizes the negative. It repeats its appeal incessantly, and it doesn't want me to look closely at its logic.*

Richard Hartnett, *The Three Inner Voices*

## Alan

Alan's girlfriend, Carolyn, complained about feeling ignored. She felt that Alan smoked too much marijuana and watched too much television. Listening to this, he felt angry. Why did she have to bother him now, while he was stoned? He slammed the door on her and watched his favorite TV show.

The next day, Alan was remorseful about his behavior. In response to Carolyn's threats to end the relationship, he bought flowers, took her out to dinner, and said how sorry he was. He vowed he was making an absolute commitment to give up his drug use.

This was not the first time that Alan had made this promise. This time, however, he demonstrated his sincerity by throwing out all of his marijuana supply and his drug paraphernalia. Carolyn felt cautiously reassured and decided that she would wait and see if he really followed through on this promise.

Over the next two weeks, Alan had apparently stopped smoking marijuana. She did find a stub of a marijuana cigarette in the car, but he insisted that it was there from several weeks ago. He reassured her he was totally committed to the promise he had made. He said he loved her and did not want to lose her. He told her that only a day ago he had refused marijuana at work and had been kidded by the others because he was letting his girlfriend tell him what to do.

Three days later, cleaning out the closet, Carolyn found a plastic bag of marijuana hidden in Alan's shoe.

# EXPERIENCING DENIAL

One of the most difficult aspects of working with people in addiction is the lies they tell you. Be certain—they will lie to protect their addiction. And be certain that you will feel like a fool for believing them. We have seen many helping professionals take this lying personally. They take it as an insult to their efforts. This is natural but unnecessary.

## Carolyn's Experience

Carolyn's response to the discovery of the marijuana was to feel hurt and betrayed. There was also a feeling of humiliation at having been deceived and manipulated. What also began to surface was rage at being made to feel this way. Carolyn clearly personalized Alan's lie and felt it was a reflection of his feelings toward her and her worth. It would be difficult for someone in her situation not to have this reaction. Carolyn had been led to believe she meant more to Alan than drugs. She did not at this point have the perspective that his loyalty was to drugs above and beyond any other feeling. She could not yet understand that he felt he had to have marijuana to feel safe in the world. She needed help in realizing this and in letting go of the fantasy that she was capable of controlling Alan's drug use. Clearly, she would need to seek guidance for herself, whether or not she stayed in the relationship. Al-Anon and other support groups specialize in helping the partners of people in addiction.

### *Experiencing Denial—The Nurse*

In working with people in addiction, the nurse needs to understand the feelings that people like Carolyn go through. The nurse will encounter many behaviors similar to Alan's manipulation. The nurse cannot take the lies and manipulations personally. Neither can the nurse take these behaviors as reflections on professional competence and skills. These behaviors are a reflection of the power of denial within the addictive process. *Denial* is, at the most basic level, the refusing of reality. If this is fully understood, then it is much easier not to personalize being treated this way. Failure to understand this can be seen in many health care professionals' negative attitudes toward helping people in addiction. Several encounters with the lies and manipulations are often enough to infuriate the professional and make him decide the person in addiction is not worth bothering with. This reactiveness is not necessary. Alan is simply protecting his coping mechanism, marijuana, that allows him to feel safe. He does not experience the lies as actions that hurt the other person, but rather as necessities so he can continue to function in the world. When he promises to stop his drug use, he temporarily means it. Unsafe feelings, however, inevitably return and seem intolerable. His promise to stop feels impossible to keep.

## *DEFINITIONS OF DENIAL*

Addiction impairs a person's functioning mentally, emotionally, physically, and spiritually. Problems in living become obvious. Relationships suffer, work issues get worse. The addicted person, to protect the addiction, denies these realities. This denial is the key obstacle to beginning the healing process.

Here are several definitions of denial:

- Continuous negative behavior in the face of obvious negative physical, emotional, and social consequences. "My girlfriend is constantly bugging me and threatening to break up with me because of my drinking. She's really got hang-ups about drinking because her father is an alcoholic."

- Prideful insistence the person has control of behaviors that are out of control. "I didn't get into that car accident because of the coke. I actually am a better driver when I've done a few lines. It keeps me alert and my reflexes are better."

- A maladaptive strategy for achieving security. "I don't really have a problem with alcohol, I just need a few drinks when I get home from work because I work the evening shift. My job is very stressful and it's hard to relax enough to fall asleep."

- The energy used to maintain a destructive lie. "I only use drugs because my girlfriend does. I can stop whenever I want."

- A narrowing of awareness to shut out anything that makes the person vulnerable. "When I get high I just don't give a damn. All this crap just fades away."

- An unwillingness to experience the feelings the truth provokes. "My boss was a total hypocrite. He was always on my case. All the guys have a few beers at lunch time. He fired me because he never liked me."

To put it simply, denial is refusing to accept reality.

## *Reality and Denial*

In reality, the person is buying more and more cocaine for the weekends. Her denial tells her she is doing this because she chooses to, and therefore she is still in control.

In reality, the person has a list of several different doctors prescribing tranquilizers for her. Her denial tells her she is taking them under medical supervision; after all, she is getting the drugs from licensed physicians "who understand these things."

In reality, she falls into bed sideways, sometimes with all her clothes on, and often wakes up in the morning exhausted. Her denial tells her a bottle of wine a night is average drinking for a hard-working executive.

In reality, she spent two hours finding a new hiding place for her marijuana. Her denial tells her her husband is upset about her drug use because he comes from an uptight, snobby family.

## *Forms of Denial*

There are different forms of denial: rationalization, suppression, projection, and repression. They are each defenses the mind can utilize to refuse reality. To protect addiction, the person will utilize these defenses frequently to try to confuse those around him.

*Rationalization* is twisting rational thought in order to lie to oneself or others. The person makes up "good" excuses for his addictive behavior.

> Nurse: Why do you drink?
> Active Alcoholic: Because my wife left me.
> Nurse: Why did she leave you?
> Active Alcoholic: Because I drink.

This dialogue may sound made up, even a joke, but it actually occurred in a rehabilitation center. The nurse made a common error as a result of inexperience in the field: she asked the addicted person *why* he is addicted. Asking why is a meaningless exercise. The person has no idea. The vulnerability at the root of the addiction is not yet known to the person. Denial is still operating as a coping skill. As Wing and Hammer-Higgins (1993, p. 17) pointed out: "The assessment of denial can be laborious because of the various aspects of denial and the obscure manner in which it can manifest itself." Perhaps, later into recovery, the question of why can be of interest, but during the active addiction, and then into the first stage of recovery, behaviors are all that matter. There are behaviors that either lead toward addiction or behaviors that lead away from addiction. Recognizing this is part of the path of healing.

*Suppression* is the active attempt to keep information out of awareness. The person consciously pushes reality away: "I don't want to think about it and I don't want to hear about it from you either!" Confrontation, pleading, nagging, and threatening are all futile if the person in addiction has chosen not to hear. This is an active, often angry, determined refusal.

*Repression* is a total numbing of awareness to certain information. It is as if the information does not exist. Reality does not even enter into awareness. The person in repression sounds completely unconscious in her thinking. You may actually feel the urge to shake her and wake her up out of her mental sleep: "I know he has a gambling problem, but he's a good person and he'll stop when we're married."

*Projection* is disowning your feelings but imagining that someone else feels that way: "My wife is weak and insecure and it makes me crazy, so I drink to relax around her." It is a dynamic whereby the person never acknowledges personal responsibility. Rather, everything is attributable to the next best cause.

In dealing with addictions, you will hear the full range of denial techniques. **Remember:** Refusing to accept reality is the key theme to all the denial techniques. The choices that keep addictions going are filled with lies. In Alcoholics Anonymous there is a frequently used slogan: "You're only as sick as your lies."

In the true story that follows, it will be hard to take in the degree of denial we see in the main character. It will be hard to realize that he does not know he is ruining his life. From his perspective, all he sees is the need to drink. What about the other people involved in this story? How can we explain their denial?

## THE POWER OF DENIAL

A story entitled *Million Dollar MDs Lost All* (*The Wall Street Journal*, 1994) appeared recently on the front page of a leading financial newspaper in the United States. Variations of this story have been repeated in hundreds of thousands of addicts' lives. Versions of it can be heard every night at AA meetings. For your study of addiction, this story is a striking example of denial engaged in by the addicted person, by his medical and business associates, and by the hospital where he was a surgeon. Incidentally, the first person to challenge the pattern of denial was a nurse in the hospital, whose warnings about the alcoholic surgeon were eventually heard. For the sake of anonymity, we will call him Dr. X.

## The First Intervention

Ten years ago, a hospital spent a great deal of money to draw new surgery patients to their medical center. Dr. X was one of the primary surgeons helping to build the hospital's reputation. He soon became a multimillionaire and lived a lavish lifestyle. Everyone at the hospital became invested in his continued success. But soon, trouble began. Dr. X was reported by a nurse to have alcohol on his breath while on patient rounds. Nothing was done about this. He was reported to have tremors while in surgery, and he was confronted about this. He reassured the hospital administration and nothing else was done. One of his fellow physicians even went out of his way to concur that the tremors were not alcohol-related.

A year later, the reports increased and Dr. X was eventually confronted by a group composed of an alcoholism counselor and several physicians. In the addictions field, this is called an intervention (see figure 3.1). An *intervention* is a planned confrontation of the addicted person by important people in his life. Interventions have saved many lives. They are planned group efforts to break through the addicted person's denial. It is presenting the person with the truth.

## Beginning Treatment

Based on the intervention, Dr. X agreed to visit a chemical dependency facility. A month later, he returned to the hospital and resumed his surgery practice. Everyone involved was happy that the news of his visit to the rehabilitation facility remained a secret, rather than becoming a cause of bad publicity for the hospital.

The problem with their happiness was their ignorance about the recovery process. Yes, Dr. X had taken a great step, but it was only a small step on a long road.

The purpose of an intervention is to present the chemically addicted person with the undeniable reality of what she is doing in a way that she can hear it. It is an assault on the person's system of denial, but not an attack on the individual personally.

To conduct an intervention, it is necessary to:

1. Assemble a group of close friends and/or family members who are concerned about the person

2. Have each group member present specific facts—behaviors and actions—the person has engaged in as a result of her addiction and then present the undeniable negative outcomes of these behaviors and actions

3. Present these examples in a firm, clear, nonjudgmental and caring manner

4. The group members should have researched and have on hand information on treatment options and resources available to the addicted person

Even if the intervention does not result in the person seeking treatment or stopping the addiction, it serves as an important commitment on the part of the caring people in the person's environment to no longer participate in the lies. It may result in the people seeking help for themselves, either through Al-Anon or through other resources.

***FIGURE 3.1    What is an intervention?***

## Relapses

Soon after he returned to his surgery practice, he again showed signs of impairment due to his alcoholism. He went back to the rehabilitation center and then once again returned to work. Within one year, this happened three times. When a hospital spokesperson was asked why Dr. X was allowed to return to performing surgery again and again, the reporter was told: "I've been here fifteen years, and we've had only four cases of substance abuse among physicians. Prior to this case, we had three complete cures." The reporter of the article makes no comment about this statement, but we must. This spokesperson's comments represent an absolutely classic example of denial about the prevalence of drug and alcohol addiction and the complexity of recovery.

## Monitoring

The surgeon's relapses led to a plan to periodically monitor his urine for alcohol and drugs. By this point, his license to practice medicine was being threatened. He faced severe economic punishment if he drank again. The monitoring was set up in an attempt to try to control him. Despite pleading from his attorney,

Dr. X refused to participate in the urine monitoring and was finally suspended from the hospital staff. In January, 1993, he again entered a rehabilitation center. Soon after he was discharged, he was arrested for a DWI (driving while intoxicated). His medical license was taken away, and there is no more information about him. We fervently hope that one day, in his recovery, he will bring his own experience to the help of other addicts.

## Group Denial

A surgeon with a substance abuse problem is a frightening thought. If you are new to the field, you may find the idea hard to accept. (Another idea that is hard to accept is substance-abusing airline pilots. We know a major hospital that has a special, confidential unit for addicted pilots.) We have to wonder how often Dr. X's substance abuse harmed his patients either on or off the operating table.

The investigative news story barely touched this powerful question. It cites vague statistics, indicating some rise in surgical fatalities. None of us wants to think of the surgeon actually operating drunk and making mistakes. We want to deny this reality. None of us wants to think that this physician had periods of blackouts, when he was not in contact with reality at all.

## Acute Abstinence Syndrome

When fellow physicians noticed he was having tremors, Dr. X assured them the tremors were unrelated to alcohol use. In reality, tremors indicated he was in an acute abstinence syndrome. *Acute abstinence syndrome* occurs when the blood alcohol level drops far below the level the alcoholic's body needs. Marked by central nervous system agitation, acute abstinence syndrome can be evidenced in tremors, hallucinations, deliriums, and convulsions (Gorski & Miller, 1982). This withdrawal syndrome reveals that the alcoholism is very advanced.

Why would Dr. X let his blood alcohol level drop down so far? Most likely, he was afraid his alcohol consumption was being noticed, so he made sure to avoid drinking on the mornings when he was scheduled to perform surgery. His body, however, was suffering withdrawal symptoms because of the alcohol-free morning, and the withdrawal was revealing itself in his central nervous system tremors. He used denial, reassuring his colleagues his tremors were not related to alcohol, and his colleagues wanted to believe him.

## Collusion

We can appreciate the surgeon's denial. It is the very power of the addiction. He is sick with the very advanced stages of alcoholism. He will defend his alcohol use to the death because he needs it. Without it he suffers agitation, fears, and panic. With it, he feels better, even if only for a short period of time. It is an inescapable loop, a sick logic that makes total sense from the viewpoint of the user. Reality plays no part in his thinking. He will lie to everyone to protect his drinking, and most of his colleagues, in an attempt to protect themselves, will accept his lie.

What reasons can there be for the colleagues' denial? Their collusion in this seems self-destructive. An intoxicated surgeon is bound to cause a tragedy at any working moment. Why would these other health care professionals let him continue to practice surgery on their mutual patients? In some cases, individuals have their own drug and alcohol problems, or someone close to them in their family does, so they feel too uncomfortable with confrontation. Or they may be afraid of being wrong, of making a mistake, of making a false accusation. They rightly feel it would be a very serious accusation to call a surgeon an alcoholic. Perhaps they could believe he only drinks because of the pressure of his work. He must not really be an addict, he really does have control.

## The Dysfunctional System

Traditionally, people who point out difficult and possibly embarrassing problems are not necessarily lauded for their integrity. So there is a complex interplay of personal, professional, legal, and institutional forces that collude to not take this problem on. It is very likely that no one ever made an explicit decision to avoid Dr. X's continued alcoholism. The system had become dysfunctional and chose to buy into the lies.

The problem is the lie does not work. The hospital administrators, nurses, physicians, and other workers must have known that they were not dealing with something that would magically go away or decrease on its own. The addictive process is chronic and progressive. Until the person stops using completely (abstinence), addiction typically only gets worse. Once the colleagues denied their own perceptions of Dr. X's addiction, they were passively agreeing to let him get worse and cause damage.

## Enabling

The lie begins to compound. Once you have chosen denial, you become even more afraid to say anything. In effect, you become a kind of accomplice to the addict's sick, irresponsible acts. This happens to the partners, wives, husbands, and children of addicts all the time. If you stay in denial, if you refuse to accept the reality of the person's addiction and its consequences, if you start to organize your life around the other's addiction, you are becoming sick yourself. The commonly used term for this process is *enabling.* You have become an *enabler,* a person who has lost all perspective and is helping the addict continue his illness. At this point, the person in addiction and you both need an intervention to break through the denial.

## Betty Ford

Betty Ford was saved by an intervention. In 1978, the former First Lady was confronted by her entire family about her addiction to prescription medications and alcohol. She was no longer able to refuse reality. She had tried to have individual family members participate in her lie, but the power of the love, concern, and strength of her entire family broke through her denial. The undeniable reality of her united family's fears for her propelled her into her own journey of recovery. As part of that recovery, she made public her addictions. She also became a spokesperson for the recovery movement, cofounding the Betty Ford Center, the hospital well-known for the treatment of chemical dependency.

## RECOVERY IS ONE DAY AT A TIME

As a health professional, it is important for you to not participate in false ideas about recovery. The person in recovery is in for a hard time. Recovery is a day-to-day process and takes years to deepen. You can see the typical newspaper stories of a famous athlete, actor, musician, or politician who has entered an addiction facility and is now "turning his life around." The stories are written as if the addiction is over and a new life is in place. The desire to believe this is strong, but there is in fact a troubling relapse rate in addiction treatment.

An addicted person has been using chemicals to alter emotions and attempt to feel safe in the world. The addict develops a powerful physical and emotional relationship to these chemicals. Then, for one day, some intervention scares her, breaks through the denial, and she tries to stop using chemicals. The first day is not the end of addiction, it is the beginning of recovery. **Remember:** she does not know how to live without these mood-altering substances. She only knows how to cope by using them. She faces an entire emotional reeducation about living in the world.

The person in addiction typically begins drug experimentation in early adolescence. In many ways, the age of onset of drug use marks the end of emotional development. Each time a chemical is used to get rid of anger, anxiety, loneliness, depression, or vulnerability, an opportunity is missed to learn how to tolerate and learn from these feelings. Learning how to live with difficult emotions is not accomplished in a thirty-day *visit* to an addiction treatment center. Our clinical experience teaches us that recovery is a *process* with early, middle, and advanced stages, a process that needs to lead, in time, to a "new consciousness" (Alcoholics Anonymous, 1978). We provide details of this new learning in Part 2, The Choices.

Dr. X's story is dramatic because it conjures up images of drunken surgery, conniving hospital administrators trying to protect their investment, ignorant or callous fellow physicians, and the addicted physician's privilege of having repeated chances that an ordinary health care worker would most likely never have. But at the heart of this story is a gravely sick person, an environment filled with ignorance, denial, and fear, and the multiple tragedies and far-reaching effects of addiction. The tragedy ends and the healing begins when the truth comes forth and the denial is broken.

# SUMMARY

The practical definition of addiction is simple: The person is using chemicals that are causing problems in his life, and the problems are being vehemently denied. If, in your role as nurse, you observe this pattern in someone, you are seeing addiction. Do not refuse your own reality. Honor your perceptions. **Remember:** The desire to deny addiction is strong, but all denial does is make everything worse.

# REFLECTIONS

Have I observed patterns of denial in my home environment?

Have I observed patterns of denial in my work setting?

Is there a way I am not being fully truthful with myself?

What steps can I take on a daily basis to honor and support my inner truth?

Am I willing to do this?

## References

Alcoholics Anonymous. (1978). *Alcoholics anonymous.* New York: AA World Services.

Gorski, T., & Miller, M. (1982). *Counseling for relapse prevention.* Independence, MO: Independence Press.

Hartnett, R. (1994). *The three inner voices: Uncovering the spiritual roots of addiction and recovery.* New York: Serenity Publications.

*The Wall Street Journal,* September 13, 1994, p. 1.

Wing, D. M., & Hammer-Higgins, P. (1993). Determinants of denial: A study of alcoholics. *Journal of Psychosocial Nursing, 31*(2), 13–17.

## Suggested Reading

Hartnett, R. (1994). *The three inner voices: Uncovering the spiritual roots of addiction and recovery.* New York: Serenity Publications.

# 4 THE CYCLE OF RECOVERY

*Miracle doesn't lie only in the amazing living
through and defeat of danger; miracles become
miracles in the clear achievement that is earned.*

Rainer Maria Rilke

## CASE STUDY | *Jack*

Jack's problem drinking went the full cycle. He began by
drinking heavily in the evenings "to sleep," but, in time,
was drinking heavily first thing in the morning "to get
going." Over the years, his alcoholism caused him to lose
his business and his marriage. His grown children moved
far away, both emotionally and physically. Jack became
a disruptive street drunk on the very street where he once
owned a hardware business. He was incoherent much of
the time, and he was misspending his government
disability check. None of these tragedies had convinced

him to stop drinking. He still had not "hit bottom." Eventually, he was arrested for public disturbance and was brought by the police to the detoxification unit, the "drunk tank," at the county hospital. After seven days of "drying out" (not drinking), he was transferred to an inpatient treatment center where he underwent six weeks of education and counseling. He was then transferred to a halfway house for a six-month period of residence, counseling, and vocational rehabilitation. Jack walked out of the halfway house his first morning there. He still had not hit bottom.

### Observation

When we consider Jack's case, we can understand why terms such as "possessed" or "dope fiend" or "demon rum" came to be associated with addictive behavior. While sounding old-fashioned and unscientific, they are certainly descriptive of Jack's self-destructive, out-of-control behavior. In his case, we can see the force of addiction and the difficulty of stabilizing in recovery.

## CASE STUDY | Alice

Alice's father died of alcoholism when she was ten. By age thirteen, Alice had begun drinking. By the age of sixteen, she noticed that she definitely drank much more than her friends. In her last year of high school, she was drunk at every party, at every football game, and at every family affair. In fact, she found a way to drink whenever she had to be with people. She tried other drugs, but their effects scared her. She liked alcohol the best. It worked for her. It made her feel more at ease in the world.

During her second year of college, Alice got very drunk at a bar and went home with a strange man. In the morning, waking up in his house, she became frightened and ran out of his home half-dressed. She cried on the street, humiliated by the passersby who were looking at her. She knew she was in deep trouble; she was becoming a drunk like her father. She had hit bottom. She went to her first Alcoholics Anonymous meeting that night.

She is now twenty-eight years old and leads a sober, conscious, and successful life.

### *Observation*

Alice's early recovery was marked by wondering if she could handle drinking again. She began to question whether she actually was an alcoholic. She thought that perhaps she was overly sensitive to the label of alcoholic because of her father. She began to think that she was overreacting to one bad experience.

Such thinking is typical when people in early recovery begin to worry about living the rest of their life without chemicals. They begin to bargain with the possibility of controlling their addiction. Sometimes they will try to engage you in such thinking and try to get you to agree with them.

In the middle of her confused thinking, Alice would then remember the searing image of herself half-naked and humiliated on the street. She stayed in recovery because of that image. That image was her picture of hitting bottom.

# HITTING BOTTOM

Recovery can be seen in three stages:

1. stopping drinking and drugging
2. healing feelings
3. increasing inner peace

The first stage, the stopping of drinking and drugging, is almost always made possible by a powerful, undeniable reality: *the addiction has become too painful to continue.* This moment is often referred to as hitting bottom. *Hitting bottom* is a moment in time when the person in addiction cannot tolerate the addiction anymore. She may have come near this moment many times before, but now she has reached a particular moment when her addiction has become unbearable. The addiction that in the past was easing the pain has now become the source of pain. Now the addiction is causing her the loss of job, friends and family, memory, sanity from the fear and humiliation, physical health, or control. She may be getting arrested, or jailed, or hospitalized. She may be feeling sick or in trouble all the time. She may have no idea of what the original pain was that motivated her addiction. That beginning is in the long, lost past forgotten by an addiction-saturated brain.

## *Different Depths*

Different people hit bottom at different depths. Some people go all the way down to dying without stopping the addiction. Others must go very close to death's door. Others can see where they are going and stop much sooner.

In Jack's case, the bottom was very low. He finally reached it when he completely misused his government check and became homeless. Drunk, incoherent, hallucinating, he was found living in a cardboard box in the woods along a highway. Even from this low point in life, the addicted person can recover. Jack's recovery is now a work in progress, one day at a time.

Sometimes hitting bottom is not as horrible as Jack's or as dramatic as Alice's. Sometimes the addicted person wakes up, feels bad, and just does not have the energy to go through another day of addiction. As is said in Alcoholics Anonymous, the person is "sick and tired of being sick and tired."

### *The Value of Education as Primary Prevention*

Is it even necessary to hit bottom? No. In part, the difference between Jack's story and Alice's story is that Alice was highly sensitized to the stages of addiction. Her father's progressive illness and death from alcoholism affected every minute of her life. She could not deny the destructiveness of his addiction, and she could not deny the deterioration it caused mentally, emotionally, physically, and spiritually. She had witnessed it all. She saw the signs of it in herself. Crying on the street, half-dressed, humiliated, she could no longer deny the signs. She was aware enough to know what the signs meant.

Over the years, we have seen an important change in awareness of addictions. We have seen younger and younger people recognize their addictions. This awareness gives them a chance to avoid the middle and later stages of deterioration. The more awareness, the more choice. Alice's story definitely makes a case for addiction education programs at the earliest possible age. For nurses, this points to the importance of primary prevention and to the need to be knowledgeable about the signs of alcohol and drug addiction.

## THE EARLY STAGE OF RECOVERY— DETOXIFICATION AND ABSTINENCE

The cycle of recovery is the exact reversal of the cycle of addiction. It begins when denial has broken down, whether through hitting bottom, exhaustion, interventions, or education and awareness.

With the late stage of addiction comprised of nervous system disturbance, using chemicals to get rid of nervous system disturbance, and resulting nervous system disturbance, the early stage of recovery consists of detoxifying, of removing chemicals from the cycle. *Detoxification* is the process of withdrawing from chemical use. We referred to this earlier as stopping drinking and drugging. Actions, not words, begin the recovery process. If you have not seen an action at this stage, then you have not seen the person start recovery yet.

## *Medically Managing Withdrawal*

What action can the person take to remove chemicals from her life? In some cases, depending on the substance and the amount being used, she can enter a detoxification unit to be medically managed through the withdrawal process. These units are often in hospitals, but may also be in free-standing clinics that are run privately or by local government drug and alcohol agencies. Medications may be prescribed to manage withdrawal symptoms.

Since the 1970s, acupuncture has been successfully used for detoxification from a broad range of drugs and alcohol (Helms, 1995; Smith, D., cited in Nebelkopf, 1981). *Acupuncture*, derived from Chinese medicine, focuses on correcting imbalances in the human energy system. Dr. Michael O. Smith at the Lincoln Detox Program in the South Bronx, New York has been a pioneer in the use of acupuncture in drug treatment. He has indicated that acupuncture has been found to be one of the most dramatic and effective natural techniques for the detoxification of people in addiction. Acupuncture, besides being effective, is simple and inexpensive to use and can be applied in a variety of inpatient, outpatient, drug-free, and medication programs (Smith, M.O., cited in Nebelkopf, 1981). Acupuncture is effective for easing the physical discomfort of detoxification from drugs as diverse as heroin and nicotine, and for restoring energetic balance to the entire physiological system.

## *Group Support*

Detoxification units often hold Alcoholics Anonymous (AA) or Narcotics Anonymous (NA) meetings on their premises. AA and NA do not do anything medical on the units. They do not hand out medications or provide medical supervision. What these groups do is to immediately welcome the newly recovering person, the "newcomer," into a community of people who know how to stay drug-free. The combination of inpatient detoxification and AA or NA is also a form of discharge planning: if the person knows about these programs while in detox, it is more likely he will attend meetings upon returning to the community.

### Challenges to AA

Some detoxification units make attendance at the AA meetings mandatory for their patients. This policy has been challenged in lawsuits as a violation of the patient's right to freedom of religion. The legal argument is that AA is a religious-spiritual organization and that individuals should not be forced into participating in religious-spiritual groups by government-funded treatment centers. This issue has also arisen when attendance at AA or NA meetings is made a condition for probation or parole.

Over the years, we have encountered many helping professionals who are wary of AA because of its "religious" nature. There are wide differences in interpretation of the concept of Higher Power as used in AA. This controversy reflects the general confusion, both in and out of the helping professions, as to the nature of human spirituality.

Human spirituality is a natural fact of human nature and an inherent aspect of human development. For some people, organized religion plays an important role in this aspect of their life. For others, their spirituality seeks expression in more individualistic forms. In either case, finding a personally meaningful way to cultivate this aspect of human nature is an essential component of mental health and recovery. This topic is covered in detail in Part 3, Increasing Peace.

## QUESTIONING AND PLANNING

In addition to detoxification, there is a need for intensive questioning and planning during this early stage of recovery. Behaviors associated with addiction are usually so thoroughly integrated into the person's life that she does not notice or recognize them as self-defeating to her recovery. These behaviors need to be identified and labeled as no longer possible.

Some of the questions to ask are:

- What was the social setting for the addictive behavior? Some people isolate in their home or car when using drugs. Others prefer group settings such as a bar or club or work environment.

- What were the rituals associated with the behavior? For example, a marijuana addict might go out and buy a supply of his favorite foods or music before using his drug. Alcoholics may find their favorite glass. There may be other drug paraphernalia and rituals of preparing the substances.

- What are the places associated with the addictive behavior? For the alcoholic, particular liquor stores or bars have especially strong memories and pulls. The neighborhood of the drug dealer or the building where drugs were shared may have the power to draw the person into relapse.

- Who are the people in the environment associated with addictive behavior? This may be the most difficult area of all. The person in recovery may realize that everyone she knows is associated with her drug use. We have had experiences with people in recovery who cannot name a single person they can count on to be drug-free on a predictable basis. The person may feel completely overwhelmed at the loss of this network of family and friends.

## *Initial Steps toward Recovery*

Based on these questions, the nurse counseling the person during her initial recovery period should focus on the following steps:

- getting rid of any remaining drug or alcohol supplies

- getting rid of any drug-related equipment

- staying away from people connected to addiction

- staying away from places connected to addiction

- going to AA meetings or other recovery groups
- going to counseling
- going to rehabilitation programs

It is a leap of faith for the newcomer to break the addictive cycle by removing chemicals from her life. She will now live, from this moment forward, without her mood-changing, feeling-altering, self-soothing addiction. What will life feel like? How bad will it get? Will she be able to tolerate it?

## CASE STUDY | *Roy*

Roy never felt comfortable in his family. He never felt comfortable in school. He was always glad when he was alone again. He used withdrawal from situations to feel more at ease. He was seen as a quiet kid. He never caused trouble. He was pleasant enough and went along with what others wanted to do. When one of the older kids bought beer, Roy tried it too. It tasted strange, but he liked the feeling it gave him. The discomfort that seemed to be built into him went away. He began to realize that, with beer, he could do more things.

To the addiction-aware observer, Roy clearly had a serious drinking problem throughout high school. By his first year of college, he was drinking daily. Currently, Roy is 31 years old and has been in recovery for two months. Looking back at those early memories, he sees a child in emotional pain who was actively searching for something to take those feelings away.

What will Roy face now? He will feel emotional pain without knowing what to do to help himself. He will have periods of racing panic. He will have many nights of lying in bed unable to sleep. He will promise to kill himself if the feelings get worse. He will enter periods of euphoria that feel disconnected and unreal. He will feel criticism burn through him: "I feel like I don't have any skin." He will see a world full of people who can drink and drug without consequences. He will feel very, very young in a world full of grown-ups, even though he is 31 years old. He will feel that AA (or some other recovery group) is for losers. They are all crazy or trying to control him. He will feel surges of irritability and restlessness. He will feel high even though he is drug free. He will feel intense boredom and fear being alone. He will feel incredibly isolated from both his addict friends and the nonaddicted people who have no idea what he is going through: "I feel like I'm from Mars, everything is so strange." He will fight many times with persuasive images of drinking and drugging again. He will feel humiliated by his vulnerability.

### Observation

In every one of these moments, Roy's survival instincts will tell him to get rid of these unsafe feelings. It feels like too much. It feels intolerable. It feels like he will die. He will not, but the unsafe feelings are very convincing. He knows how to get rid of this feeling by using chemicals, and the simplicity of using chemicals is compelling. He does not know any other way. Remember, he has medicated himself on a daily basis for more than half his life. All through adolescence, all through young adulthood, when he should have been learning about his emotions and who he is, he was numb.

## Emotional Skill-Building

The emotional skills you learned to deal with anxiety, insecurity, depression, and disappointment are not available to Roy yet. He does not know what causes these feelings, nor does he know how to help himself. Now, having started a chemical-free life, Roy must enter emotional school. To do well in this school, he must be willing to ask for help from teachers. The teachers, the people who help in recovery, are everywhere. As a nurse, you are one of his teachers.

## The Power of Community

At this early stage of recovery, it is our strong opinion that Alcoholics Anonymous is invaluable. Roy walks into a room full of people who have gone through this early stage, have lived to tell about, and are experts on how to do it. We have heard many people like Roy describe the first moment they felt the power of community support in an AA meeting. Roy says now that it is the power of that community support, more than any specific advice, that is getting him through the bad times of recovery.

## Irritability and Insomnia

It is important to realize that the physiological effects of the alcohol and/or drug usage continue beyond the initial period of withdrawal or detoxification. These effects are seen in the heightened irritability of the nervous system and the residual effects of the nutritional deficits that usually accompany the addicted lifestyle. Difficulty sleeping is common. As part of this initial healing process, it will be important for Roy to develop some strategies for calming the mind and body, such as meditation, imagery, and self-hypnosis. *Meditation* is a conscious choice to focus attention, which leads in turn to a state of dynamic stillness. *Imagery* is the conscious use of the power of the imagination. *Self-hypnosis* is the conscious choice of entering a relaxed state and suggesting new thoughts to the mind. Additionally, a nutritional and dietary consultation is advisable.

# RELAPSE

In every stage of recovery, relapse is an ongoing issue. *Relapse* is the breaking of abstinence and the return to drinking and drugging, even if on one occasion.

In AA, there is a saying: "The further you are from your last drink, the closer you are to your next." The danger of relapse, the return to chemical use, is particularly acute in the early stages of recovery. Roy does not yet have new living skills in place. The wild swing of feelings described in the previous section causes him to desperately want relief. It is estimated that up to 75 percent of people in recovery relapse within the first year. It is significant to note that the figure is estimated to be even higher, up to 90 percent, for women with a history of sexual abuse and trauma. In *Counseling for Relapse Prevention*, Gorski and Miller (1982) outlined the signs that lead back toward addiction. As a nurse, you can use this list to notice a relapse trend in the person's recovery process. Paraphrased from Gorski and Miller, the signs leading to relapse include:

- active denial in many areas of life
- convincing others of the need for sobriety
- defensiveness
- compulsive behaviors
- impulsive behaviors
- tendencies toward isolation and bitterness
- tunnel vision
- loss of a sense of future
- idle daydreaming and wishful and magical answers to complex problems
- hopelessness
- immature wish to always be happy
- consistent periods of confusion
- irritation with other people's limits

- easily angered
- irregular eating habits
- listlessness
- irregular sleeping habits
- progressive loss of daily structure
- irregular attendance at treatment meetings
- development of an "I don't care" attitude
- open rejection of help
- self-pity
- thoughts of social drinking as manageable
- conscious lying
- complete loss of self-confidence

None of these signs inevitably lead into relapse. They are warning signs that can be responded to constructively. To one degree or another, such thoughts and feelings will recur throughout Roy's life. Each time he lives through the experience and finds that it passes, each time the feeling is effectively tolerated and responded to in a healthy manner, recovery and satisfaction in living is deepened.

## *Step by Step*

The most familiar AA aphorism is "One day at a time." When working with Roy through difficult times, it may be necessary to break this down even further, to "One hour at a time," or even "One minute at a time." This concept addresses the tendency in addictive thinking to view things in terms of extremes, all or nothing, black or white, good or bad. This plays out in feelings of panic at the enormity of the idea of never being able to use drugs or alcohol again and the fear that if he does not do something right now to alleviate this emotional pain, he will freak out, or lose his mind, or die. The idea of "never" can then become a reason to use, because thinking in terms of being deprived forever is too enormous.

# ENTERING MIDDLE RECOVERY

The stopping of drinking and drugging is often motivated by hitting bottom. The person in the cycle of addiction has reached a place in life where the addiction is too painful to continue. Roy reached his bottom when he got into a violent confrontation with fellow workers and was fired from his job. He left feeling insane and frightened for his life. He knew he needed help and he knew his drinking was destroying him. This initial decision to try to stop brings Alcoholics Anonymous into the picture as a primary treatment modality. The nurse's role at this early phase, especially in outpatient treatment, is to engage the person in the support and expertise of AA.

## *Physical Healing*

With the removal of chemicals, with the end of drinking and drugging, the nervous system begins to recover. The progression of neurological and other physical damage is halted, and with the introduction of health-promoting behaviors such as a nutritious diet supplemented with vitamins and minerals and adequate rest and exercise, the body's natural healing and restorative mechanisms are supported.

## *Slow, Steady Progress*

The middle stage of recovery takes many years. The person who fails to appreciate the slow, steady, middle stage is in trouble. The cycle of addiction is breaking down, but it is not broken simply by removing drugs and alcohol. Remember, the middle cycle of addiction looks like this:

- unsafe feelings
- using chemicals to get rid of the feelings
- nervous system disturbance
- unsafe feelings

In this part of the addictive cycle, the unsafe feelings start the process. With the chemicals gone, with the nervous system getting back in balance, it is the unsafe feeling that still remains. Now a new set of responses for feeling unsafe must develop. To develop these new responses, the person in recovery must become educated emotionally. She must become capable of recognizing what this feeling is. To do this, she must be willing to tolerate the feeling long enough to know it. This is the key breakthrough in the middle stage of recovery. In particular, the unsafe feeling must become a center of attention and care. The feeling must be recognized for what it is at its core: *vulnerability.*

## SUMMARY

The cycle of recovery must start with an action. The action is to stop the drinking and drugging. This early step often occurs after the person has hit bottom. At this early stage, community support is helpful, thus the need for AA and other peer support groups and programs. Moving into the middle stage of recovery begins the process of healing feelings. This process of healing will be examined in detail in Part 2, The Choices.

## REFLECTIONS

What pattern in my life would I like to change?

What is the first action I must take in order for this to happen?

Which people in my life will support me in this change?

### References

Gorski, T., & Miller, M. (1982). *Counseling for relapse prevention.* Independence, MO: Independence Press.

Helms, J. M. (1995). *Acupuncture energetics: A clinical approach for physicians.* Berkeley, CA: Medical Acupuncture Publishers.

Nebelkopf, E. (1981). Drug abuse treatment. *Journal of Holistic Health, 6,* 95–102.

### Suggested Reading

Gorski, T., & Miller, M. (1982). *Counseling for relapse prevention.* Independence, MO: Independence Press.

# 5 | THE VULNERABILITY MODEL OF RECOVERY

*The blue sky opens out farther and farther, the daily sense of failure goes away, the damage I have done to myself fades, a million suns come forward with light, when I sit firmly in the world.*

Kabir, translated by Bly, 1971

## Tony

It is New Year's Eve. Tony, a 39-year-old recovering addict, sober for eight years, is getting ready to go out. Tonight many people all over the city will drink as much as they can.

As Tony leaves his apartment and walks down the street, he notices that the liquor stores are crowded with people buying alcohol for parties. He is going to a party where there will be no alcohol. All the people at his party are in recovery from addiction. The uniqueness of their lifestyle, the dramatic difference between them and the "normal" people, is exaggerated on a night like this.

Tony feels secure in his recovery. He could go to parties where alcohol is served. He could stand by and watch other people drink, smoke marijuana, snort heroin or cocaine without fearing he would relapse. He could stand by and watch other people begin to slur their speech, lose their coordination, and behave erratically as the drugs begin to affect them. He would not feel threatened by any of this. He is in recovery long enough to know that alcohol and drugs are not a choice for him. But he also has no need to test his sobriety. Tonight it feels just fine to be at a sober party with conscious people.

As Tony and his sober friends reflect on the New Year, they wonder what really led them to addiction. As they talk, the common answer begins to reveal itself. They try to put it into words. They decide it is this: they never felt they were enough; they never felt safe in the world. Alcohol and drugs got rid of the feeling for a while, but it always came back. Simply put, Tony says his addiction was based on "I'm not enough." Even in recovery, he and his sober friends continue to confront that vulnerable feeling again and again.

# VULNERABILITY—THE KEY TO ADDICTION AND RECOVERY

Vulnerability is described in many ways by clients. They say it is a feeling of uneasiness, or of sensing something is wrong, of feeling unsafe in the world or on edge, of "waiting for the other shoe to drop," of something bad about to happen. It is also described as feeling at risk from some unknown danger, or feeling weak and ungrounded, or feeling they do not belong in the world. More intensely, clients describe the experience as one of sheer panic, of feeling unable to go on another second. They may describe feeling close to annihilation and not wanting to experience another moment of this terror. These agonizing vulnerable moments happen often in recovery, especially in the early phase.

## The Human Condition

Vulnerability is anxiety ultimately rooted in the human condition of being conscious, separate, and mortal. The *human condition* refers to the actual facts of human existence. As such, this vulnerability is a normal emotion, an elemental aspect of our actual human situation.

As the theologian Paul Tillich put it, "To be aware is to be anxious." We all share a common consciousness of our human situation. We all realize the conditions of our life—we are separate from each other and we are temporary. Adolescents act as if they are immortal and do risky things without a second thought. As we get older, however, we become more and more aware of our mortality. We experience the deaths of friends and relatives and begin to see ourselves aging. Deaths of younger people shock us, as if somehow such things are not supposed to happen. Despite some heroic mental efforts at denial, we all come to realize we live in a transitory situation in this life.

## Death Anxiety

This basic anxiety, this basic vulnerability, is considered to be, at its root, the fear of death. What else besides a threat to our very survival could have such emotional power? Psychiatrist Aaron Beck, the renowned innovator in the development of cognitive therapy, views fear of death as the cause of all of the anxiety disorders, including generalized anxiety disorder, panic disorder, obsessive-compulsive disorder, and the phobias (Beck & Emery, 1985). However, during intense vulnerability, even death itself (the imagined end of all feeling) can be desired over the continuation of the vulnerability.

Perhaps the supreme contemporary study of vulnerability is Ernest Becker's *Denial of Death* (1973). The book was written while Becker was dying of cancer and seeking answers to his anxiety:

> The individual has to protect himself against the world, and he can do this only as any other animal would: by . . . shutting off experience, developing an obliviousness both to the terrors of the world and to his own anxieties. Otherwise, he would be crippled for action . . . In order to function

normally, man has to achieve from the beginning a serious constriction of the world and of himself. We can say that the essence of normality is the refusal of reality. What we call "neurosis" [or "addiction"] enters precisely at this point: some people have more trouble with their lies than others. The world is too much with them, and the techniques that they have developed for holding it at bay and cutting it down to size finally begin to choke the person himself" (1973, p. 178).

# THE HEALING POTENTIAL
# OF VULNERABILITY

Fortunately, vulnerability is not all bad. In fact, it is a state with great potential. John Welwood, a psychologist and meditation teacher, described ". . . utter vulnerability . . . as the essence of human nature and consciousness . . ." (1982, pp. 132–133). Welwood thinks that vulnerability has the potential for being valued as our basic emotional experience, as our basic aliveness. Vulnerability is therefore a common bond among all people. Potentially, it is an emotional bridge between ourselves and anyone we meet. If we try to get rid of our vulnerability, it is lost as a way to connect at a basic level with ourselves and others. When we recognize our vulnerability and treat it with respect, it immediately connects us with our world.

For Tony, choosing to go to the sober party was an act of acknowledging his vulnerability, both to himself and to others. Looking around the room at other sober people, he knew they were vulnerable, too. He could feel safe and open his heart in this environment. His ease and honesty at the party pleased him and made him feel at home in himself. Such a sense of serenity and oneness was a million miles away from the severe isolation and disconnection of his addictive and early recovery days.

## Vulnerability and Love

The Vulnerability Model of Recovery includes Welwood's thinking and goes further. Vulnerability, at its heart, is not rooted in death anxiety. We emphasize instead that it is the deep love of life and the fear of its loss that is the root of vulnerability. It is not death itself we fear; it is the loss of this life. The heart of the matter, then, is that vulnerabilty is rooted in love.

This great love of life is innate in us. It is reflected in every one of our physiological systems. If our life is threatened, our entire self activates to protect it. Survival is the most essential emotion we have.

These two basic truths about our life—our transitoriness and our love—do not blend easily. Instead, these difficult and contradictory truths cause our deepest anxiety. The dilemma we then face is that we cannot live successfully if we are too sensitive to these realities. We would be, as Ernest Becker put it, "crippled for action" (1973, p. 178). We would be afraid to leave our home and, in fact, some people develop exactly such a disorder—fear of leaving their home (agoraphobia). Others develop similar vulnerability fears: fears of driving over bridges or through tunnels, of riding in elevators or flying in airplanes, of germs, of social gatherings or crowds, of bad thoughts. The list of fears can go on and on. Remember the conclusion Tony and the other people in recovery decided upon to explain their addictions: the fear of not being enough.

## *Vulnerability and Addiction*

These human fears unite us all, but a crucial distinction exists in regard to addiction. Some people's defenses simply do not suppress these fears enough. Instead, they remain sensitive and vulnerable to these fears and need extreme ways to reduce these fears in order to live.

This insight into the root nature of addiction takes all the pointless moral judgment out of addiction. Dropping moral judgments about addiction is an important step to take for the nurse working in this field. Clinical experience alone convinces us that people in addiction have simply come up with ways, maladaptive as they may be, to try to survive without too much pain.

## *Addiction as Avoidance*

From the perspective of the Vulnerability Model, addiction is not stressed as an attachment or as a habit, as it is most commonly thought of. What is emphasized instead is that addiction is an act of avoidance. The person is attached, habituated, addicted to the Valium because: 1) she feels afraid and 2) Valium makes her feel safer. Valium allows her to avoid her experience of vulnerability. Vulnerability and the desire to get rid of it are of primary treatment importance. The means (Valium) by which the person gets rid of vulnerability is of secondary importance.

## *Addictive Process*

Addictive process as a repetitive avoidance of vulnerability can therefore be seen as a defense similar to denial and repression. Denial and repression also get rid of vulnerability. Denial and repression, however, numb vulnerability. In addictive process, another experience is substituted. This substitution can include the following forms:

- repetitive thoughts (e.g., grandiose fantasies)

- repetitive acts (e.g., compulsive lying about self, cruising for sex)

- repetitive substance use (e.g., stimulants, depressants, opiates)

Such elaborate acts of substitution point to a core insight about addictive process: the enormous amount of mental-emotional-physical energy it uses. Add to this the rituals many people develop around their addictions and one can see how addictive process absorbs consciousness. It is clear why Alcoholics Anonymous stresses a new consciousness as necessary for recovery. *New consciousness* is a reorienting of life away from addictive thinking and toward an understanding of life's purpose or a higher power's will.

## VULNERABILITY AND CHOICE

Why does one person need to avoid vulnerability to the point of developing an addiction? We discussed possible explanations for this in Chapter 2, Models of Addiction. However, no single type of addictive personality emerges from these models.

There are common themes of the addictive process itself and of addictive behaviors: they are in fact totally predictable once you have heard enough histories. However, the individual who develops addiction is complex and diverse. What these individuals do have in common is a new need: a need to be able to choose new responses to vulnerability.

Vulnerable moments challenge recovery. The old coping skill, addiction, suggests itself as the answer to the vulnerable feelings. Recovery is learning new, drug-free responses.

## *Justina*

Justina is a thirty-two-year-old woman who has been drug and alcohol free for ninety days. She travels on the public bus to go to work. Whenever the bus gets stuck in traffic, she feels an uneasiness and a buildup of panic. Her mind begins to race from one thought to another. First she thinks the uneasiness means something bad is about to happen. Then she thinks the feeling is a symptom of a serious illness. Her next thought is an image of herself stoned in her room, a memory of her addiction days. Her mind then races forward to imagining she will be late for work and the boss will yell at her. She next thinks of how much she hates working and wishes she could take it easy all day. She then feels herself getting angry at the bus driver, as if somehow he has caused her to be trapped in her situation. She feels emotionally chaotic and senses a small voice inside her telling her to go back to drugs. She wants to cry, but suddenly becomes intensely self-conscious, fearing she must be looking crazy to other people on the bus.

Justina could not admit to herself why the bus ride was so difficult. She blamed it on the bus driver and on the city for not doing something about the traffic. Her own turmoil was lied about, even to herself. This lie to protect herself is understandable. She was still using denial as a primary coping skill. She was still too early in recovery to realize the bus experience was an example of her extreme vulnerability. Later, as she continued in recovery, she began to realize her vulnerability was triggered by any situation in which she could not exert complete control. In time, she began to understand that her childhood home was a place of implied violence all the time and that she had grown up in a constant state of vigilance.

## The Lie Technique: Lies as Information

Such new learning becomes part of the recovery and healing process. To assist Justina's healing, even her lies became a source of new learning. A lie may seem like an untruth, but in fact lies frequently reveal basic truths about underlying feelings. For Justina, her compulsion to lie about the simplest things became a signal for her that she was denying some deeper emotional truth. To assist in investigating the emotions hidden in lies, the authors have developed an imagery exercise entitled The Lie Technique. The *lie technique* is a nonjudgmental way of studying lies for the sake of new learning.

---

## EXERCISE

## The Lie Technique

In one simple technique, vulnerability can be discovered by studying a lie. Take a few moments to experience this method personally. Make some notes on what you discover in this process.

**1.** Recall the last time you told an insignificant lie about yourself. (Insignificant lies, despite their seeming harmlessness, often hide deep fears.)

**2.** What was the immediate reason for the lie? (In most cases, the immediate reason for the lie is to "look good" or to "not look bad.")

**3.** Now in your imagination step back from your immediate reason for telling the lie. Examine what it is about yourself that you were trying to protect.

**4.** Spend some time with this part of you and see it fully. What are your feelings and reactions to this part of you?

**5.** Thinking about it now, what purpose did the lie really serve?

### Discussion

The nurse therapist listened to Justina tell the story about how angry she was at the bus driver. The nurse asked Justina to step back from her anger and to see if there was more to the experience. Justina answered that she was in fact upset about the possibility of being late for work. She was afraid to "look bad" to the boss. The nurse had already arrived at Step 3 of the exercise: she asked Justina to step back from the fear of looking bad to the boss and to examine what else she was trying to protect. Justina saw a memory of her angry father out of control. She was now touching the root of her charged and vulnerable experience on the bus that morning. This was still very new learning for her, but it gave Justina the awareness that she needed new skills for such difficult moments. The nurse therapist explained to Justina that learning relaxation and stress management skills would provide necessary tools for her recovery from addiction.

---

### The Recovery of Choice

Nurses in any phase of addiction work need to help their clients choose new thoughts and new behaviors. The ability to make new choices is the key to recovery.

In order to make new, healthy choices, clients in recovery must first learn about vulnerability. Vulnerable moments challenge recovery. The clients know their old way of handling vulnerability—drugs. In recovery, they must respond in a new way. Every time clients skillfully manage a vulnerable moment, recovery strengthens. It is important for nurses to have a deep understanding of vulnerability since it is the key emotional state that triggers the cycle of addiction.

In Tony's vignette, we can see someone who is now comfortable with his sobriety. That was not true earlier in his recovery. At that time, New Year's Eve was torturous for him. He would think all evening about relapsing back to addiction and would feel strong urges to go out to his old drinking places. He would sometimes pray to God to make New Year's Eve pass quickly.

## The Liberation of Choice

As defined by Alcoholics Anonymous, addiction is a mental obsession and a physical compulsion. An *obsession* is a thought or urge that will not go away. It locks itself into a person's mental life. A *compulsion* is an action that cannot be resisted. Even today, Tony has occasional thoughts of drinking again. However, he now can choose not to focus on the thought and feels no urge to act on it. He has arrived at this level of sobriety by constantly making healthy choices for himself. He has accomplished this with the help of professionals and AA members over many years.

Recovery from addiction is the recovery of choice. *Choice*, in regard to addiction, is the freeing of the person's consciousness from mental obsessions and physical compulsions.

Choice is the basic principle of all recovery techniques:

- It stops obsessive thinking and directs the mind toward healthier thinking.

- It stops compulsive urges before they become actions.

Every time the person steps back from the obsessive thinking and is able to observe it, rather than mindlessly act on it, the recovery gets stronger. Every time the person steps back from the compulsive urge and chooses a new and life-affirming action, recovery gets stronger. This process of liberation of choice occurs one step at a time, moment to moment.

## The First Choice: Addiction Is not a Choice

The first choice to be made is to accept that addiction is not one of the choices. The following choices need to be made over and over again:

- to move away from the people involved in addiction

- to move away from places involved in addiction

- to move away from attitudes involved in addiction
- to move away from things involved with addiction

There is no neutrality in this process, no possibility of nonchoice. The person in recovery needs to recognize that he is making choices all the time.

***H.A.L.T.*** This choice process is clearly reflected in the slogans of Alcoholics Anonymous. For example, AA uses the slogan "H.A.L.T." **H.A.L.T.**, referring to *H*ungry, *A*ngry, *L*onely, *T*ired, is an acronym to remind the person in recovery of the typical situations that reactivate the desire to use drugs. Each of these feeling states can activate the "I'm not enough, I'm unsafe" experience that Tony and his friends identified as the trigger for addiction. The first choice becomes HALT, not moving toward addiction to get rid of the vulnerable state. The second choice becomes responding in life-affirming ways to the vulnerable feelings; eating if hungry, telephoning someone in AA if angry or lonely, getting rest if tired.

## SUMMARY

Nurses play a key role in helping a person in recovery to identify and respond to vulnerable moments. At one level, nurses can reinforce basic self-care skills:

- eating meals regularly
- not isolating
- not holding resentments
- not getting overtired

Healing from addiction occurs in these small steps, in making these moment-by-moment life-affirming choices. In time, these small steps begin to create in a person the sense that she can live without chemicals, that she can take care of herself.

This developing sense of trust in self brings with it a compassion for all of the suffering and vulnerability she has experienced. At this level, nurses are assisting a healing process that goes far beyond stopping drinking and drugging. They are assisting people in recovery to develop what AA calls a new consciousness. It is important for nurses to hold this big picture of healing addictions. The beginning small steps of recovery are the movement toward a sense of wholeness.

# REFLECTIONS

Can you remember a time when you felt very vulnerable and shared your feelings with someone else? What was the outcome of this?

Can you remember a time when you felt very vulnerable but kept the feelings to yourself? What was the outcome of this?

## References

Beck, A., & Emery, G. (1985). *Anxiety disorders and phobias: A cognitive perspective.* New York: Basic Books.

Becker, E. (1973). *The denial of death.* New York: Free Press.

Welwood, J. (1982). Vulnerability and power in the therapeutic process. *Journal of Transpersonal Psychology, 14*(2), 125–139.

## Suggested Reading

Becker, E. (1973). *The denial of death.* New York: Free Press.

# 2 | THE CHOICES

# WILLFULNESS, WILL-LESSNESS, AND WILLINGNESS

---

*Think. Decide. Act.*

Slogan in Alcoholics Anonymous

## "THE INNER TYRANT"

Addictions specialist Richard Hartnett (1994) identified the "*inner tyrant,*" a self-attacking, destructive mental pattern in the addicted person's thinking process. He sees this inner tyrant as a key aspect of addiction and, therefore, as a key aspect of recovery. To recover, Hartnett sees the absolute need for the tyrant to yield to a more balanced, more compassionate inner voice—the "healthy self." The "*healthy self*" is an inner voice that is a source of guidance and wisdom. Without the development of this "healthy self," the tyrant will continue to cause the kinds of feelings that lead into relapse of the addiction.

## CASE STUDY | *Ed*

Sitting on the bus, Ed observes the other passengers and finds something wrong with each one of them. In his mind, he silently insults their facial expressions, their ethnic category, their clothes, and so on. He has been sober for twenty years. He resents most people and sometimes wonders if he should drink and say to hell with everyone.

### *Observations*

It is important to understand Ed's use of his mind. Such mental hostility toward others, such silent attacks on everyone for the most petty reasons, serves an important function for him. By continuing to feed his anger, he avoids how he really feels, unstable and afraid. His mind is used to scan, assess, criticize, and ridicule others in order to make them unimportant and harmless. He never tells anyone how he thinks. He would be too worried about anyone finding out. He keeps the "inner tyrant" a secret.

At times, this inner tyrant turns inward, towards Ed, and reminds him of missed opportunities, of mistakes, of humiliations. Some of these memories will be from forty or even fifty years ago. He still has not let go of them, still has not forgiven himself or others for these long-gone events. In these moments, he moves from anger to remorse. He moves from being an angry man to being a sad, self-pitying victim. This feeling then carries him all the way back to his boyhood sixty years ago, visualizing himself as the fat little kid who stayed by himself. He does not look back with compassion, but instead turns his mental attack, his inner tyrant, on the child of his memory.

At age 68, after twenty years of sobriety, Ed felt like a fraud. He would tell everyone about the wonders of sobriety and all the benefits he had gotten from AA. He had gotten benefits—sobriety and sanity—but in some ways he felt like he had not changed at all. He could no longer stand his hostility, his unhappiness.

He first chose to start a new AA meeting. He designed it for people like himself in long-term recovery. He rightly made the assumption that there were other people in recovery like him who still needed more, who still were searching for more. (The autobiographical stories of Bill Wilson, one of AA's founders, are characterized by his lifelong search for more wisdom and peace.) Secretly, Ed hoped that the new meeting would help him feel safe and happier inside. Unfortunately, he conducted them with his edge of hostility. He was using the meeting to feel good about himself but was not touching the source of his hostility.

## THE NEED FOR A SECOND RECOVERY

Ed required recovery from his brutal childhood as well as recovery from addiction. He had used alcohol to protect himself. Then, in recovery, he used hostility as protection. Now his protection was harming him. When you encounter a person in recovery with Ed's level of anger and self-pity, remember that you are dealing with someone who is very afraid. You can treat it as a formula that such anger reveals, just below the surface, great vulnerability.

He was still reactive and fearful in very young ways. He needed what we call "a second recovery." *Second recovery* is the need to recover from childhood trauma as well as from addiction. (More on the second recovery is discussed in chapter 9.) When the new meeting did not alleviate his unhappiness, he finally decided to go to counseling with a nurse therapist. In all of his years of sobriety, he had always been against counseling. He had felt that AA would take care of everything for him. He also shared the animosity and the mistrust that some AA members feel towards professionals.

His decision to go to counseling was very brave. He was in essence going with the knowledge that he would probably have to give up his primary protection of hostility. This would in turn mean he would have to face his vulnerability and admit it to the nurse. At age 68, Ed began another healing.

## Tomeka

Tomeka has been sober for eight years. She needs to make an important phone call regarding work. Instead, she goes to the video store and rents ten videos. She tells herself that she just needs to take it easy for a while. There is nothing bad expected in the work phone call, but she just wants to stay away from it as long as possible. She reasons that she has already paid for these video rentals, and so it would be a waste of money not watch the films. She never makes the call. The next day, she goes to work, nervously expecting something bad to happen.

Tomeka proceeds to have a miserable day at work. The failure to make the phone call has resulted in more work for herself and her coworker. She avoids her supervisor all morning. She quietly berates herself, saying, "I'm unbelievably stupid." This thought makes her feel like isolating even more than she has been.

At lunch time, Tomeka makes a healing choice. She walks out of her office into a beautiful, sunny day. The warmth of the sun lifts her mood, and she feels ready for a change. She is so tired of her old patterns and behaviors. She decides to take a long walk. While on the walk, she resolves to face her fears. She will speak to her supervisor when she gets back from lunch. She also chooses to break her isolation by calling a friend and making plans for the weekend.

## THE SPECTRUM OF CHOICES

Choice is the key recovery technique. It is therefore crucial to assess the kinds of choices people in recovery are making in response to vulnerability.

Our ability to choose is our free will. We say, for example, that we are "willing" to do something. That means we choose to give our energy to the situation. At other times, we are "unwilling" to become involved. In such a case, we withhold our energy. We may also find ourselves at times being "willful." We might also call this using our willpower. In such situations, we are forcing our energy into a situation. Alternatively, we may at times feel we have no will, no choice. We feel powerless. In the late stage, addiction is an experience of no will.

## *Willful, Will-less, Willing*

We can say, then, that we can choose to use our energy in three different ways: willfully, will-lessly, and willingly. As addiction psychiatrist Gerald May (1988) put it: "Willingness and willfulness become possibilities every time we truly engage life. There is only one other option—to avoid engagement entirely [will-less-ness]." *Willfulness* is a forceful use of our energy. *Willingness* is a balanced use of our energy. *Will-lessness* is a complete withdrawal of our energy.

Willfulness shows itself when we make the following choices:

• power
• force
• exertion
• strain
• contraction
• constriction
• compression
• violence
• manipulation
• drivenness
• control

If we think in terms of the fight or flight reaction to fear, then willfulness is the fight reaction to vulnerability. Ed, sitting on the bus, uses his "inner tyrant" to attack people.

Will-lessness shows itself when we make the following choices:

• numbing
• collapse

- escape

- withdrawal

- giving up

- immobilization

It is the flight reaction to vulnerability. Tomeka, sitting in her apartment watching one of her ten videos, escapes from making the phone call. She has withdrawn into her safe, circumscribed space.

**Dangerous Choices**   Tomeka is getting rid of her vulnerability by making herself numb. Ed is getting rid of his vulnerability by trying to feel powerful. Both have made choices. For the person in recovery, they are both dangerous choices. They are dangerous because they cover up the vulnerability that is being experienced. Tomeka and Ed may not be using drugs or alcohol, but they are still using denial. Neither of them has yet acknowledged the truth of their vulnerability. This is very important to see. Made repeatedly, willfulness or will-lessness puts the person further and further away from the real emotional work of recovery—responding effectively to vulnerability.

**Mood Swings**   Made repeatedly, willfulness and will-lessness also set up a pattern of mood swings. *Mood swings* are rapid shifts in emotional states. Willfulness is exertion, and in time the willful person in recovery exhausts her energy. She then commonly swings toward lethargy, will-lessness. Ed swings from mental hostility toward others to a sinking, hopeless feeling that he cannot adjust to the world. He feels as afraid as when he was a boy. Will-lessness is stagnant energy. It is a nondirected struggle. In time, it fills the person in recovery with a panicky sense of dread. She will then swing toward forcing herself to take action in an urgent way. Tomeka swings temporarily from numbness staring at the videos to a mood of anger and paranoia about something that was said to her yesterday at work. Her mind drifts off from the video to a daydream of getting revenge.

These swings only worsen normal vulnerability. They keep the person feeling out of balance. They cause a kind of chronic instability. It is therefore crucial to assess if the person in recovery is making repeated willful and will-less choices.

## A Holistic View

Framing the behaviors in this way is very helpful for the person in recovery. It makes sense, in a nonjudgmental way, of behaviors that are familiar and readily identifiable. Using a holistic approach, we can observe the manifestations of willfulness and will-lessness on the mental functioning, emotional responses, physical states, and spiritual life of the individual. A *holistic approach* is a bio-psycho-social-spiritual view of the person, consistent with traditional nursing philosophy.

## THE UNIVERSALITY OF WILLFULNESS AND WILL-LESSNESS

As we enter this discussion on willfulness and will-lessness, it is important to understand the commonality and universality of these patterns. They are not only seen in people in addiction and recovery. They are seen in everyone in every circumstance. They are universal patterns of reactivity to unsafe feelings. They can be seen in the animal world as clearly as in the human world. When trapped, some animals will get violently aggressive (willful), while others will freeze and "play dead" (will-less). These reactive patterns are rooted in our instinctive, fight/flight impulses. Their entire intention is to protect ourselves, to survive. From this viewpoint, there is no judgment about the nature of these patterns. They are natural attempts to preserve life and should be respected. Our argument is simply that, made repeatedly, these patterns put us out of balance and cause harm to ourselves and others. There will be times when willfulness is the healthiest reaction to have. There are other times when will-lessness is the best choice by far.

### EXERCISES

### Willfulness and Will-lessness

In the next chapter, we will explore the spectrum of willful and will-less choices seen on the mental, emotional, physical, and spiritual levels. These exercises will give you some personal information for reflection as you go on to the next chapter.

Read the suggested willful images, go through them in your imagination, and then make some notes for yourself. Do the same with the suggested will-less images.

## *Willfulness*

**1.** Follow your breathing . . . let it center you.

**2.** Once you are feeling centered, close your eyes and imagine a willful person that you know . . . Notice the effect the willful person has on your centered feeling.

**3.** Now notice what you feel as you imagine that willful person approaching you.

**4.** Can you identify with this person's way of being or is it totally foreign to you?

## *Will-lessness*

**1.** Follow your breathing . . . let it center you.

**2.** Once you are feeling centered, close your eyes and imagine a will-less person that you know . . . Notice the effect the will-less person has on your centered feeling.

**3.** Now notice what you feel as you imagine that will-less person approaching you.

**4.** Can you identify with this person's way of being or is it totally foreign to you?

## *Discussion*

We each tend to choose one style of will again and again. For one person, a moment of vulnerability leads to two days of withdrawal (will-less). For another person, a moment of vulnerability leads to anger and violent fantasies (willful) that go on for hours after the minor incident is over. Becoming self-aware of our style, our habitual choice, gives us the option of considering other uses of our will. With awareness, our choices increase. Without awareness, our habits deepen.

# SUMMARY

Human will is the directing of consciousness, intention, and energy. Consciousness, intention, and energy can be utilized for or against the person's health and development. In recovery, the utilization of human will can be seen in the choices a person is making. The choices can lead toward deeper recovery or toward inner struggle and relapse. The nurse can assist the person in examining and optimizing the choice process.

# REFLECTIONS

Do you make any addictive choices? What are they?

What are your healing choices?

### References

Hartnett, R. (1994). *The three inner voices.* New York: Serenity Publications.

May, G. (1988). *Addiction and grace.* San Francisco: Harper.

### Suggested Reading

Assagioli, R. (1974). *Act of will.* New York: Penguin Books.

Hartnett, R. (1994). *The three inner voices.* New York: Serenity Publications.

# 7 | WILLFULNESS

*Despite your wishes, you were conceived.*
*Despite your wishes, you were born.*
*Despite your wishes, you live.*
*Despite your wishes, you die.*
*Despite your wishes, you are destined to deal*
   *with the consequences of your actions.*
*So get on with it.*

Rabbi Eliezar ha Kappar

Willfulness can pervade inner and outer behaviors in every aspect of life. We can operationalize the specific behaviors, attitudes, and responses that are associated with this way of being. Figure 7.1 (see page 85) illustrates the spectrum of willfulness.

## MENTAL WILLFULNESS

Mental willfulness is the misuse of the mind to feel power and control.

## Marshall

Marshall is a 40-year-old man eight years in recovery from alcoholism and marijuana addiction. He was a college graduate who had at one time taught high school math. He lost his job as a teacher fifteen years ago because he was caught smoking marijuana in his car on his lunch break. He never accepted the fact that this was inappropriate behavior for a high school teacher, maintaining that the principal and other teachers were jealous of him. He pridefully insisted that he was the most popular teacher in the school because he could relate to the kids. He never returned to teaching because he said the system was filled with losers and control freaks.

Marshall worked intermittently in construction, and his wife provided the primary family income working as a waitress. He constantly found fault with any authority figures, and in fact discouraged his wife from completing college because she was only buying into the system. He finally joined AA at his wife's insistence and stopped his substance abuse, but never changed his thinking. He continued to earn a minimal and unreliable income, frequently losing jobs because of conflicts with supervisors. His only socializing was with a friend from AA, and their usual conversation was about how they had been victimized by the system just because they had refused to fit in. After Marshall's wife left him, Marshall moved back to his hometown and lived with his recently widowed mother.

## *Rigidity*

Mental willfulness is characterized by rigidity of thinking. If we understand that the intention underlying willful thinking is to ward off vulnerability, then it makes sense that forming rigid, dogmatic attitudes would be one way to create an illusion of power. The person always has the answer. There are no unexplainable questions. The refusal to tolerate ambiguity, confusion, or relativity results in a reliance on a black-and-white view of the world. Consequently, judgmental attitudes and intolerance of indecision are common characteristics. Extremes of this result in prejudice, racism, and fanaticism.

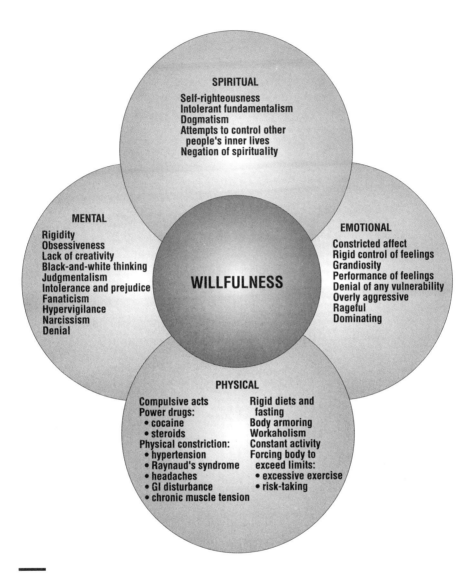

**FIGURE 7.1    *The spectrum of willfulness***

Marshall never felt capable of, nor did he ever succeed in, making it on his own. He was dependent on his wife. When she left, he returned to being dependent on his mother. This vulnerability was never acknowledged by Marshall. Instead, he built walls of rigid and hostile thinking around himself.

## The Dry Drunk

In AA, there is a personality pattern referred to as the dry drunk. The *dry drunk* is not drinking (is therefore "dry") but has retained all the mental characteristics of his substance-abusing days. A person such as Marshall is exhibiting the classic pattern of acting like the world's greatest expert or a grandiose know-it-all. He has remained fixated at the very first level of recovery, abstinence.

## Obsessing

Mental rigidity can also be seen in obsessive and hostile thought patterns. Like Ed in chapter 6, the person may ruminate about past injustices and embarrassments. Commonly, the person continues the patterns of projection and denial that protected his addiction. We can observe that Marshall removed substances from the picture, but these mental mechanisms are being used to justify why he is not succeeding in his present life.

## Lack of Creativity

Absence of creativity, poor adaptability, and paucity of problem-solving skills all result from this constricted thought pattern. The mind is preoccupied by vigilance and anger. It is not given the ability to relax, to imagine, to intuit. The person is cut off from some of the most resourceful and adaptive qualities of the mind.

# EMOTIONAL WILLFULNESS

Emotional willfulness is the misuse of feelings to gain power and control.

## Dennis

Dennis is a 38-year-old married man with two teenage daughters. He had been an alcoholic for over twenty years and stopped drinking four years ago. During his active alcoholism, he had never been physically violent, but his seething, underlying rage was expressed through his demeaning and sarcastic comments to his wife and daughters. This behavior continued after he stopped drinking. As his daughters were approaching adolescence, he insisted on unreasonable and punitive restrictions on their social life. He was constantly finding fault with their friends. When he was angered by something "stupid" his wife or daughters had done, he would show it by giving them the silent treatment, at times refusing to speak to them for as long as a week.

## Rage

Dennis displays classic characteristics of emotional willfulness. This is a man who had stopped using substances; that was the full extent of his recovery. He had not allowed himself to acknowledge any vulnerability. Instead, he had intensified the wall around his emotions, occasionally allowing for explosive verbal displays of rage that were then "resolved" by silence. His refusal to acknowledge his own fears of being out of control resulted in him projecting these feelings onto his daughters.

### Constricted Affect

Another variation of emotional willfulness is constricted affect. The person exerts control over expression of any feeling. This is Dennis's silent treatment which he exhibits after his outbursts of rage.

### Performance of Feelings

*Performance of feelings* is an insincere, false, contrived, and seductive emotional style used by the person to manipulate and control others. This inauthentic display of emotions can be very convincing. For the person who uses it, it can become so deeply habituated that she loses awareness of any genuine emotional experience.

### Grandiosity

Grandiosity is a prime willful emotion. It heightens the person's mood through (1) inner fantasies of self-worth and (2) criticizing the worth of others. Since grandiosity is not based on anything real, it eventually collapses, usually through a slight or criticism. Then the person swings into the will-less emotion of humiliation. This is a classic emotional pattern found in many people in recovery. The root of the pattern is humiliation and vulnerability, but the grandiosity (the defense) will be more obvious and on the surface. If you are dealing with a person in recovery who displays grandiosity, you can predict with absolute certainty that he is easily humiliated.

## PHYSICAL WILLFULNESS

Physical willfulness is the misuse of the body's energy in a forceful, strained, constricted way to exert power and control. Within the addictions, examples of physical willfulness can be seen in:

- anorexia
- power drugs such as cocaine, steroids, amphetamines
- addiction to exercise
- forcing the body to exceed physical limits
- addiction to excitement and adrenalin through physical risk-taking behaviors

### Gloria

Gloria is a 30-year-old nurse recovering from cocaine addiction. During her adolescence, she had been preoccupied with her weight, often taking nonprescription dieting aids or laxatives. When she went to college, she started using cocaine on a daily basis. She liked it because it made her feel confident and it reduced her appetite. Gloria stopped using cocaine six months ago and has taken up jogging to prevent her from gaining weight. She also loves the high she feels when she runs. Gloria has to run at least eight miles a day even when she has injuries; if she does not, she feels her sobriety is threatened.

## *Physical Symptoms of Willfulness*

Physical willfulness is characterized by physical strain, exertion, force, and inflexibility. These ways of being in the body result in physical constriction. There are a range of medical problems that result from this constriction:

- the constriction of blood vessels leading to hypertension
- Raynaud's syndrome
- headaches
- muscle spasms
- gastrointestinal disturbances

## *Physically Willful Acts*

Physical willfulness is also expressed through physical activities that are attempts to use, control, or manipulate the body in ways that create feelings of power or invulnerability. Behaviors such as excessive exercising, as seen in Gloria, create the illusion that one can exert control over life. Gloria will force her body to bend to her will. It will not be stopped by fatigue, injury, bad weather, or the pressure of other responsibilities.

Typical manifestations of physically willful acts include:

- rigid diets, excessive fasting, and anorexia
- risk-taking behaviors such as driving a car aggressively and recklessly
- participating in dangerous sports
- the extremes of bodybuilding

These behaviors are often treated with pride as indications of mastery and victory. Even though they may bear a resemblance to athleticism and health-promoting activities, they are in fact damaging and destructive to the body. The body's signals are ignored and defied.

## Willful Drugs

Physical willfulness also expresses itself in the attraction to drugs that increase energy and a sense of power. These drugs include cocaine, steroids, methamphetamines, and caffeine.

A recent *New York Times* article ("Good People," 1996) described an increase in methamphetamines used to stay awake for days on end and to create feelings of euphoria and energy. It was also described as particularly popular with long-haul truckers and factory workers who had to force themselves to stay awake through tedium, boredom, and excessively long hours.

## Body Armoring

Another form physical willfulness can take is body armoring. *Body armoring* is the conscious and unconscious control of the body as a major coping style, resulting in rejection of the body as a source of pleasure or contact. This is often present in people who have experienced physical or sexual abuse. Extreme control of the body is an attempt to ward off the profound vulnerability that the abuse has created. In such cases, it is important to remember that a second recovery is necessary.

Recovery from addiction will be the first step in this healing process, but not all subsequent symptoms and struggles should be related to postaddiction issues. There are many people in drug treatment who require attention to their second recovery issues. Second recovery is discussed in more detail in chapter 9.

## Drivenness

Finally, physical willfulness is seen in *drivenness,* the desperate need for constant activity and busyness, done with a sense of time urgency (sometimes referred to as hurry sickness). It is clearly seen in workaholism. The dilemma with many of these physically willful behaviors is that they are admired and rewarded by the popular culture. Extremes of this include the anorectic fashion models who sustain their appearance by starvation, nicotine addiction, and other drug use, or the workaholic businessperson who is so successful that he has no time for a personal life or meaningful intimate relationships.

## SPIRITUAL WILLFULNESS

Spiritual willfulness is the misuse of spirituality to feel power and control. Such willfulness is often the cause of the abuse that can take place in religious and spiritual groups.

### Barbara and Peter

Barbara, a 42-year-old woman in recovery from alcoholism, spoke to Peter, a clergyman she met through AA. She was seeking some spiritual guidance. Barbara remembered that her spiritual life had been important to her as a child. She wanted to revive it as part of her healing. She had heard a lot about spirituality in AA, but she had doubts about how real it was for her.

She spoke to Peter about her most personal spiritual feelings. She described visiting a cathedral in Italy and being moved to tears by the beauty of the place. She described walking along the beach early in the morning, watching the sun rise, and feeling incredibly joyful. She talked to him about her love of singing, feeling herself merge and lose herself in the music. She described these experiences as her sense of spirituality and explained that these were the kinds of experiences that gave her peace. She also talked about her struggle with the structure of organized religion.

Peter seemed to be listening thoughtfully and intently. Suddenly, he interrupted her and told her, "Spirituality is more than just your female hormones acting up." He went on to tell her the only true higher power was Jesus Christ, and she should stop wasting her time and his time trying to make up her own spirituality.

## Shame Reaction

Barbara, new to recovery and unsure of herself in every area of her life, was at first devastated by what Peter said. She ended the meeting and went out to the street, feeling lightheaded and ungrounded. She also felt great shame, as if she had done something very wrong. Her mind did not really agree with Peter, but for a while her mind was overwhelmed by her feelings. Her feelings told her she was bad and stupid. She felt very, very young, a 42-year-old child ashamed of herself, walking down the street in a world of adults.

A *shame reaction* is exactly this, the state of feeling bad about yourself even though you did nothing wrong. For people like Barbara, it is important in time to realize that shame is distorting their thinking.

## Self-Care Skills

Barbara did know enough at a moment like this to find someplace where she could be quiet for a moment and focus on her breathing. The nurse in the rehabilitation center had taught her breathing techniques as a way to center herself in moments of stress and vulnerability. *Centering* is the conscious act of quieting and focusing the mind and body.

Barbara remembered those teaching lessons with great affection. Frightened about life, frightened by her unreadiness for living without alcohol, she remembered the moments of peace that would come to her as she followed the nurse's instructions. As the nurse, you must remember that you are not only teaching recovery skills, you are teaching life skills. Those brief lessons in breathing as centering had now become a basic self-care skill for Barbara.

Barbara decided to find a cafe where she could sit, do her breathing exercise, and have some soothing chamomile tea. She sat at a corner table and began to recall the nurse's instructions to turn her attention to her breathing, to notice it just the way it is, and to let all other thoughts and feelings fade into the background of her awareness. As she did this, she began to feel more present, more grounded, less frightened. Her mind, her thinking, began to become more available to her.

Barbara imagined the scene of talking with Peter. She imagined his face as he was interrupting her and scolding her.

She realized that *scolding* was the right word; that was actually how she felt. She was being scolded for having done something wrong. As she imagined Peter's face, she saw the desperation in it. She saw his need to be the one who knows, the one who must be listened to. Barbara began to understand Peter's urgent need to be the expert. She also began to understand why some people in AA thought Peter knew everything and why others would not go near him. She felt some anger for what he had done to her, and with the coming of the anger the shame began to fade. Her anger was intelligent; it was the emotion that rose up to defend her.

Having centered, having taken time out to reflect, she decided that she would find someone else to talk to about her recovery and her spirituality. She did not have to get revenge or argue with Peter. She needed to move forward in her recovery.

Anger can help the person go beyond her fear. Then the person must get on with the business of living and let the anger go.

## Peter's "Expertise"

Peter, two blocks away, was still busy in his mind thinking of his conversation with Barbara. People like her infuriated him. He was convinced that they did not know what they were talking about.

Spiritual willfulness asserts itself in the same way as willfulness expressed mentally, emotionally, and physically. It moves into control, power, anger, and manipulation. People like Peter clearly cannot tolerate ambiguity. Everything must be one way, their way. They cannot tolerate doubts. Peter sounded as if he had all the answers, but in fact what he had was a fear of not knowing.

If we could enter his mind, we would find swings from absolute knowing to absolute self-doubt. We encountered this same pattern in the discussion of grandiosity and humiliation as a pattern within emotional willfulness. Peter's swings from all-knowing to knowing nothing are the spiritual equivalents of swinging from grandiosity to humiliation emotionally. For Peter, he simply could not spend much time not knowing. Not knowing was too vulnerable. It gave him the sense he was lost in a large world. When this vulnerability was touched, he quickly swung back toward spiritual grandiosity, back toward being the spiritual expert. He imposed this "expertise" on Barbara.

Spiritual willfulness similar to Peter's can manifest itself in the following forms:

- self-righteousness
- fanaticism
- attempts to monitor other people's inner lives
- the intolerant forms of fundamentalism and dogmatism

There can be tolerant forms of fundamentalism and dogmatism. The person can accept such spirituality for himself but not impose it on others.

# Victor

Victor was a 35-year-old recovering alcoholic diagnosed as HIV positive. He had been in counseling for the past year to help him with his fears and his declining energy. He had been a professional singer for many years. He had a great love of art and integrated many creative activities into his life.

In addition to counseling, his nurse therapist had introduced Victor to meditation as an adjunctive help for his fears. He had many interesting experiences through meditation and discussed them in his counseling sessions. He felt supported by the nurse in his meditative explorations and also felt the meditation contained even more potential for the difficult days he knew were ahead for him.

One of his most fascinating meditative experiences was a sense that his consciousness could travel and experience other dimensions of reality. (**Note:** Larry Dossey's book *Recovering The Soul*, 1989, has an especially grounded discussion of the possibilities of consciousness.) This sense of the expansion of consciousness was reassuring to him when contemplating his own death.

Victor had very limited financial resources and had lost his health insurance. He became aware of a research project at a major medical center that was exploring the relationship of stress reduction with long-term survival for HIV patients. In exchange for participating in this project, he would receive free medical care. He eagerly joined the program. The treatment modality was a psychotherapy approach to stress management.

In his first session with the new therapist, Victor enthusiastically told him about his meditation practice and all he had learned about an expanded sense of reality. The therapist listened with disdain to Victor's descriptions. The therapist could barely tolerate such ideas and felt completely certain that Victor was indulging in wishful thinking and escapism. While the therapist tried to appear as if he were still listening to Victor, his mind was in fact preparing to confront Victor's thinking process as irrational. The therapist had no doubts about his own opinion and was unable to give Victor's perceptions any respect. The therapist himself had had no such meditative experiences. In fact, he rejected the whole idea of meditating. He also had never read any spiritual literature. Despite this, he was sure, almost aggressively absolute, about his viewpoint on what Victor had experienced.

## Negation of Spirituality

A very different manifestation of spiritual willfulness is observed in people who refuse to consider any concept of a higher power, universal reality, or larger sense of life's purpose, cycles, and processes. They display a prideful insistence that their logic can understand everything. As with Victor's new therapist, they demean and dismiss any consideration of spiritual reality as irrational or illogical. They aggressively reject anything that has not yet been proven by science. Recently, the psychological literature has begun to support meditation practice for its physical, mental, and emotional benefits (Kabat-Zinn, 1991; Levey, 1987; Murphy, 1993; Schaub, 1995a, 1995b).

# SUMMARY

Willfulness is characterized by rigidity and the need to control self and others. At its core are fears of loss of control and the unknown. The control is an attempt to wall off conscious awareness of the essential vulnerability. The resulting effect is the loss of creativity, the loss of openness to possibilities, the loss of meaningful relationships, and spiritual isolation. This pattern, like will-lessness, prevents the person in recovery from experiencing her full healing potential.

# REFLECTIONS

Do you recognize any patterns of willfulness in yourself?

Are there any people in your life who are very willful? If so, what effect do they have on you?

## References

Dossey, L. (1989). *Recovering the soul.* New York: Bantam.
Good people go bad in Iowa, and a drug is blamed. (1996, February 22). *New York Times,* A1–A19.
Kabat-Zinn, J. (1991). *Full catastrophe living.* New York: Delta.
Levey, J. (1987). *The fine arts of relaxation, concentration and meditation.* London: Wisdom Publications.
Murphy, M. (1993). *The future of the body.* Los Angeles: Tarcher.
Schaub, R. (1995a). Alternative health and spiritual practices. *Alternative Health Practitioner, 1*(1), 35–38.
Schaub, R. (1995b). Meditation, adult development, and health. *Alternative Health Practitioner, 1*(3), 205–209.

## Suggested Reading

Dossey, L. (1989). *Recovering the soul.* New York: Bantam.

*Chapter*

8 WILL-LESSNESS

*Those who stay awake too late at night
    neglect the body;
Those who walk alone
    neglect the heart;
Those who allow the mind to be idle
    neglect the soul.
All these forfeit life—
Even while they live, they are dead.*

Rabbi Chanina ben Chachinai

Willfulness is about power. In contrast, will-lessness is about numbness. Vulnerability is avoided by behaviors that are diffuse, chaotic, ineffectual, confused, escapist. Acts of will-lessness look on the surface to be without choice. The nurse, however, should be aware that choice is very much involved in will-lessness. Figure 8.1 illustrates the spectrum of will-lessness.

## MENTAL WILL-LESSNESS

Mental will-lessness is the misuse of the mind to feel numb. The forms of mental will-lessness include:

- chronic refusal to decide
- numbing of mental processes through disconnection and disassociation
- unthinking acceptance of others' thoughts and desires
- victimized thinking

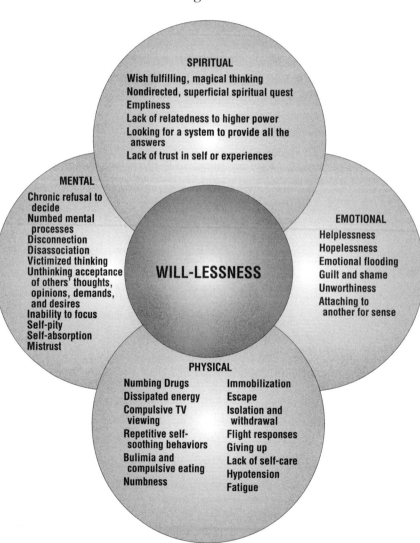

*FIGURE 8.1    The spectrum of will-lessness*

## CASE STUDY | *Wayne*

After alcohol detoxification and a thirty-day rehabilitation program, Wayne briefly attended AA. He did not like the spiritual language and stopped going. He then found out about a private recovery group through someone at work. The person told Wayne that the group leader was keeping a lot of people sober. This should have been a sign to Wayne that something was wrong. The group leader was not keeping anyone sober. No one keeps another person sober. No one makes another person relapse back to drugs. People in recovery stay sober because they have made an inner decision.

Wayne attended a meeting and was impressed by the group leader. The leader had ten years of sobriety and appeared to be confident, successful, and relaxed in the world. Wayne desperately wanted to feel this way himself. He saw such a possibility as very far away. He had no idea how to get to this goal. Wayne hoped that by being with the leader, he would also begin to feel like the leader seemed to feel. The other people in the group also seemed to feel the leader had some secret of living that they wanted.

During many of the group sessions, the leader gave ultimatums to the members. For example, he would announce that one of the members was sure to drink again if he stayed married. Another member, after reporting that her brother had concerns about the group leader's tactics, was told by the leader that her brother was compromising her sobriety and was obviously sick himself. She was then told to cut off all contact with her brother.

The group leader also pressured them to recruit members for the group. As a result of this pressure, some members would recruit their spouses or partners or relatives or coworkers. Wayne had been recruited this way. The recruitment was given special status as proof that the group members were truly committed to their own sobriety. This lead to some group members seeming to have the group leader's affections, while other members were openly labeled as sicker and less committed to their own health.

When anyone complained about this favoritism, the group leader would challenge the ability of their druggy minds to know anything. The group leader was clearly using the members' fear of relapse as a way to keep them dependent on him. He constantly challenged their judgment and told them to listen to him.

After being in the group for three months, Wayne felt in turmoil about his experience there. He was not drinking, so perhaps the group was helping him. On the other hand, he had begun to hate to go to the groups. Was that because he secretly wanted to drink again? Wayne went to an individual meeting with the group leader and told him that he was thinking of quitting the group. The group leader got angry and announced Wayne's worst fears—leaving the group now was a sure sign that Wayne would relapse.

Wayne visited his former rehabilitation program and spoke with the nurse there. He said his group therapist was angry at him. Why was his therapist angry? Because Wayne said he might leave therapy. Why would this make the therapist angry? Wayne did not know. Why was Wayne thinking of leaving therapy? Because the therapist ran groups in which he controlled and humiliated people. So why did Wayne stay? Because he might have a relapse and drink again. Why did Wayne think he would drink again? Because the therapist told Wayne that if he left him, it was a sure sign that Wayne would have a relapse. Wayne was oblivious to the blatant manipulation in this situation.

### Observations

In Wayne's case, his fear kept him from thinking his experiences through to their conclusion. His perceptions of the manipulations and humiliations in the group were definitely disturbing him. He was just not willing to let his perceptions tell him what to do. He was just not willing to let his mind fully process what he was experiencing. Fear did not make this processing impossible, but it certainly did make it more difficult. Wayne chose not to focus his mind on his perceptions. He distracted himself whenever he began to try to think the situation through and make a decision.

## Disconnecting from the Mind

Mental activity includes the processing of our rational thinking, our images and imagination, our intuition, our memories, our emotions, and our physical sensations. We instinctively try to synthesize all of these complex experiences and, in time, try to derive learning from the experiences.

We think of the mind as a way to understand things better. But often, in fact, the mind is utilized as a way to know nothing, to avoid, to be numb, to experience oblivion.

Mental will-lessness is a way of refusing to use the mind. A person like Wayne is refusing to learn from experience. Mental will-lessness is the choice of disconnecting from the mind.

## The Need to Trust Instincts and Intuition

At least Wayne's instincts were working for him. By bringing up the subject with the nurse at the rehabilitation center, he was engaging another mind to help him process the experiences. The nurse listened carefully. She was deeply experienced in drug and alcohol rehabilitation. She knew there are a wide range of treatment approaches. She knew that some of them are confrontational with people in recovery, and she balanced out her experience of these confrontational approaches with what she was hearing about Wayne's group. It was clear to her that this group was abusive. She guided Wayne to follow his instincts and perhaps to look into other groups or counseling.

Wayne went back to the group for one meeting. The consultation with the nurse was still fresh in his mind. In fact, he experienced the group as if the nurse were sitting there with him. We could say that he borrowed her mind to help him see clearly. He let himself experience how bad it felt to be there in the group, and he decided to leave.

Years later, he looked back on that period of indecision as a classic example of not trusting his intuition. Eventually, his intuition told him to consult with the nurse, and he chose to act on this. This, in turn, set in motion a healthy decision to leave an abusive situation.

## Chronic Refusal to Decide

Chronic refusal to decide includes the following strategies:

- procrastination
- distraction
- denial

Procrastination is a primary method of protection used by many people in and out of recovery. What does someone accomplish by procrastinating, by staying away from an action or a decision? One avoids setting in motion an unpredictable response to the action or decision. Procrastination is influenced by a foreboding feeling that something bad will happen if the decision is made or the action is taken. Something bad includes rejection, failure, incompetence. No one wants to experience such things. If such negative outcomes are expected, then they can only be avoided by not taking the action or making the decision. If you recall the vignette of Tomeka (chapter 6), she rented ten videos to avoid a single phone call. The belief built into procrastination was that she would be postponing negative outcomes.

## Unthinking Acceptance of Another's Thoughts and Desires

This form of will-lessness is oriented around avoiding conflict at all costs. By agreeing with things that she does not agree with and by accepting things that are unacceptable, the person in recovery seeks to keep others placated. This is a skill learned by children of alcoholics to keep their father or mother calm. The outer conflict is avoided. The inner conflict is not. The person using this form suffers greatly inside while at the same time feeling some relief that she has kept everyone else happy and, therefore, not angry at her.

## Victimized Thinking

*Victimized thinking* is a mental pattern pervaded by self-reference, self-absorption, and self-pity. It often disguises anger at others and anger against the self for being so fearful. It often leads to a decision to do nothing or to justify self-destructive behavior.

## Jane

Jane expressed despair about world politics. She said that nothing ever changes, and that good people are always crushed by power-hungry leaders. She concluded that her relapse to smoking cigarettes (nicotine addiction) was a minor matter compared to the sick world she has to live in. Within an attitude of hopelessness, this makes perfect sense: the world is a terrible place, it makes her upset, she needs something, give in, smoke, it does not matter anyway.

### Observations

Jane views the world as something being done personally to her. She rationalizes that she cannot fight all the depressing realities of life. This kind of thinking can pervade a person, fostering a sense of powerlessness. It also serves as an excuse for not taking any healthy actions. It reflects the chronic self-absorption that is part of the addictive process.

# EMOTIONAL WILL-LESSNESS

Emotional will-lessness is an emphasis on hopeless and helpless feelings and moods in order to be too numb to make decisions and take actions.

### Evelyn

Early in Evelyn's recovery from addiction to pills, she began a relationship with Frank, a much older man she had met at AA meetings. Evelyn felt enormous relief in dating someone who was sober. She felt Frank totally understood her and could take care of her. She became dependent on him. At the same time, she panicked at any hint of problems in the relationship, believing she was too weak to stay sober without Frank's help.

We said that mental will-lessness is refusing to participate in mental processing. Emotional will-lessness is feeling at the mercy of every passing mood, impulse, and reaction. The person is easily overwhelmed in this state. She may have great difficulty in recognizing she has the capacity to step back and make a different emotional choice.

## *Attaching to Another for Sense of Self*

Evelyn's story is typical of early recovery in which women are very vulnerable to any sexual relationship seen as rescuing. This dynamic is recognized as a problem in AA and is referred to as thirteenth stepping. The AA advice is not to enter into any new relationship in the first year of recovery.

Evelyn's attachment to pills had been very intense. Removing them from her life left her with a sense of emptiness, a void. She was preoccupied with anxiety and vulnerability. This made it impossible for her to feel any new sense of herself. Anxiety kept her just trying to survive. In Frank, she saw someone she could be—Frank's girlfriend. She projected onto him what she needed in order to go through early recovery. She did not have any particular feelings for him. In actuality, she was emotionally numb as often as she could be in order to blunt the anxiety.

## *Guilt and Shame*

In chapter 7, Barbara was described in the vignette regarding Peter's spiritual willfulness. Barbara left her meeting with Peter full of guilt and shame. He had been insulting and dogmatic, and yet she felt as if she had done something wrong.

There are of course many causes of guilt and shame. In large part, these feelings are conditioned in children in order to make them conform. These feelings are often intensified in recovery when the person begins to recall the self-debasing behaviors that occurred during addiction.

## *Depression*

Other emotions associated with will-lessness are feelings of hopelessness, helplessness, and unworthiness. These feeling states are classically associated with clinical depression.

## PHYSICAL WILL-LESSNESS

While physical willfulness is characterized by strain, exertion, force, compression, constriction, and rigidity, physical will-lessness is characterized by:

- numbness

- collapse

- escape

- withdrawal

- immobilization

- giving up

- flight responses

These choices can lead to symptomatic levels of:

- hypotension

- loss of libido

- bulimia and compulsive eating

- lack of self-care and attention to personal hygiene

- repetitive self-soothing behaviors such as sexual compulsivity

These symptoms are all related to withdrawal of energy. Hypotension can be thought of as insufficient energy being exerted within the circulatory system. Likewise, a lack of energy and engagement with the world is an aspect of loss of libido. This absence of passion can be reflected in every part of life. Mindless self-soothing such as compulsive masturbating is numbing and enervating. The self-soothing aspect of compulsive food bingeing and purging also brings on a numbness. Again, energy is drained from the person. People often describe feeling lightheaded or stoned after an episode of purging, while overeating results in feeling bloated and lethargic. Lack of attention to personal hygiene reflects withdrawal of energy from even the most basic physical activities.

# *Warren*

Warren, a 58-year-old man, had been sober for fifteen years. He had three grown children who were living on their own, and he lived with his wife. He had worked for a local utility company for the last twenty-five years.

Warren stopped drinking because his boss confronted him with a threat of job loss. His wife had confronted him many times before that, but her threats did not have as much meaning to him. He did not go to any counseling, rehabilitation program, or Alcoholics Anonymous. (**Note:** As was the case with Warren, it is surmised that many people stop addictions without any treatment.)

Warren worked the night shift because there was usually very little work to do at that time. He was often able to nap or watch television during his shift. When he got home from work, he would put on the television to help him fall asleep. When Warren was awake, he kept the television on constantly even if he was occupied with some other activity. Warren's wife complained that he might as well be drinking. He was just as unavailable to her as he had been during his drinking days.

Since the children had moved out of the house, Warren's wife was more upset than ever about his behavior. She had been pressuring him to go to couples' counseling. He was not drinking and he did not understand why his wife had a problem with his behavior.

## *Numbing Behaviors*

Warren displayed lethargy, excessive sleeping, and compulsive TV watching. These are all will-less physical acts performed to avoid any awareness of his feelings. Someone like Warren is no longer drinking alcohol but continues to choose behaviors that are numbing. This choice fits right in with the reason people drink in the later stages of addiction—to experience oblivion.

Warren had started drinking in early adolescence. He had been a shy, lonely, isolated child, and it was only through drinking with friends in junior high school that he started to feel more comfortable. Ending his alcoholism at age 43, he again displayed the emotional development of a shy, lonely boy. His recovery had not included any emotional education or healing of feelings. He had achieved abstinence. He was "dry."

Television is the perfect vehicle for this will-less behavior:

> Not unlike drugs or alcohol, the television experience allows the participant to blot out the real world and enter into a pleasurable and passive mental state. The worries and anxieties of reality are as effectively deferred by becoming absorbed in a television program as by going on a "trip" induced by drugs or alcohol. And just as alcoholics are only vaguely aware of their addiction, feeling that they control their drinking more than they really do . . . people similarly overestimate their control over television watching (Winn, 1977, pp. 24–25).

## SPIRITUAL WILL-LESSNESS

In spiritual willfulness, a person's energy is caught up in knowing all the answers to life's questions. In spiritual will-lessness, the dissipated energy is not enough to even engage in struggling with spiritual questions and answers. The will-less person looks exclusively to others as sources of guidance. She looks to others to provide the energy for the quest.

Will-lessness in spiritual life is characterized by nondirected, immature, magical, superficial, and unfortunately empty attempts to satisfy natural spiritual feelings and impulses.

According to AA, and in accord with the Vulnerability Model, spiritual development is crucial to recovery. It has great relevancy for people in recovery because of their struggle to be at ease in the world, and because of their mistaken attempt—addiction—to avoid feeling vulnerable in the world.

Spiritual will-lessness is therefore a serious problem for the person in recovery.

Spirituality is more general than religion. *Spirituality* is the innate impulse in each person to know about the universe they were born into. Landrum, Beck, Rawlins, Williams, and Culpan (1984) indicated

> Spirituality is at the core of the individual's existence, integrating and transcending the physical, emotional, intellectual, and social dimensions . . . A person's spiritual dimension encompasses much more than, . . . doctrine established by others. This dimension allows one to experience and understand the reality of existence in unique and direct ways that go beyond one's usual limits (p. 303).

# Jessica

Jessica, 46 years old, had abused alcohol, marijuana, and tranquilizers since college. Sober for eighteen years, she attended Alcoholics Anonymous meetings on an infrequent basis. She was married and had a successful business as an interior decorator.

As a child, Jessica had been enriched by her church attendance. Soon after her marriage, however, she stopped going to church. Her husband had always been critical of the churches she attended, finding fault with the minister or the other parishioners. She finally gave up on trying to go because she did not want to go alone. At the same time, she did not want to deal with her husband's negativity.

Jessica was attracted to the spirituality of AA. During the past eighteen years, she had explored many different spiritual practices and philosophies. Each time she found a new spiritual book or group, she would wholeheartedly embrace this new perspective as the answer she had been searching for. She would use her latest spiritual insight as the answer to everything. However, she never followed through on any deeper exploration or practice. She said she could not because her husband would undermine her interests or get angry about them. At the heart of these repeated capitulations was a belief that she could never achieve true insight and knowledge. She believed she was too damaged mentally and emotionally. What would happen if she really tried to develop spiritually and failed? Consequently, she settled for living with a profound sense of emptiness.

Jessica's vignette demonstrates:

- magical thinking
- emptiness
- lack of relatedness to God or some concept of a higher power

## *Magical Thinking*

*Magical thinking* is a child-like belief in having immediate, wish-fulfilling, and simplistic answers to the complex situations of life. In someone like Jessica, magical thinking is based on expecting all the answers to come from outside of herself. As a result, when Jessica found a spiritual method or system of thought, she immediately and without discernment started applying that system's answers to all of her personal problems and her spiritual questions. She wanted desperately to have a system to identify with so that her searching could be over and she could feel safe.

This approach is destined to be unsatisfying, however, because the person never personalizes or integrates any system. She never makes it her own. In Jessica's case, she tried to memorize the ideas and vocabulary of the systems she read about. She quoted spiritual systems without knowing them.

The heart of her magical thinking was hoping a system would have all the answers so that she could avoid the issues of her depression, her poor relationship, and her vulnerability.

## *Lack of Confidence*

Jessica's magical thinking was partly the result of having no confidence in her intelligence. She was a good worker, had friends, and was interested in art and culture, yet she lived with great doubt about her mental ability. She found it difficult to defend her thinking in the face of any conflict. In other words, when she felt anxious and vulnerable, she became mentally will-less. Behind her desire to have a system that had all the answers was her inability to feel confident in her own answers.

## *Emptiness*

A second important factor contributed to Jessica's desire for a system that had all the answers: she was desperate to fill an emptiness. *Emptiness* is an emotional experience marked by absence, longing, varying degrees of numbness, and feeling that something essential is missing. She found it hard to describe this emptiness since it was characterized mostly by what was not there. This specific feeling is actually very well-known to people in AA: it is referred to as the "God hole." The God hole is often described to be in the middle of the chest. This longing for something more was poignantly described by the Indian mystical poet Kabir. Kabir (cited in Bly, 1977) speaks of the longing in this way:

> We sense that there is some sort of spirit that loves
>     birds and animals and the ants—
> perhaps the same one who gave a radiance to you in
>     your mother's womb.
> Is it logical you would be walking around entirely
>     orphaned now?
> The truth is you turned away yourself,
>     and decided to go into the dark alone.
> Now you are tangled up in others, and have forgotten
>     what you once knew,
> and that's why everything you do has some weird
>     failure in it (p. 23).

Written in the fifteenth century, this poem sounds as if it were written for modern people in recovery trying to reestablish their spiritual life.

Mainstream western psychology has shown minimal interest in spirituality and typically interprets such feelings as fixations from childhood. In Part 3, Increasing Peace, we study this feeling for its definite relevancy to the person in recovery.

### *Lack of Relatedness to God or Higher Power*

As a child, Jessica had strong feelings of contact with God. She stopped going to church to avoid conflict with her husband. As an adult, she had not experienced any of the relatedness to God that she enjoyed in childhood. *Relatedness to God* is a feeling of living with a deeper presence in the self and in the world. The lack of this feeling was a loss of major proportions for her.

Jessica offers an example of someone who is blocked from spiritual development by emotional, psychological issues. Most directly, she is cut off from worship because of her fears of her husband's anger. These fears are the result of childhood fears of her father. She cannot assert her spiritual needs with her husband. She never commits herself to regaining or renewing her spiritual life.

## *OBSTACLES TO SPIRITUAL DEVELOPMENT*

Jessica needs the nurse's assistance in recognizing how her spiritual will-lessness keeps her from deeper healing. Spiritual will-lessness is an example of an obstacle to spiritual development. *Obstacles to spiritual development* are emotional attitudes and fears that block the opening of the personality to spiritual consciousness.

*Blocks to spiritual development* are emotional and social fears and attitudes that hinder contact with or expression of the person's innate spirituality. Addressing blocks to spiritual development may sound like territory beyond the nurse's role, but, in fact, the opposite is true. In *Mental Health*

*Psychiatric Nursing* (1984), Shannon, Wahl, Reha, and Dyehouse argued, however:

> . . . the nurse needs to be able to assess the individual's spiritual needs and incorporate them in the nursing care plans. The term spiritual refers to the search for a meaning in life and a belief in powers greater than oneself. In assessing the spiritual dimension, the nurse uses all of her interpersonal skills: listening, communication, observation, and interviewing. Because spiritual needs are often expressed subtly instead of overtly, the nurse needs to be sensitive to detect the expression of spiritual needs (p. 215).

Many people in recovery suffer from blocks to this development and cannot reach this degree of emotional healing. As Landrum et al. (1984) advised:

> The spiritual dimension is the most elusive for many people because of the individual nature of spirituality for each person and because of the tendency, particularly in Western culture, to emphasize what is tangible. Our spiritual dimension deals with a reality that is not tangible and that is more than what we are able to perceive through our senses (p. 303).

People in recovery can move from living in vulnerability to living in wisdom and compassion through their spiritual development. The goals of spiritual development are therefore not abstract or esoteric. They are emotional and practical. Spiritual development is the deeper part of emotional healing: feeling at one in the world. After listening to hundreds of people in recovery over many years, that is the most frequent desire expressed: to feel at ease, centered, and at one in the world.

## SUMMARY

Will-lessness is a choice. Made repeatedly, it does not work. Nevertheless, it must be understood as an attempt to manage vulnerability. In this regard, it needs to be honored. Of course, there are always exceptions. There are times when will-lessness is exactly the best choice, the most intelligent survival technique. The nurse can teach the person in recovery about will-lessness. His understanding of its manifestations on the mental, emotional, physical, and spiritual levels can guide the person to make the healthiest choices possible.

## REFLECTIONS

How do you feel when you experience will-lessness in a person?

Has will-lessness felt like an obstacle for you personally? If so, what forms does your will-lessness take?

### References

Bly, R. (1977). *The Kabir book.* Boston: Beacon.

Landrum, P., Beck, C., Rawlins, R., Williams, S., & Culpan, F. (1984). The person as a client. In C. Beck, R. Rawlins, & S. Williams (Eds.), *Mental health psychiatric nursing: A holistic life-cycle approach* (pp. 286–331). St. Louis: C.V. Mosby.

Shannon, C., Wahl, P., Reha, M., & Dyehouse, J. (1984). The nursing process. In C. Beck, R. Rawlins, & S. Williams (Eds.), *Mental health psychiatric nursing: A holistic life-cycle approach* (pp. 198–236). St. Louis: C.V. Mosby.

Winn, M. (1977). *The plug-in drug.* New York: Penguin.

### Suggested Reading

Schaef, A. (1989). *Escape from intimacy: Untangling the love addictions.* San Francisco: Harper & Row.

# 9 WILLINGNESS

*God grant me the Serenity to accept the things*
  *I cannot change,*
*Courage to change the things I can,*
*and Wisdom to know the difference.*
*Living one day at a time;*
*Enjoying one moment at a time*
*Accepting hardship as the pathway to peace.*

Reinhold Niebuhr

*Although the clear light of reality shines inside their*
*own minds, most people look for it outside.*

Padmasambhava

## *Bill*

Bill was having trouble with his small business. He daydreamed about doing violent things to his competitor. He also daydreamed about letting his business fail and going off to a foreign country and starting life over. What should he do? Should he actually carry out his illegal daydreams or should he get out of business altogether? His feelings went back and forth.

In counseling, it was explained to him that he had to tolerate the uncertainty and ambiguity of his situation. He had to be willing to stay with the discomfort of not knowing. For Bill, this was an emotional challenge. His daydreams of violence and of going off to a foreign country were both impulsive ways to get rid of the uncertainty of his situation.

In his recovery from heroin, he was beginning to learn that there is a middle way in most circumstances. He had to be willing to tolerate ambiguity, one day at a time.

### Observations

The desire to get rid of a feeling is part of the addictive cycle. Bill's impulsive choices, violence or move away, are ways of thinking left over from his addiction. They are self-destructive fantasy answers, having enormous consequences for himself and others. People in addiction make such choices all the time.

The alternative answer, to be willing to struggle with the uncertainty until a good answer emerges, is unattractive. It takes longer, its outcome is uncertain, and it does not get rid of the unpleasantness of the situation. In other words, it extends the duration of the vulnerability. For someone like Bill, this is a key moment for deepening emotional recovery by learning new ways to work through his business troubles.

## WILLINGNESS AS A CHOICE

It bears repeating that willfulness and will-lessness are attempts to maintain health in the face of vulnerability. The fact that you can observe people swinging back and forth between these two ways of being can be recognized as the attempts to achieve homeostasis. The desire is to experience a balanced sense of self, not too anxious or too depressed, not too angry or too afraid. A balanced sense of self has the qualities of feeling centered, grounded, at ease, stable. In this state, you feel you have your inner resources fully available to you. You trust yourself. You feel you can act effectively in the world.

In the face of this desire for a balanced sense of self, the willful and will-less responses need to be honored, not judged as pathological. They simply turn out to be poor choices because, over time, they do not work. Bill swings from impulses toward violence (willfulness) to impulses toward escaping to a monastery (will-lessness) to resolve his business anxieties. Made repeatedly, these swings increase vulnerability and instability. In our model, willingness is seen as the better choice.

## *The Experience of Willing*

The transpersonal psychiatrist Roberto Assagioli said that the inner experience of willing takes place

> . . . During periods of silence and meditation, in the careful examination of our motives, in moments of thoughtful deliberation and decision, a "voice," small but distinct, will sometimes make itself heard, urging us to a specific course of action, a prompting which is different from that of our ordinary motives and impulses. We feel that it comes from the central core of our being (1974, p. 9).

## *Dynamic Balance*

Willingness is not a static state. It is an active balancing between the extremes of willfulness and will-lessness. This ideal of dynamic balance is spoken of in various spiritual and philosophical teachings. It is analogous to:

- the balance of yin and yang energies in Taoism
- the Soto Zen way of effortless effort
- the concept of passive volition in biofeedback training
- the Greek ideal of the golden mean
- the Buddhist path of the middle way
- the AA advice of finding a place of wisdom from which to know when to change something and when to accept something
- Roberto Assagioli's concept of the balance and synthesis of opposing impulses in the personality
- the profound common sense of moderation in all things

## THE SPECTRUM OF WILLINGNESS

Willfulness and will-lessness are extremes. That is why both of those choices in time exhaust the person. Willingness is a balanced, easier, more adaptive response to life. Willingness can be seen in mental, emotional, physical, and spiritual responses. See figure 9.1 for examples of each of these manifestations of willingness.

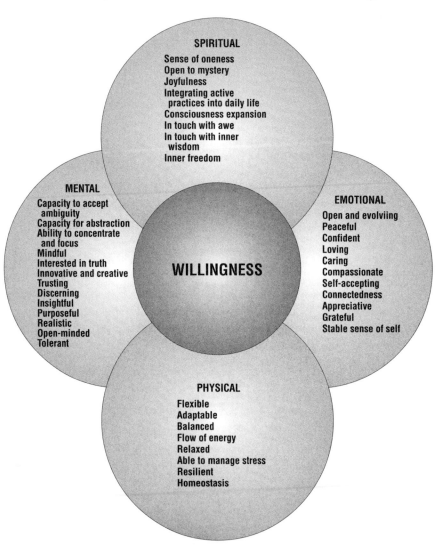

**SPIRITUAL**
Sense of oneness
Open to mystery
Joyfulness
Integrating active
 practices into daily life
Consciousness expansion
In touch with awe
In touch with inner
 wisdom
Inner freedom

**MENTAL**
Capacity to accept
 ambiguity
Capacity for abstraction
Ability to concentrate
 and focus
Mindful
Interested in truth
Innovative and creative
Trusting
Discerning
Insightful
Purposeful
Realistic
Open-minded
Tolerant

**WILLINGNESS**

**EMOTIONAL**
Open and evolviing
Peaceful
Confident
Loving
Caring
Compassionate
Self-accepting
Connectedness
Appreciative
Grateful
Stable sense of self

**PHYSICAL**
Flexible
Adaptable
Balanced
Flow of energy
Relaxed
Able to manage stress
Resilient
Homeostasis

**FIGURE 9.1    The spectrum of willingness**

# THE THREE ACTIONS OF WILLINGNESS

*A.A.A.* refers to the three actions that lead to living with willingness: *attention*, noticing what is *actually* happening, and choosing a life-*affirming* response.

1. *Attention.* This refers to turning our attention toward an inner experience. The inner experience might be a thought, an image, an urge, an impulse, a sensation, a mood. This stresses the point of not turning away from our experience, trying to ignore or avoid it. The spirit of this step is to be open to our experience.

2. *Actually.* This refers to the action of keeping our attention on the experience long enough to discern what is actually happening.

3. *Affirming.* Having taken the preceding two actions, we now have enough information to be able to choose a positive, affirming thought or behavior in response. It is important to note here that we cannot choose how to feel. We can choose how to think and act, and these thoughts and actions will produce new feelings.

## The First Action: Turning our Attention toward Ourselves

In recovery, the first action of willingness is to turn attention toward vulnerability. This is directly in line with the first step of AA: to admit powerlessness over alcohol and to admit that "our lives have become unmanageable" (AA World Services, 1976). Hitting bottom, as discussed in chapter 4, is often the convincing reason for the person to admit to powerlessness. The alcohol, however, is not the root cause of the unmanageability: "In many cases, personal unmanageability was present many years before chemical addiction" (Hazelden Foundation, 1987, p. 8). Recovery does not get rid of this unmanageability: ". . . even when sober . . . the least amount of agitation or disruption . . . causes an extreme reaction" (Hazelden Foundation, 1987, p. 9).

   Once the drug addiction is gone, the person must now face the vulnerability that was there before his drug addiction. The first

120 PART 2: The Choices

action, turning attention toward the vulnerability, is an admission that vulnerability is important. This sets in motion the powerful second act.

## The Second Action: Discerning what Is Actually Happening

The second action is to keep our attention on the thought or feeling long enough to truly know it. This action counteracts the tendency to immediately get away from the vulnerability. Instead, with attention kept on it long enough, the need to get rid of it is replaced by insight into the vulnerability.

The key insight, which is experienced and learned over and over again, is that the vulnerability is tolerable, normal, and passes without anything bad happening. This is the key emotional fact for the person in recovery. Shinzen Young, a meditation teacher with many former addicts as students, agrees the key insight into addiction is to realize these vulnerable feelings can be tolerated. According to Young, once it is realized the vulnerable feelings are tolerable, ". . . a whole new world of possibilities opens up" (1988).

## The Third Action: Choosing an Affirming Response

Tolerating vulnerability could be seen as a goal. A healthier goal is to develop new, life-affirming responses to vulnerability. The third action of willingness is exactly this: a new response. We define the new responses as choosing a life-affirming thought or behavior in the face of a vulnerable moment. For example, when the person in recovery responds to an urge to get high by calling someone in AA or by practicing a relaxation technique, she has chosen a life-affirming behavior. When she responds to an urge to get high by telling herself the urge will pass and she will be safe, that is a life-affirming thought.

These are basic self-care skills. They may sound obvious as alternatives to reacting to vulnerability self-destructively. We must remember, however, that the person in recovery never learned healthy self-care during all the years of addiction.

# EXERCISE

## Willingness

The following imagery exercise explores the experience of willingness.

1. Take a few moments to reflect on a goal you have for yourself. It can be any kind of goal as long as it is a real possibility and not just a fantasy.

2. Close your eyes and bring attention to your breathing.

3. In your imagination experience a path extending from where you are to the top of a tall hill . . . Now imagine your goal and place it on the top of the hill.

4. Now, starting from where you are, experience yourself willing to travel along the path . . . As you move along, become aware of the obstacles that try to pull you off the path . . . Notice these obstacles . . . Now reconnect with your sense of purpose and your willingness to reach your goal.

5. Experience yourself on the top of the hill and fully identify with the goal . . . Allow yourself to feel what it is like to have achieved the goal.

6. When you feel ready, make some notes.

## Discussion

This exercise can clarify the following issues:

• the goal

• the inner obstacles to the goal

• the inner strengths for achieving the goal

• the potential for staying on the path despite the obstacles

• the possibilities of achieving the goal

• the rewards for achieving the goal

These clarifications enhance willingness. They give the person specific information. Without specifics, the person is often blocked by vague doubts and moods, and the goal can seem hopelessly remote. The person experiences a non-directed struggle, a generalized frustration. For the person in recovery, these feelings only exaggerate the belief that "I'm not enough."

The willingness exercise can bring the nondirected struggle into focus and give it direction. Obstacles can be identified as specific problems to be addressed on the way to the goal. Vague feelings of incompetence can be replaced by directed actions to solve specific problems.

---

## Taking Actions

By taking actions, feelings change. A common mistake in early recovery is to wait to feel better before taking an action. This is an attempt to keep feelings in a comfortable zone. The person feels too vulnerable to tolerate any more unsafe feelings. Early recovery is unsafe enough.

Implicit in this thinking is the belief that the action will be difficult and painful. Often, the belief is that the action will not succeed and, worse, will lead to rejection. To keep from being rejected, the person does not take the action.

This thinking is based in the belief that "I'm not enough." Lack of safety, difficulty, pain, fear of rejection all follow from this basic negative belief.

In the face of this belief, taking an action is almost an act of faith. In our terms, it is an act of willingness. It is a willingness to test the vulnerability and find out that it is tolerable. Often, when the action is taken, it turns out to be not as bad as anticipated. As a result, the negative belief is proven untrue.

Taking actions and experiencing the results becomes an important aspect of emotional development throughout recovery. To make this process more effective, certain self-care skills are extremely helpful.

# THE THREE SKILLS OF SELF-CARE IN RECOVERY

The following three skills begin the process of the deeper healing work for the person in recovery. Each of these requires a new willingness to care for oneself:

- making contact
- stress management
- new thinking through emotional education

## *Contact*

Feeling different, separate, and isolated from other people is a common powerful emotion in people who develop addictions. To protect themselves from feeling this too much or too often, addicted people will stay away from others. They will isolate in order to protect themselves from feelings of isolation, from vulnerability. In isolation, private and secret thoughts build up extra power and seem to have a reality of their own.

In recovery, breaking down this isolation is a key step. Making contact with another person, calling a friend or someone who will understand, is an entirely new response for the person in early recovery. This contact immediately modifies the vulnerability and therefore sets up a choice of contact, rather than isolation, the next time vulnerability is strong.

Such willingness to make contact and to reveal vulnerability involves moving past self-judgments and shame about one's feelings. This sharing, rather than secretiveness, is a crucial act of recovery. AA recommends finding a sponsor, a person who is willing to be available at any time to listen and offer guidance. The sponsor is not a trained professional. The sponsor uses her own experiences of staying sober as the basis for guiding others in the process.

Contact seems to work almost every time. There is even current medical research on the physiological benefits of opening up and telling another person a secret (Penebaker, 1990). But contact, of course, is not always possible. The person in recovery may be traveling or may be at work and unable to make personal calls. In such moments, self-help stress management techniques are crucial to know.

## Stress Management

AA uses the slogan H.A.L.T., which is an acronym for Hungry, Angry, Lonely, Tired. It reminds the person in recovery to question if they are in any of these states. These states are especially stressful because they intensify the person's natural vulnerability. The life-affirming response to any of these states is to halt them by eating if hungry, making contact with a friend if angry or lonely, or getting rest if tired. The destructive response would be to halt these states by using drugs. As a stress management technique, H.A.L.T. gives the person in recovery a way to identify a difficult feeling state, "I'm in HALT," and a prescription for practical responses.

Such stress management and self-care techniques can include meditation, prayer, physical exercise, and other quieting and grounding practices. The nurse as health care educator can teach these techniques at any point in recovery treatment. It is not too early to teach them in the detoxification or inpatient unit.

***Focusing on Breath***    Each of these stress reduction exercises starts out with focusing on breath. Two of the practices work exclusively with breath. All of these have the potential to enhance consciousness as well as provide relaxation.

Meditation teacher Lama Govinda (1990) wrote:

> . . . Breathing is the only vital function which, in spite of its independence from our normal consciousness and its self-regulating and self-perpetuating subconscious character, can be raised into a conscious function, accessible to the mind. Due to this double nature, breathing can be made the mediator between mind and body, or the linking between our conscious and unconscious, . . . volitional and automatic functions, and therefore the most perfect expression of the nature of all life (p. 115).

Breath is literally a potential source of inspiration.

## EXERCISE

### Centering for Stress Reduction

One simple technique to learn, practice, and teach others is counting breaths. Counting breaths is a first step in many forms of meditation.

1. Ask the person to notice his breathing.

2. Instruct the person to count his next out-breath as one.

3. Instruct the person to continue to count his out-breaths until he reaches ten.

4. Let the person try this.

5. Discuss the person's experience together.

### Discussion

One of the first physiological responses to stress is alteration of breathing patterns. Typically, the alteration is toward becoming more shallow and rapid. The simple act of centering by bringing attention to breathing tends to bring the breath back into a more relaxed rhythm. The relaxation is enhanced by the fact that the mind is being given a simple focus. For many people, this centering can be a dramatic revelation of their ability to shift out of a stress state and into a relaxed state.

As with all stress management techniques, this works best for the people who use it on a regular basis. This represents a challenge to the nurse to motivate people to develop regular stress management practices.

It is always easier to sell a product that you truly believe in. We cannot emphasize enough the importance of the nurse working with these techniques personally in order to motivate others.

## EXERCISE

### Imagery for Stress Reduction

The imagination is a powerful force in human nature. It can bring back the past, picture the future, bring creativity into the present.

It can also dream up magically ideal wishes as well as the worst catastrophes. In this exercise, the power of the imagination is directed toward communicating calm to the body.

**1.** Ask the person to notice her breathing.

**2.** Instruct the person to begin to imagine a safe place.

**3.** Instruct the person to imagine what it feels like to be there.

**4.** After some time, discuss the person's experience together.

**5.** Help the person to recognize that this safe place is available to her in her imagination whenever she is in need of it.

### Discussion

In utilizing the imagination, the nurse should be aware that people do not have to "see" the imagined scene in order to gain the benefits of imagery. Some people may experience this safe place with a visual imagination. Others may think about it or feel it. The imagination can be present in any of our senses and emotions. This is an important point to explain to the client.

---

## EXERCISE

### Centering for Sleep Difficulties

Many people in recovery report sleep difficulties. Disruptions in the sleep cycle are a great source of stress and increased vulnerability. This exercise, adapted from yoga, is a breathing technique to help the person fall asleep and to sleep more deeply. Many people fall asleep doing this exercise, which is of course the point. Try it out for yourself several times so that you can feel confident introducing it to the person in recovery.

**1.** Do all breathing through the nose if possible, counting the duration of your inhalations and exhalations, and allowing yourself to exhale for twice as long as you inhale . . . Do not strain . . . Do this easily . . . Pay close attention to the feeling of your breathing . . . Let it be smooth . . . Do not have any pauses or stops between the inhale and the exhale . . . One continuous cycle, but done easily.

**2.** Do ten cycles of breathing on your back.

**3.** Do twenty cycles of breathing lying on your right side.

**4.** Do twenty cycles of breathing lying on your left side.

## Discussion

When breathing through the nose, the inhalation activates the sympathetic nervous system. The exhalation through the nose activates the parasympathetic nervous system. This balancing, homeostatic effect is present in all the systems of the body. It is helpful to explain to your client that the sympathetic system is the one that is activated with stress: it is the activation of the fight/flight response. The parasympathetic system is the counter-balancing, or quieting, of this activation. Therefore, in doing this one-two breath rhythm, you are providing twice as much activation to the quieting, parasympathetic nervous system. For some people, this scientific explanation engenders confidence in utilizing this technique.

___

## EXERCISE

## Progressive Muscle Relaxation

Progressive muscle relaxation originated in hatha yoga and has been modified by many Western health professionals to release muscle tension. A typical way to guide the client may sound like this:

> Lie down on the mat (floor, couch, bed) and begin to focus on your breathing . . . I will guide you as we begin to focus on different muscle groups . . . This exercise asks you to tighten and relax muscle groups. You will tighten each muscle group, hold the tension for a brief time, and then release the tension . . . Now turn your focus to your feet and calves . . . Tighten them as much as you can . . . Now let the tension slowly dissolve and feel the difference in your lower legs and feet . . . Let your attention move up to your knees and thighs and begin to tense those muscles . . . When you are ready, release the tension.

The exercise then progressively goes to the following areas: hips and buttocks, abdomen and lower back, chest and upper back, shoulders and biceps, forearms and hands, neck and shoulders, jaw and tongue, and finally the face.

## Discussion

This exercise is a more active, more physical technique, especially good for people who are tense, anxious, or agitated. It should be used with caution if the person has hypertension, back pain, or other evidences of constriction.

---

***Stress Management and Fear of Loss of Control***    Stress management techniques such as the preceding exercises are clearly designed to reduce stress. The nurse should be aware, however, that some people can experience an increase in stress from such practices. This can be particularly true for some people in recovery. The reduction of stress and the increase in relaxation can be the first time the person has lowered his defenses. The result can be:

- a flooding of traumatic memories

- an intense episode of vulnerability

- a feeling of having no defenses available

These reactions tell us how much control the person needs to feel safe. One person described it as being naked in front of the nurse. Such feelings should be respected. Over time, however, the person will suffer the consequences of such an intense preoccupation with control and fear of letting go. The first step in dealing with such a reaction is to talk through the person's experience. Examine the fears together. Often, once the mind has acknowledged the fears, the technique can be modified and tried again with less fear.

***The High***    A very different negative reaction can occur in response to stress management techniques. The person can experience a high from such techniques. This high may simply be a sense of relaxation, release, or inner ease. The person in recovery, however, may only associate such a feeling with the effects of drugs. Especially in early recovery, any feeling that mimics a drug experience can provoke a fear of relapse. This too can be effectively dealt with by talking through the fear together. The goal would be to discern the clear difference between a self-help technique and a return to drugs and self-destruction.

People in recovery who used many hallucinogenic drugs are particularly susceptible to another type of fear. With hallucinogenic drugs, they had many abrupt and vivid alterations and expansions of consciousness that were not within their control. Consciousness expansion is coming in contact with energetic, informational, and imaginal states not readily available or recognized in ordinary awareness. Centering, imagery, and progressive relaxation can evoke states of consciousness that are reminiscent of such experiences. A fear of loss of control may occur in response to any alteration of consciousness, even though the person is in control of the situation when practicing these techniques.

McPeake, Kennedy, and Gordon (1991) argued that the part of drug use that is seeking a high is not in itself pathological or self-destructive. They advocate the use of safe, nondrug consciousness altering techniques for people in recovery. McPeake et al. indicated that a clear difference can be discerned between seeking consciousness expansion and drug addiction. They even speculate that one of the reasons for the high relapse rate in drug treatment is that people are not taught healthy ways to alter their state of consciousness.

***Diet and Stress*** In stress management, it is also important to uncover any dietary contributions to stress. Any foods or additives that overly stimulate the nervous system can contribute to feelings of vulnerability. Caffeine, nicotine, and sugar are the three most common stimulants to ask about. These often contribute to sleeplessness at night and anxiety during the day. As one example, a person in long-term recovery complained of symptoms of panic attacks and feeling that his sobriety was threatened by these episodes. He thought very seriously of drinking just to get rid of the building sense of panic. Upon questioning him, the nurse discovered that he had gone on a diet six months ago, had lost a lot of weight, and was trying to maintain his weight loss by drinking large amounts of diet cola. The nurse educated him about the caffeine in the soda and recommended that he detox himself from all caffeine. Upon follow-up with him two weeks later, the nurse learned that all symptoms of panic had abated.

Remarkably, AA allows smoking, coffee drinking, and the use of sugar at their meetings. This, however, is changing as more and more people become aware of the relationship between food intake and mood changes.

Many people in recovery have reduced their stress by changing their diet. Some theorists advocate that nutritional deficiencies are at the core of addiction and recovery (Milam & Ketcham, 1988).

***Nutritional Depletion***     Chronic use of alcohol or other drugs results in serious nutritional depletion. Drugs interfere with absorption and metabolism through chemical interaction with essential nutrients. Alcohol and drugs also cause damage to mucous membranes. The B vitamins—thiamine, riboflavin, niacin, pyridoxine, pantothenic acid, biotin, folic acid, cobalamine, choline, inosital, and para-aminobenzoic acid (PABA)—are all seriously depleted by alcohol consumption. Supplements of these vitamins, as well as zinc, potassium, and magnesium, are all recommended for recovering alcoholics (Mason, 1985).

People dependent on drugs or alcohol suffer from serious nutritional deficiencies because they have neglected themselves. For example, alcohol is very high in calories, but it has no nutritional value. For this reason, a thorough nutritional evaluation is an important aspect of early recovery.

***Medications and Stress***     It is important to find out about any medications the person in recovery is using. Some people in AA counsel against most medications for fear of reactivating chemical use in general. In the more extreme view, the use of any psychoactive medication is viewed as a relapse. This leads some people in recovery to refuse painkilling medications. Others in AA counsel that a medication, properly used under professional supervision, is not a threat to recovery. Drugs obtained from a doctor or a nurse-practitioner do not of course guarantee the patient will use them properly. Appropriate use of medication depends upon the person's degree of honest desire to stay sober. The use of painkillers after dental surgery, for example, can lead to brief and necessary relief from excessive pain or it can weaken the person's resolve to remain drug-free in general.

This entire topic of medications in recovery can be a great source of stress. The answer to this dilemma, as to all questions in recovery, can only be based on what has worked for people in advanced recovery. Some of them use medications when medically necessary without activating any desire to move toward addiction. Others still sense the wisdom of staying away from any highs from medication. The answer for the person in recovery, therefore, rests in knowing herself and what is the best choice for self-care.

In terms of stress management, the nurse needs to determine if commonly used medications such as birth control pills or antihypertensive drugs are having stimulant or depressant side effects. The person in recovery may believe he is experiencing an unbalanced emotional state when in fact it may be the side effects of medication.

## EMOTIONAL EDUCATION

*Emotional education* refers to increasing awareness of feelings, impulses, urges, moods, reactions, and inner resources.

## CASE STUDY | *Theresa*

Theresa, a 43-year-old woman, has been sober for ten years. She sobered up without any professional treatment, but did have sporadic involvement with AA. Her earliest memory of drinking was at age eleven. She remembers coming home from school and sneaking into her parents' liquor cabinet. She was addicted to alcohol and sedating drugs by early adolescence. Interestingly, in her path to sobriety, Theresa first gave up pills, then alcohol, and finally cigarettes. It was her smoking addiction that was the most difficult to stop.

Theresa was the oldest of four children. Her youngest sister, Kelly, was diagnosed with leukemia at age two. Kelly was a loving child, and Theresa spent a lot of time with her. When Kelly was first diagnosed, Theresa and the other children were only told Kelly was sick. Over the next two years, Kelly was hospitalized many times. The parents never allowed the other children to see Kelly in the hospital and often made up stories about where she was. Theresa, therefore, never knew about the seriousness of Kelly's condition. One day, when Kelly was away, Theresa and her other siblings were sent to stay with their aunt. When they returned home two weeks later, all of Kelly's things were gone from the house. Kelly was not seen again, nor was her name mentioned by her parents.

It was not until after ten years of sobriety, and in psychotherapy, that Theresa realized her drinking had begun only months after Kelly's disappearance. This awareness brought intense feelings of sadness and mourning. Theresa also felt shame that she was feeling so much pain about events from so long ago. She needed encouragement to finally allow that eleven-year-old child to sob and be comforted in her pain. She needed help in having compassion for the part of her that is still a frightened eleven-year-old girl.

### Observations

The loss of her sister is not the explanation for Theresa's addiction. But the increase in awareness of this loss gives her a new view of her addiction and her struggles. The new view gives her the possibility of forgiving herself and respecting herself more.

For the nurse, it is important to place addiction within the larger view of human struggle. The constricted symptomatic model of thinking only of addiction, divorced from human struggle, is not real.

---

## The Vulnerable Moment

Vulnerability is a time of great uncertainty, of fearing the worst is about to happen. Emotional education points to the need to learn everything one can about these difficult vulnerable moments. Through emotional education, the person can move from a vulnerable moment to a recovery moment. Accomplished often enough, this movement from vulnerability to a new response deepens the person's confidence in being able to meet the difficulties of life.

## Facilitating Emotional Education

Emotional education can be helped by the nurse through open curiosity. As you listen to someone like Theresa describe a vulnerable moment, ask every question you can think of. Get every detail you can. Do not hold back any questions for fear of disturbing her. Your questions will not disturb her. It is the fear of the next vulnerable moment that is disturbing. Your questions open up possibilities.

You definitely want to identify these aspects of the vulnerable moment:

- what the body feels like
- what the mood or emotions feel like
- what the mind is thinking or imagining

Through the nurse's questioning, Theresa began to see that her vulnerability was filled with a sadness she carried everywhere with her. She then could trace her sadness back to her sister's disappearance and see how her drinking, at age eleven, began a few months after the loss.

Questions are quests. They help get to the essence of the experience and build the ability to look at oneself, to self-observe. By recognizing the origins of vulnerability through self-observation, the person in recovery begins to be able to name his feeling states and to identify vulnerability more quickly. The person also begins to realize he goes in and out of vulnerability often, which in turn means he is capable of surviving these moments.

This is what Shinzen Young meant about realizing that these feelings are tolerable. With self-observation and the learning of self-care skills, the person begins to have new possibilities for those difficult moments. This all begins with awareness, and your questions are the way to increase awareness. Your questions begin to liberate the possibility of choice in the face of vulnerability. Choice is the central tool to early and middle recovery.

**Feelings Aren't Facts**     There are several key emotional education concepts to teach the person in recovery. The single most important, and the most difficult to integrate, is said succinctly in an AA phrase: "Feelings aren't facts."

The phrase "Feelings aren't facts" separates internal emotional reality from external reality. Emotional reality may be a feeling of fear even when the situation is not dangerous. A classic example of this is the fear of being criticized. Many people in recovery, as well as outside of recovery, are controlled by this fear. It keeps them from making important phone calls, from trying to do new things, from asking for help. What is the power of criticism? It is not actually dangerous.

"Feelings aren't facts" is a succinct way of saying that our biological flight/fight mechanism is not always right. It goes off, signaling danger and sending adrenalin and anxiety through our system, even when the situation does not call for it. In short, just because the person is feeling frightened does not mean he is in danger. Just because he is feeling hopeless does not mean a situation is hopeless. Just because he is angry at someone does not mean the person did anything to him. Just because he feels like escaping does not mean he has to go anywhere.

This does not suggest ignoring feelings. Quite the contrary: the first action of willingness is to turn directly toward feelings. In the second action of willingness, you keep your attention on them long enough to discern what is happening. In this second action, the person can see that his flight/fight reactivity is usually way out of proportion to the situation. He does not have to fight and he does not have to flee. He can stay and make a life-affirming response.

**Second Recovery**    Second recovery is the need to recover from trauma as well as from addiction. Second recovery is typically not dealt with by alcohol and drug treatment centers. It is not mentioned in Alcoholics Anonymous, even though many AA members could be helped by it.

If the nurse learns of trauma in the person's history, it is important to distinguish it from the problems of addiction itself. It is a great relief to the person in recovery to have this distinction made for her. This provides her with a better understanding of her struggles and a perspective on why her treatment program is not resulting in her feeling more at ease in the world.

We wonder if the need for second recovery is a reason for such a low rate of success in drug treatment. We wonder how often the pain in addiction can actually be placed on addiction itself. In how many cases is addiction really a person self-prescribing medication for traumatized feelings?

Second recovery requires intervention by professionals with specific understanding of trauma and posttraumatic stress disorders' symptomotology.

**The Recovery of Intuition**    Another important factor in emotional education is the recovery of intuition. Intuition, the sixth sense, is an inner guide in all situations. It originates in a place of deep inner wisdom and instinct. Intuition gives us an instant sense of what is happening. The rational mind and our emotions can then sort through what our intuition told us. In many instances, our intuition is completely accurate. How many times do you tell yourself that you should have followed your intuition? The very question reflects the fact that many people ignore their intuition.

The person in addiction goes beyond ignoring his intuition. He puts his intuition into the service of his drug use. He uses his sixth sense to focus on getting drugs and on keeping his drug use going. He uses his intuition to figure out how to manipulate others into cooperating with his addiction. The people he manipulates often become emotionally unbalanced themselves. Self-help groups such as Al-Anon teach the relatives and friends of addicts how to stop cooperating with the addictive thinking and behaviors. In addition, they learn to keep the focus on their own recovery from the damaging effects of having been caught up in the cycle of self-defeating and self-destructive behaviors.

Intuition in the service of living is a distinct goal for the person in recovery. In your clinical work, you can consistently ask the person, "What is your intuition on this?" As with any human skill, intuition can return if given enough practice. In early recovery, the person looks for answers from others, and often her recovery depends upon accepting those answers. It is too early for her to be thinking correctly. At the same time, she can be guided to turn toward her intuition. In time, each person can begin to identify those experiences that are distinctly coming from a place of intuition. For some, intuition is felt as a clear body energy shift. For others, it is a thought or image accompanied by an emotional change.

In encouraging the return of intuition, there needs to be discernment. Impulses, urges, wishes, and guesses mimic intuition but are inferior to it. Impulses usually come from passing physical sensations. Intuition comes from a wisdom center in the human being. We will discuss this wisdom center in depth in chapter 10.

***The Normalcy of Shifting Feelings***   The next factor in emotional education is to understand the normalcy of shifting feelings. Often the person in recovery can barely keep up with all the emotions he is going through on a moment-to-moment basis. The shift from peace to despondency, from confidence to humiliation, can happen with a word or glance from another person. This instability, in the extreme, can cause him to relapse (refer back to the section on relapse in chapter 4).

As the person's mind begins to clear through being clean and sober, his thinking can begin to help his feelings. He is often amazed to learn that even "normal" adults have feelings that shift and change throughout a day, an hour, or a minute. The changing weather is often a good analogy to use. The weather is always in a process of change, and yet the blue sky is still up there. Your feelings are always in a process of change, and yet your sanity and sobriety are still there.

## SUMMARY

Willingness is about aligning the energies of the person with a healthy, life-affirming intention. There are a number of life skills that the person in recovery must learn in order to make this possible. It is the nurse's role to educate the person in these skills.

In summary, the healing process is facilitated by developing the ability to:

- move from isolation to contact with others on a healing path

- recognize and manage stress in healthy ways

- recognize, understand, and develop strategies for dealing with unsafe feelings

## REFLECTIONS

What are the ways in which you manage your own stress?

Is there a network of healthy support in your life? If there is, how do you nurture it?

If there is not, what steps can you take toward creating one?

Do you feel a willingness to grow and develop throughout your life?

### References

AA World Services. (1976). *Alcoholics anonymous* (3rd ed.) New York: AA World Services, Inc.

Assagioli, R. (1974). *Act of will.* New York: Viking.

Govinda, L. (1990). *Creative meditation and multi-dimensional consciousness.* Wheaton, IL: The Theosophical Publishing House.

Hazelden Foundation. (1987). *The twelve steps of alcoholics anonymous.* New York: Harper/Hazelden.

Mason, L. J. (1985). *Guide to stress reduction.* Berkeley, CA: Celestial Arts.

McPeake, J. D., Kennedy, B. P., & Gordon, S. M. (1991). Altered states of consciousness therapy. *Journal of Substance Abuse Treatment, 8,* pp. 75–82.

Milam, J. R., & Ketcham, K. (1988). *Under the influence.* New York: Bantam Books.

Penebaker, J. (1990). *Opening up.* New York: Avon Books.

Young, S. (1988). *Overcoming compulsive behavior.* Oakland, CA: Thinking Allowed Productions.

## Suggested Reading

Assagioli, R. (1974). *Act of will.* New York: Viking.

# 3 | INCREASING PEACE

# 10 THE SPIRITUAL ASPECT OF RECOVERY

*Every individual is made up of physical, mental, and spiritual components. One cannot be separated from the other without losing one's identity.*

Agnelo Dias

## *SPIRITUALITY AND NURSING PRACTICE*

The spiritual aspect of the person has always been a part of nursing philosophy and practice. Spiritual development is a practical, clinically relevant issue for the nurse to assess and assist in the person's recovery.

## *Daniel*

Daniel stopped using pills a year ago. He experiences anxiety often, sometimes feeling he is on the edge of a panic attack.

In sobriety, he is learning the self-care skills of contact, stress management, and emotional education. Sometimes none of these work. In very anxious moments, he needs to feel part of something

more, something greater. For Daniel, the figure of Jesus represents
something greater. When Daniel is feeling very nervous on the
subway, he imagines Jesus is on the subway car and immediately
calms down. The thought of Jesus fills him with a certainty that all
of these anxieties, all of these struggles, are manageable. Daniel does
not understand this. In fact, he would much prefer to always be
comfortable and never have to struggle again. He has a magical
wish that life would never touch him, never get to him. But he
knows this is not possible. He knows he will struggle. When he
thinks of Jesus, Daniel's sense of struggle eases and lightens. He
thinks of the struggles and humiliations Jesus suffered. In those
moments, Daniel feels compassionate toward Jesus.

Among the many interesting aspects of this inner relationship
with Jesus is the fact that Daniel was not raised a Christian. He
did not have formal training in Christianity and never converted to
Christianity. He does not read the Bible or go to any church.
When he heard about Jesus through friends, he remembered an
instant connection. In his recovery, he draws upon this connection
for support, courage, and inspiration to stay free of drugs.

# Vicki

Vicki has no interest in religion. She was turned off by the religious
language in AA and never went back there. Her father was religious
and cruel, and she saw no evidence that religion changes people for
the good. She loves nature. Whenever she needs to reaffirm her commitment to stay sober, she sits by a tree or walks in the park. She loses
her small sense of self and expands into a feeling of being part of
something more. She feels lighter, clearer, more connected, and calm.

In such a state, the thought of putting alcohol, which is really
a poison, into her body is repellent to her.

## *Ray*

Ray prays everyday. He was taught in AA to try to understand God's will. Ray has no idea what this means, but he prays because he wants to stay sober. After prayer, he feels calmer, but this does not last long. As soon as he goes to work, all of his vulnerability gets activated by criticism and pressures. Inside, though, he can sense a resolve to get through all of these difficult feelings. He feels a basic desire to choose sanity after fifteen years of insane living as a heroin addict. He wonders if this desire, this basic sense of real sanity, is somehow God's will.

## THE PRACTICALITY OF SPIRITUAL DEVELOPMENT

As we said at the start of this book, we choose to stay entirely practical. Just as you do, we face people in addiction and people in recovery everyday who are suffering. We do not have time for abstractions or nice ideas. When we consider a concept or method, we ask the quintessential American philosophical question: Does it work? If something works, we use it and encourage it. If it does not work, we let it go.

Spiritual development has proven itself clinically. This conclusion is based on thirty years of clinical practice. It is based on practical wisdom. We have seen over and over again the vast difference between a person in recovery who has developed spiritual consciousness and one who has not. The founders of AA discovered this for themselves and passed it on to others.

We have no particular bias in favor of spirituality or AA. If they did not work for our clients, we would ignore them. They work. Spiritual development evokes latent potentials inside the person, the perspective of wisdom and the emotions of compassion and peace. This new consciousness helps the person realize she is participating in a larger life than the separate, threatened, anxious, self-absorbed personality. Disconnected from the larger life, the personality is in a constantly vulnerable state. Daniel experiences this larger life when he transforms from isolative fear to compassion for suffering. Vicki experiences this realization in nature. Ray experiences it whenever he sees the desire for more and more sanity.

### Moving from Vulnerability to Peace

Spiritual consciousness is the only healthy response to our vulnerability. The development of spiritual consciousness is therefore a practical and intrinsic part of our Vulnerability Model of Recovery. The challenge of the Vulnerability Model is whether to live in vulnerability or to live in wisdom, compassion, and peace. The founders of AA referred to this as achieving serenity. To understand the development from vulnerability to peace, let us first consider ways to appreciate spirituality.

## THE SPIRITUAL ASPECT OF HUMAN NATURE

Dossey, Keegan, Guzzetta, and Kolkmeier (1995) indicated there are three defining characteristics of spirituality:

> (1) Unfolding mystery, (2) inner strengths, and (3) harmonious interconnectedness. Unfolding mystery refers to one's experiences about life's purpose and meaning, uncertainty and struggles. Inner strengths refer to a sense of awareness, consciousness, self, inner resources, sacred source, unifying force, inner core, and transcendence. Harmonious interconnectedness refers to interconnections and harmony with self, others, higher power/God, and the environment (p. 22).

In *Mental Health Psychiatric Nursing: A Holistic Life-Cycle Approach* (1984), Landrum, Beck, Rawlins, Williams, and Culpan indicated:

> Throughout the ages, a recognition of the spiritual dimension has been present as people have contemplated their place in the universe and their relatedness to others

and to nature. Each of the major religions recognizes the spiritual dimension as basic to fostering a sense of hope . . . meaning . . . (p. 290).

Landrum et al. go on to make a distinction between religion and spirituality:

> Organized traditional religions tend to adhere to the revelations of one or more persons that are passed along to those who follow . . . A person's spiritual dimension encompasses much more than these revelations, more than established doctrine introduced by others. This dimension allows one to experience and understand the reality of existence in unique and direct ways that go beyond one's usual limits. Hence spirituality is not completely synonymous with religious belief (p. 303).

The world's religions are evidence of people's attempts to understand the universe they are born into. Freud (1964) saw religion as an attempt to feel better in the face of our helplessness, our vulnerability. This has some truth, but Freud also ignored a major factor of human experience: people in every culture and every time have had direct experiences of deep knowing and deep feeling about the universe. These mystics, saints, sages, scientists, and artists all made contact with a level of knowing that transcends what society says life is. And all cultures throughout history have tried to capture these transcendent experiences in symbols, ceremonies, paintings, poems, songs, and dance. These expansive experiences go beyond the personality. They tell us there is more to human nature than just the personality trying to fit into society. These experiences are direct evidence of a transpersonal (beyond personality) aspect of human nature. The spiritual aspect of human nature is, simply, a fact.

## *Spiritual Experiences*

Ferrucci (1982, pp. 130–131) offered a list of spiritual experiences. Paraphrased, they include:

- a transfigured vision of external reality
- the apprehension of some truth concerning the nature of the universe

- a sense of unity with all beings
- illumination
- an extraordinary inner silence
- waves of luminous joy
- liberation
- cosmic humor
- a deep feeling of gratefulness
- an exhilarating sense of dance
- resonating with the essence of beings
- loving all persons in one person
- feeling oneself to be the channel for a stronger force to flow through
- ecstasy
- an intimation of profound mystery and wonder
- the delight of beauty
- creative inspiration
- a sense of boundless compassion
- transcendence of time and space as we know them

Gifford-May and Thompson (1994, pp. 124–129) offered a list of subjective reports of meditative phenomena. Paraphrased, the list includes:

- you become a field of energy
- you merge with objects
- you forget who you are
- you become conscious of being conscious
- your arms extend to the reaches of the universe
- you experience immeasurable distance
- your head feels incredibly expanded
- you have a sense of being enormous and yet not out of your body

- you expand in all directions
- you have no sense of yourself
- you are a field of awareness that is cosmic
- you are just awareness, endless, boundless, oceanic
- you are falling without hitting bottom
- you are like a very still pond
- you have a sense of space
- you experience nothingness as enormous
- you experience great love
- you are utterly serene and content
- you experience emotional expansiveness, laughing in a very deep way
- you experience joy bubbling up, joy quietly pervading all things

There could be many additions to this list. One key addition is the experience of the higher self. The *higher self* is the inner source of wisdom and guidance which becomes more available as the person develops deeper levels of self-awareness.

## THE HIGHER SELF

The higher self is a phenomenon that has been recognized and validated by every wisdom tradition on earth (Dossey et al., 1995). The higher self is the person's ". . . synthesis or realization of individuality and universality" (Assagioli, 1965, p. 87). If the client is religious, he may already have a name for the higher self. If the client has no religious system, he may accept the idea that there are many organizing processes in nature, and that the higher self is one such process in people, perhaps there for evolutionary reasons.

Terms to indicate the higher self include:

- the soul (Judeo-Christian)
- the guest (Sufi)

- the still voice within (Quaker)
- the big mind (Zen)
- the self (Jung)
- the higher self (psychosynthesis)
- the higher power (Alcoholics Anonymous)

In these and many other approaches, the higher self is understood as the experience of inner wisdom and the emotions that come with it. The source of the wisdom is depicted in many ways. For example, in Italian Renaissance paintings, words and images travel through the air from angels to humans. In the Renaissance understanding, this is a symbolic depiction of information moving from one level of human nature to another level of human nature.

## *Daniel's Inner Experience*

The higher self represents a major developmental step beyond the ego self. In Daniel's case, he makes the developmental step beyond ego with the help of Jesus. How can we understand what is happening inside him?

We have said that the higher self is a term referring to the worldwide recognition of a natural knowledge, an innate wisdom, a basic sanity, an inner purpose in human nature. When Daniel imagines Jesus, he evokes this wisdom nature. He does not understand this. He just knows that the thought of Jesus evokes some important part of him.

When this wisdom is evoked, compassion naturally accompanies it. Wisdom provides us with a perspective that alleviates our personal fears. With our fears reduced, our innate love of life can then come more easily to the surface of our emotions. When we are looking from a place of wisdom, the compassionate form of love becomes available to us. In such moments, Daniel feels compassion not only for himself but also for Jesus' suffering.

This interaction between thinking of Jesus and the changes that take place in Daniel are of profound importance. Enough emphasis cannot be put on this. In such moments, someone like Daniel transcends his vulnerability, transcends his suffering. Instead of suffering, he feels wisdom and compassion.

Through thinking of Jesus, Daniel is transformed. The person makes conscious contact with spiritual qualities, wisdom and compassion, that are available in latency.

Implicit in this is a potential: if wisdom and compassion are so available, then they could be made available more and more often. Daniel is not merely comforting himself with thoughts of Jesus. Daniel is not simply escaping from his helplessness momentarily by imagining a powerful figure. Instead, Daniel is making contact with a part of human nature that exists in latency. Through thoughts of Jesus, Daniel is developing access to the spiritual consciousness inherent in human nature. For Daniel, Jesus becomes the way.

### The Interplay between Vulnerability and Spiritual Consciousness

Daniel's vulnerability will of course return again and again. It is the emotion of our desire to survive. This interplay between our vulnerability and our spiritual consciousness is at the heart of deeper recovery. The spiritual aspect of our nature can transform our vulnerability, but it cannot make it disappear. This means that we will live in a constant interplay between our vulnerability and our spiritual possibilities. Turned into a course of health and development, we can use a moment of vulnerability as a signal to evoke wisdom and compassion in ourselves. By extension, this suggests the possibility of evoking wisdom and compassion toward others.

Imagine the difference: living in vulnerability or living in wisdom and compassion. This is the challenge of spiritual development, of the spiritual aspect of recovery.

## ALCOHOLICS ANONYMOUS AND SPIRITUALITY

The emphasis on spiritual development is the core of Alcoholics Anonymous and the Twelve Steps. AA advocates moving from a self-will run riot to seeking an understanding of God's will. The Twelve Steps of AA are overtly spiritual. (See appendix 5 for the text of the Twelve Steps). The first step advocates reorientation of the self toward surrender. The second and third steps advocate a spiritual view of life. The fourth through tenth steps advocate introspection, honesty, confession, and forgiveness; the eleventh step advocates prayer and meditation; and the twelfth step advocates service as a result of a spiritual awakening. *Spiritual awakening* is a phrase used in AA to refer to a realization that the isolated individual is in fact participating in a universe of divine intention and order.

## Support for AA's Spirituality

Whitfield (1985), Sparks (1987), and other addiction authors support the AA use of spirituality. Sparks, for example, focuses on substance abuse as a mistaken acting out of an innate spiritual impulse to go beyond the limited sense of self. To respond to this spiritual or transpersonal impulse, Sparks advocates drug-free techniques that provide experiential expansion beyond the personality. In this regard, Sparks is following the lead of one of AA's founders, Bill Wilson, in pointing to spiritual awakening as an underpinning of recovery. Bill Wilson's awakening is referred to later in this book when we examine models of consciousness.

## Antagonism toward AA's Spirituality

It is important to note that most recovery programs are not spiritual. Despite its recognition, the Twelve Steps of AA may not even be the most effective program (McCrady & Irvine, 1989). Furthermore, some newer models of recovery, such as Rational Recovery, actively oppose the spiritual orientation of AA. Buxton, Smith, and Seymour (1987) cited Albert Ellis, Rational Recovery's mentor, as saying that all spiritual language in AA should be eliminated. Buxton et al. commented: "Many within the drug treatment field and in the recovering community supported this stand" (p. 278).

To understand why this antagonism toward AA's spirituality exists, a brief history of addiction treatment is necessary. The self-help, twelve-step programs developed out of a failure of the medical community to be of help in alleviating addiction (Sparks, 1987). AA grew out of an unmet need. As a result, the AA community had and still has a distrust of professional treatment, feeling that professionals do not understand addiction. Some AA members feel that only a fellow alcoholic can help them. The religious and spiritual emphasis in AA then adds another dimension to the gap between AA and professionals. (The religious and spiritual language exists in AA because spiritual experiences of the early founders lead to their conviction that they could live a saner life. There is a fuller discussion of this in chapter 11.) Typically, anything religious has been treated with neglect or worse by the professional community in its emphasis on being scientific.

The conflict between AA and the professionals has lessened over the years. The authors, however, still meet addiction professionals who see AA's spirituality as crippling and AA members who see professionals as ineffective and misinformed about the nature of addiction and recovery.

The reality is that both sides offer the other a possibility of strengthening the entire treatment of people with addictions. The professional community can offer insights into human development necessary to deepen recovery and can offer research breakthroughs on the nature of physiological and genetic components of addiction. The AA community can continue to offer insights into exactly how recovery works.

AA success is not measurable, since AA is anonymous and keeps no records on anyone. The authors express confidence in AA because our clinical practice shows us that AA provides structure, support, and techniques for recovery passed on by experts, the people who have already recovered. We know of no greater source of addiction specialists.

# THE NURSE AND SPIRITUAL PRACTICES

The spiritual aspect of the person has always been a part of nursing philosophy and practice. It is logical that the nurse should develop skills in assisting this aspect of the person.

## CASE STUDY | *Charles*

Charles was terminally ill from AIDS. He had acquired AIDS through heroin addiction and sharing hypodermic needles with other addicts. The AIDS virus had by now led to neurological damage. Charles was unsteady on his feet, and his speech was beginning to slur. His memory was slipping away from him.

This case study describes a creative meditation session with Charles. (Creative meditation is described in more detail in chapter 12.) The session took place in his apartment as he was lying in bed in severe discomfort from skin rashes and from the side effects of his medications. Under these circumstances, it would be hard to imagine how meditation could help. In fact, this single session provided Charles with wisdom and compassion that helped him throughout the dying process.

(**Note:** As a nurse, you may not know what the effect of these interventions will be. You can offer them, not expect any particular outcome, and be open to what they do for the person you are helping.)

Charles knew the nurse well and trusted her as much as he trusted anyone. This certainly contributed to the depth of the experience. The nurse asked Charles to close his eyes and follow her voice. The nurse asked him, despite the severe itching, to try to bring his attention to his nostrils. She then talked to him about how to follow his breathing. She suggested that he not try to do anything special to it; not to try to make it rhythmic, not to try to make it more noticeable. Instead, just let it be the way it was. She then asked him to imagine that each breath had the potential to take him deeper and deeper into calmness, as he gave permission to his breath to do this for him. (***Note:*** This is a standard relaxation technique in imagery and hypnosis.)

The nurse noticed that Charles's chest was in a slower breathing pattern. This suggested that Charles was responding to her directions and was experiencing a more relaxed, more inwardly absorbed state. The nurse next suggested that he continue to follow his breathing and listen to her at the same time. The nurse talked slowly about the fact that in all times and in all cultures, people have prepared themselves for meditation in exactly the same way Charles was now doing. She spoke about meditation as an ageless practice for realizing inner wisdom. She then wondered if Charles could begin to notice someone in another time and culture following his breath and going toward wisdom, just as Charles was doing now.

The nurse saw Charles's chest slow down even more. Her own personal experience in meditation and her clinical uses of meditation told her that at that moment Charles had deeply let go. She said nothing else. She silently meditated by his bedside, keeping her eyes open to observe any changes in him.

Twenty-five minutes passed. The nurse felt a peace palpable in the room. Charles slowly opened his eyes. He began to tell the nurse what he had experienced:

> I felt my body sink deep in the bed. I felt a great heaviness and peace. The itching was gone, and it's still gone. I saw an image of a young man. I saw him become ill and saw his flesh begin to fall off him until he became a skeleton.

Then his flesh reappeared, and his life force returned. He was the same healthy young man I first saw.

Soon, the flesh began to come off him again, his life force left him, and he became a skeleton again. At that point, I saw an old man behind him, and I realized that as the old man moved his hand to the left, the flesh came off the young man, and as the old man moved his hand to the right, the life came back to the young man. I watched this with great feelings of peace. I felt something very important was being taught to me. I can't even say the peace was in me, because by the time I was watching this I had absolutely no sense of my body at all. My body was gone. My body had dropped away. I was free, I was floating free. I had no fear at all. I was free.

Charles closed his eyes and went back into meditation. The nurse sat quietly, not wanting to say anything.

When the nurse visited Charles a week later, he had invited three friends to be at the session. He wanted them to experience the meditation, so that they could learn it and practice it with him whenever they visited. Charles felt he had found a way to help himself.

In a month, Charles could no longer manage at home. He was hospitalized, and after a few days he stopped communicating. He was not in a coma, but his attention was definitely elsewhere. Visitors would talk to him, not get a reply, and then leave. The nurse visited him, and the same process happened. Everyone began to accept this as either a neurological and/or emotional consequence of his dying process.

The nurse found out from his friends that Charles had made them promise to guide him to his inner wisdom if he was near death. Finding this out, the nurse intuited that Charles was not communicating because he had determined to keep his consciousness focused inward. The friends had agreed to the promise, but they all felt embarrassed about the thought of guiding Charles in the hospital room with other patients and other visitors around.

One evening, his friend, Paul, was visiting him at the hospital. As Paul was about to leave, the floor nurse told Paul that this was probably Charles's last night. Charles's vital signs and her long clinical experience told her so. Paul became upset and started toward the elevator to go outside. He suddenly remembered the promise to Charles, to guide him to inner wisdom in the event he was about to die.

Paul went back to the hospital room. There was Charles, still, uncommunicative. His silence had continued throughout his hospitalization. Feeling self-conscious, Paul leaned close to Charles's ear and began to instruct him on the creative meditation process he had learned from the nurse. Charles continued to lie there, unresponsive. Nevertheless, Paul continued to guide Charles to follow his breathing and begin to imagine a wisdom figure from another time and place also following his breath, to imagine both Charles and the wisdom figure meditating together, and to be open to any communication from the wisdom figure.

Paul finished the guiding. To Paul's great surprise, Charles spoke. Charles said, "Don't worry, Charles is already gone." Paul began to both cry and feel happy. He did not know what was happening to him. He felt the need to go outside for some fresh air. Charles died thirty minutes later.

### *Observations*

In this case study, the nurse played three important roles. First, she was a *practitioner*. She assisted Charles in experiencing deep relaxation, new learning, and new coping skills for his transition through the dying process. She was able to do this because she had explored these techniques for herself. Intuitively and through personal experience, she knew they would be clinically helpful. (The clinical uses of imagery and meditation can be learned at the New York Psychosynthesis Institute in New York City, where highly experienced professionals study and teach these techniques. *Psychosynthesis* is a school of psychology developed by Roberto Assagioli, M.D., that recognizes and studies the spiritual dimension of human experience. For a full description of psychosynthesis, see chapter 11.)

Second, she was a *health educator*, teaching her patient and his caregivers ways to utilize meditation in the dying process.

Third, she was an *important role model*. She took a spiritually based helping technique and applied it clinically to a man in great suffering. She knew clinically that creative meditation had the potential for deepening relaxation. She also knew it had the potential to open Charles to the transpersonal aspect of his nature. This spiritual aspect of his nature did become available to him. This had never happened before in his years of recovery from addiction. Now he was experiencing the inner peace that came with conscious contact with this part of his nature. The nurse had provided intelligent, responsible, professional guidance for Charles that helped him to experience spiritual awakening at a desperate time in his life.

## HEALTH PRACTICES AND SPIRITUAL PRACTICES

In using meditation clinically, the nurse was taking part in a recent trend in health practice. There is an increase in acceptance of alternative health practices as adjuncts to mainstream modern health care. The origins of these alternative practices are in spiritual traditions (Schaub, 1995a). The trend is an interesting cross-fertilization between health care and spiritual practices.

These alternative practices include:

- meditation (Kabat-Zinn, 1990; Schaub, 1995b, 1996)

- biofeedback (Green & Green, 1977)

- prayer (Dossey, 1993)

- imagery (Schaub, Anselmo, & Luck, 1991)

- music therapy (Schroeder-Sheker, 1994)

- therapeutic touch (Salewski, 1993)

- yoga (Ornish, 1990)

Major teaching hospitals have begun to open centers specializing in these practices. Large insurance companies, responding to consumer demand and cost benefits, are now reimbursing for some of these practices. An example of this is the Dean Ornish approach to reversing coronary artery disease (1990). His program is a combination of yoga stretching, imagery, meditation, diet, and exercise.

This cross-fertilization of health care and spiritual practices has a uniquely American character. Our guaranteed religious freedom and our independent spirit, along with our vast information systems and the emigration of many spiritual teachers to America, have resulted in American health professionals having access to the entire world's meditative and spiritual insights and practices. The nurse that worked with Charles had studied meditation practices from Roman Catholicism, Tibetan Buddhism, Theravada Buddhism, Sufism, and western imagery teachers before synthesizing her own approach to help Charles.

The key aspect of this cross-fertilization is outcome. As we said earlier, we advocate spiritual development in recovery because of the outcome: it works, it helps. These spiritual practices, applied clinically by nurses and other professionals, will prove either to work or not work. Through research trials and clinical applications, the world's spiritual practices are being put to test to see if they reduce our patients' suffering. Clearly, in Charles's case, the outcome was profoundly healing.

### *Cautions with Spiritual Practices in Health Care*

The nurse must observe several cautions in assisting in spiritual development and utilizing spiritually based practices:

1. The nurse must have extensive personal experience with spiritual development and practices.

2. The nurse must have examined the growing research literature now available on practices as a result of this trend of cross-fertilization.

3. It is not appropriate for helping professionals to direct patients to specific spiritual or religious organizations (Smith, 1986), although it is appropriate for the patient to discuss such interests with them.

## *SPIRITUAL ASSESSMENT*

Dossey et al. (1995, pp. 20–21) provided a series of questions to assess, evaluate, and increase spiritual awareness in the nurse and patient (figure 10.1). We would suggest you select from this assessment tool the questions most appropriate to your setting. Overall, this questioning process can evoke new thoughts and behaviors to increase active spiritual development.

## *SPIRITUALITY AND SUFFERING*

In a crisis, we feel fear move through us. This fear has different degrees of intensity. Sometimes it is everything. Our mind cannot focus, our mind races, our hands have no strength, our legs are shaky, our feet do not feel solid on the ground. At other times, the fear is on the edge of awareness, with the feeling that it might become stronger soon. In crisis, we always have at least one eye on the fear. It is very difficult to rest. Under these conditions, we do not have our full self available to us. We do not have our reason, our intuition, our spiritual qualities. Fear makes us contract. Perceived threats to survival make us retreat to the limited survival emotions of flight or fight.

---

**Meaning and Purpose**   These questions assess a person's ability to seek meaning and fulfillment in life, manifest hope, and accept ambiguity and uncertainty.

• What gives your life meaning?
• Do you have a sense of purpose in life?
• Why do you want to get well?
• How hopeful are you about obtaining a better degree of health?
• Do you feel that you have a responsibility in maintaining your health?
• Will you be able to make changes in your life to maintain your health?
• Are you motivated to get well?
• What is the most important or powerful thing in your life?

**Inner Strengths**   These questions assess a person's ability to manifest joy and recognize strengths, choices, goals, and faith.

• What brings you joy and peace in your life?
• What can you do to feel alive and full of spirit?
• What traits do you like about yourself?
• What are your personal strengths?
• What choices are available to you to enhance your healing?
• What do you believe in?
• Is faith important in your life?
• How has your illness [addiction] influenced your faith?
• Does faith play a role in regaining your health?

*continued*

---

**FIGURE 10.1   Spiritual assessment tool for nurses. From Holistic Nursing: A Handbook for Practice *(2nd ed.), by B. Dossey, L. Keegan, C. Guzzetta, and L. Kolkmeier, 1995, Gaithersburg, MD: Aspen Publishers. Copyright 1995 by Aspen Publishers. Reprinted with permission.***

**Interconnections**    These questions assess a person's positive self-concept, self-esteem, and sense of self; sense of belonging in the world with others; capacity to pursue personal interests; and ability to demonstrate love of self and self-forgiveness.

- How do you feel about yourself right now?
- How do you feel when you have a true sense of yourself?
- Do you pursue things of personal interest?
- What do you do to show love for yourself?
- Can you forgive yourself?
- What do you do to heal your spirit?

These questions assess a person's ability to connect in life-giving ways with family, friends, and social groups and to engage in the forgiveness of others.

- Who are the significant people in your life?
- Do you have friends or family in town who are available to help you?
- Who are the people to whom you are closest?
- Do you belong to any groups?
- Can you ask people for help when you need it?
- Can you share your feelings with others?
- What are some of the most loving things that others have done for you?
- What are the loving things that you do for other people?
- Are you able to forgive others?

These questions assess a person's capacity for finding meaning in worship or religious activities and a connectedness with a divinity or universe.

- Is worship important to you?
- What do you consider the most significant act of worship in your life?
- Do you participate in any religious activities?
- Do you believe in God or a higher power?
- Have you ever tried to empty your mind of all thoughts?
- Do you use relaxation or imagery skills?
- Do you meditate?
- Do you pray?
- What is your prayer?
- How are your prayers answered?
- Do you have a sense of belonging in the world?

Specific answers to these questions can clarify the thinking and behaviors necessary to make the person's spiritual development an active, conscious process.

---

**FIGURE 10.1    *continued***

## *Perceived Threats to Survival and Fight/Flight Reactiveness*

Most suffering is caused by the brain's excessive perception of threats to survival. Many events that set off fight/flight reactions are not true threats at all (Green & Green, 1977). A simple criticism can set off our entire neurochemical and cardiovascular reaction as if a monster was about to eat us. These fight/flight reactions only create more fear, which in turn creates more fight or flight reactions. The fear itself needs to be healed.

In the language of the Vulnerability Model of Recovery, fight reactions are willful acts, and flight reactions are will-less acts. Fight reactions take the form of:

- exertion
- strain
- force
- control
- drivenness
- punishment
- contraction

Fight reactions can reach problematic levels of:

- hypervigilance
- rage
- bitterness
- distrust
- judgmentalism
- fanaticism
- grandiosity
- anorexia
- workaholism
- use of stimulant drugs (e.g., cocaine, crack, steroids, methedrine)

Flight reactions take the form of:

- collapse
- numbing
- escape
- chaos
- confusion
- loss of control

Flight reactions can reach problematic levels of:

- overeating
- obsessing
- worrying
- agitated depression
- dissociation
- indecisiveness
- victimization
- scapegoating
- extreme clinging and dependency
- helplessness
- hopelessness
- apathy
- humiliation
- lack of self-care
- sexual compulsivity (as a soothing technique)
- use of sedating, numbing drugs (e.g., alcohol, barbiturates, heroin, tranquilizers)

## *Perceived Threats to Approval*

Fear, however, is not limited to perceived threats to survival. Our survival also depends on others accepting us, including us, liking us, validating us, approving of us. If we are disapproved of, we are excluded from connection, from work, from opportunities. We are not self-sufficient: we are not living off the land, unaffected and indifferent to how others feel about us. We must interact in order to be part of the marketplace, in order to obtain our food and shelter.

Beyond the economic implications of disapproval, approval is human emotional food. We cannot thrive without it. Clinically, we can see the suffering every day of people who feel they are not good enough, who have not received enough attention and validation of their worth. Remember the vignette of Tony and his friends at the New Year's Eve Party. When they tried to agree on one reason they had all become addicted to drugs, it was because of the feeling "I'm not enough."

Perceived threats to approval produce the same instinctual responses of fight and flight as in perceived threats to survival.

Fight reactions to perceived threats to approval can reach problematic levels of:

- competitiveness

- hostile disregard for others

- shameful joy (enjoying tragedy in other people's lives)

- workaholism

- mental abuse of self and others

- judgmentalism

- the use of stimulant drugs

Fear reactions to perceived threats to approval can reach problematic levels of:

- shyness

- shame and embarrassment

- self-defeating beliefs

- severe self-criticism

- emptiness

- perfectionism

- people pleasing

- feelings of incompetence and failure
- feelings of being unlovable
- the use of numbing drugs

### Learned Self-Hatred

Disapproval produces learned self-hatred. *Learned self-hatred,* originating in messages of disapproval from others, becomes our own feeling about aspects of ourself. We say "learned" self-hatred because self-hatred is not an innate human condition. It is a learned feeling.

Self-hatred need not be the result of trauma, abuse, or loss. It can be learned in any of the normal settings of social conditioning: the family, the church, the school, the popular culture. Self-hatred is suggested to the person through cultural messages of disapproval: one epidemic example in American culture is women's self-hatred of their body types.

Other messages of disapproval can involve:

- skin color
- socioeconomic status
- ethnic category
- religious category
- age
- gender
- emotional style
- health status
- sexual orientation

The resulting self-hatred goes either against the self or against others.

## THE GOOD EGO

Perceived threats to survival and learned self-hatred produce massive suffering around the world. These are threats that go beyond stopping drinking and drugging. These threats are inherent in the human condition, and biologically based flight/fight reactions make the suffering worse. How can the person in recovery manage the suffering from these basic dilemmas?

The current model of mental health offered to reduce suffering is the development of a good ego. The ego is seen as an inner organizing process that puts together our self-images and feelings and gives us an individual sense of self. This sense of self then gives us ". . . the capacities for action in the environment . . ." and gives us the experience of ourselves as . . . "someone who persists through space and time, who endures as a unique entity . . ." (Masterson, 1988, pp. 23–24). This ego self is thought to have the defenses and stability to maintain itself without too much anxiety or too much depression. In this model, it is failure to develop a good sense of self that exposes the person to instability and maladaptive responses to reality. The many problems of an unstable self are defined in the DSM-IV (American Psychiatric Association, 1994) under the categories of:

- anxiety disorders
- somatoform disorders
- dissociative disorders
- eating disorders
- impulse-control disorders
- adjustment disorders
- substance-related disorders
- personality disorders

## *Limitations of the Ego*

In mainstream psychology, the development of the ego self is seen as the ultimate mental health goal. With an enduring ego self, the person is considered able to:

- defend against both biological and social threats
- maintain stability
- avoid problematic levels of fight/flight reactiveness

The good ego certainly reduces suffering. A person suffers badly when her ego cannot organize her into a coherent self and cannot use defenses to protect her from instability. In ego psychology, for example, the stages of borderline self and narcissistic self are used to categorize underdeveloped egos and the suffering that comes from these stages (Masterson, 1988).

But the good ego cannot "endure" as a "unique entity" (Masterson's language cited earlier) and cannot solve the dilemmas of biological and social realities. Even the good ego cannot deny reality. The person's ego self sees undeniable proof that in fact it will not endure, that it will die. The person's losses in life begin to teach this fact to the ego: the losses and deaths of others; the diminishing of sexual attractiveness, of mental sharpness, of dreams about life, of business pursuits, of vocational choices, of physical stamina, and so on. The enduring self is confronted with a loss of belief: it can no longer believe in itself.

The breakthrough of this fact into full awareness can motivate spiritual development or induce despair. This is a challenge for every adult, whether or not they are in recovery. The person faces the choice of (1) continuing to participate in the denial of reality, no matter how unsatisfying and desperate the denial becomes (Becker, 1973), or (2) going beyond the ego sense of self.

## BEYOND THE EGO

From the perspective of psychosynthesis (Assagioli, 1991) and other transpersonal psychologies, the ego self is not the end point of adult development (Wilber, Engler, & Brown, 1986). In these schools of thought, development only to the ego level is seen as a guarantee of more vulnerability and suffering.

To go beyond the ego assumes there is more to go to. Fortunately, the good ego has never been convincing as the ultimate reality for some people. Explorers, spiritual seekers, meditators, scholars, healers, artists, theologians, mystics, and scientists in every culture and across all time have found methods to go beyond the social, ego self and experience extraordinary feelings and perspectives on reality. These methods have included prayer, meditation, drugs, ethics, study, debate, fasting, journeys, pilgrimages, rituals, and physical training. As a result of these experiments, we have available to us vast information about the beyond-ego level of our nature. In this book, we have referred to the beyond-ego level as the development of spiritual consciousness.

Spiritual consciousness helps each person to realize he is an individual participating in a universal life. Each individual is also a universal. The movement is ". . . from the pain of our personal . . . fragmentation towards the direct intuitive understanding of our wholeness and potential as human beings" (Levey, 1987, p. 90).

To begin the movement from individual to universal consciousness, we need a good map. Roberto Assagioli's work is the most clear and comprehensive map we have found so far. In the next chapter, we will discuss his model of consciousness and its application to recovery.

# SUMMARY

The spiritual aspect of the person has always been recognized in nursing philosophy and practice. Spiritual development is a practical, clinically relevant issue for the nurse to assess and assist in the person's recovery. The scientific community has neglected or ignored spirituality, but the recovery field has long held the importance of spiritual development for well-being.

In the view of the Vulnerability Model, spiritual development can move the person from living in vulnerability to living in wisdom and compassion. This development is dynamic and a daily possibility.

# REFLECTIONS

Are you comfortable with participating in your patient's spiritual development?

How do you encourage your own spirituality?

What are the obstacles to full expression of this part of you?

# References

American Psychiatric Association. (1994). *Diagnostic and statistical manual of mental disorders.* Washington, DC: American Psychiatric Association.

Assagioli, R. (1965). *Psychosynthesis.* New York: Penguin Books.

Assagioli, R. (1991). *Transpersonal development.* London: HarperCollins.

Becker, E. (1973). *Denial of death.* New York: Free Press.

Buxton, M., Smith, D., & Seymour, R. (1987). Spirituality and other points of resistance to the 12-Step recovery process. *Journal of Psychoactive Drugs, 19*(3), 275–286.

Dossey, B., Keegan, L., Guzzetta, C., & Kolkmeier, L. (1995). *Holistic nursing: A handbook for practice* (2nd ed.). Gaithersburg, MD: Aspen Publishers.

Dossey, L. (1993). *Healing words.* New York: HarperCollins.

Ferrucci, P. (1982). *What we may be.* Los Angeles: Tarcher.

Freud, S. (1964). *The future of an illusion.* Garden City, NY: Doubleday Anchor Books.

Gifford-May, D., & Thompson, N. (1994). Deep states of meditation. *Journal of Transpersonal Psychology, 26*(2), 117–128.

Green, A., & Green, E. (1977). *Beyond biofeedback.* Fort Wayne, IN: Knoll Publishing.

Kabat-Zinn, J. (1990). *Full catastrophe living.* New York: Delta.

Landrum, P., Beck, C., Rawlins, R., Williams, S., & Culpan, F. (1984). The person as a client. In C. Beck, R. Rawlins, & S. Williams (Eds.), *Mental health psychiatric nursing: A holistic life-cycle approach* (pp. 286–331). St. Louis: C.V. Mosby.

Levey, J. (1987). *The fine arts of relaxation, concentration and meditation.* London: Wisdom Publications.

Masterson, J. (1988). *The search for the real self.* New York: Macmillan.

McCrady, B., & Irvine, S. (1989). Self-help groups. In R. Hester & W. Miller (Eds.), *Handbook of alcoholism treatment approaches* (pp. 153–170). New York: Pergamon.

Ornish, D. (1990). *Dr. Dean Ornish's program for reversing heart disease.* New York: Ballantine Books.

Salewski, R. (1993). Meeting holistic health needs through a religious organization. *Journal of Holistic Nursing, 11,* 183–196.

Schaub, B., Anselmo, J., & Luck, S. (1991). Clinical imagery: Holistic nursing perspectives. In R. Kunzendorf (Ed.), *Mental imagery* (pp. 207–213). New York: Plenum Press.

Schaub, R. (1995a). Alternative health and spiritual practices. *Alternative Health Practitioner, 1*(1), 35–38.

Schaub, R. (1995b). Meditation, adult development and health. *Alternative Health Practitioner, 1*(3), 205–209.

Schaub, R. (1996). Meditation, adult development and health: Part two. *Alternative Health Practitioner, 2*(1), 61–68.

Schroeder-Sheker, T. (1994). Music for the dying. *Journal of Holistic Nursing, 12,* 83–99.

Smith, J. (1986). *Meditation: A sensible guide to a timeless discipline.* Champaign, IL: Research Press.

Sparks, T. (1987). Transpersonal treatment of addictions. *ReVision, 10*(2), 49–64.

Whitfield, C. (1985). *Alcoholism, attachments and spirituality.* East Rutherford, NJ: Thomas Perrin, Inc.

Wilber, K., Engler, J., & Brown, D. (1986). *Transformations of consciousness.* Boston: New Science Library.

## *Suggested Reading*

Ferrucci, P. (1982). *What we may be.* Los Angeles: Tarcher.

# 11 | A MODEL OF CONSCIOUSNESS

*From the eternal, to the present, for the future.*

Roberto Assagioli

## Fred

Fred, a 40-year-old recovering heroin addict who has been sober for ten years, walked down the hallway to the presentation meeting. As he became aware of his feelings and thoughts, he recognized a sense of panic in the pit of his stomach and images of going into the meeting and making a fool of himself. He imagined hostile faces evaluating his proposal and noticed the fantasy of turning around, leaving the building, and going to get heroin.

He recognized these thoughts and feelings for what they were—his old tapes, the inner voice that mocked and discouraged him. In his mind, Fred was able to observe this pattern. He chose to have compassion and love for what he understood to be the "frightened child" part of his pysche.

This feeling of love expanded as he realized that anyone looking at him at this moment would be unaware of this part of him. He appeared confident and purposeful. He smiled inwardly at his secret, knowing that the people at the meeting had their vulnerabilities hidden, too. Again, he connected with feelings of love and compassion, and relaxed.

In this state, he found that his mind was clear and that his creativity was available to him. As a result, the presentation went well. This confirmed for Fred the importance of awareness and choice.

### Observations

How can we understand the process that brought Fred from heroin addiction to the life-affirming transformation described in this vignette? Like many others, he was certainly helped by many of the basic principles of recovery. The potential also exists for everyone in recovery to mature spiritually. Part of maturing spiritually means cultivating the higher human qualities of love, compassion, creativity, and purposeful living.

# ASSAGIOLI'S MODEL OF CONSCIOUSNESS

Roberto Assagioli, M.D. developed a comprehensive model of consciousness and the human psyche that offers an understanding of Fred's experience. Assagioli was a colleague of Freud and Jung and the first psychoanalyst in Italy. He developed this model to address what he perceived as the limitations of psychoanalytic and other western psychological models. The focus in these models is on the influence of early problems and deprivations in nurturance and the resulting fixations and limitations in adulthood. The therapeutic goal is to develop a good-enough ego structure to be able to deal with the conflicts between survival drives and what is necessary to function within the rules and structures of society. Assagioli recognized the value of these therapeutic goals, but thought they were just one aspect of human development and potential.

## The Neglect of Spirituality in Traditional Psychology

Assagioli felt strongly that the spiritual aspect of human beings is a real and vital one. He saw the neglect and outright dismissal of this component of human experience within traditional psychological thought as a serious deficit.

Robert Coles, in his book *The Spiritual Life of Children* (1990), wrote about how his traditional psychoanalytic education dismissed the religious and spiritual interests of his child patients as defenses against their sexual and aggressive impulses. Coles described having a transformation in attitude through his extensive work with children. He concluded his book with this reflection on his work:

> So it is we connect with one another, move in and out of one another's lives, teach and heal and affirm one another, across space and time—all of us wanderers, explorers, adventurers, stragglers, and ramblers, sometimes tramps or vagabonds, even fugitives, but now and then pilgrims: as children, as parents, as old ones about to take the final step, to enter that territory whose character none of us here ever knows. Yet how young we are when we start wondering about it all, the nature of the journey and of the final destination (p. 335).

## *A Holistic Model of Consciousness*

In the spirit of openness to exploring this reality inherent in human beings, Assagioli cultivated a lifelong interest in spirituality and was a student of the world's wisdom traditions. His appreciation of the literature and practices of yoga, Buddhism, Judeo-Christian teachings, and western and eastern esoteric traditions led him to articulate a holistic model of consciousness that integrated the spiritual aspect of human experience. He called his model psychosynthesis. He carefully designed it to be neutral in its language so that it would be useful and meaningful to people from all spiritual perspectives.

Assagioli used a simple diagram to illustrate his theory (figure 11.1). This diagram should be thought of as three-dimensional and dynamic, representing the full potential of the human being at any given moment in time.

Imagery exercises are included in this discussion of the holistic model of consciousness so that you will be able to personalize each part of the model. We have used all of these

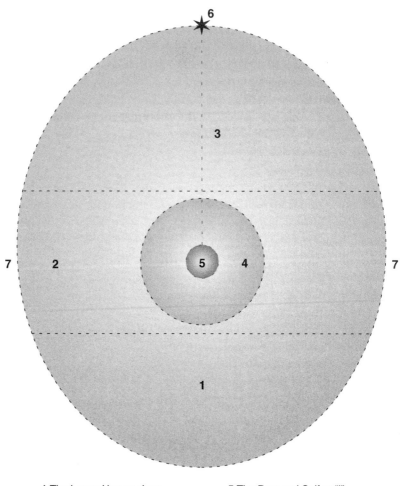

1.The Lower Unconscious        5.The Personal Self or "I"
2.The Middle Unconscious      6.The Transpersonal Self
3.The Higher Unconscious       7.The Collective Unconscious
4.The Field of Consciousness

**FIGURE 11.1** *Assagioli's holistic model of consciousness.*
*Adapted from **Psychosynthesis**, by R. Assagioli, 1965,*
***New York: Penguin.***

exercises clinically for many years with our clients in recovery. It is essential for you to work with this imagery personally before using it with clients. A deep personal understanding of these different states will make you far more effective in teaching others.

# THE LOWER UNCONSCIOUS

The *lower unconscious* (number 1 in figure 11.1) represents the sum total of our past biological and psychological conditioning, as well as genetic and parental influences. When Fred started to feel terror in the pit of his stomach, his life was not in danger, yet his entire autonomic nervous system was surging with a fight or flight response. This primitive biological response is based on the body preparing for physical attack. Fred's instinct was to suppress this fear in the way he had in the past, with heroin. The time orientation of the lower unconscious is to the past, to what has happened. Fred's biological response was activated by feelings from his childhood, such as fear of being ridiculed and shamed or fear of being punished and beaten if he made a mistake. All of these feelings can be relived in the present moment, yet they are not about the present reality.

## EXERCISE
### Images of Childhood Survey

We have developed this exercise to demonstrate how childhood emotions can enter the present in an instant. This is important emotional education for the person in recovery. It helps support the understanding that present feelings are not necessarily the result of present facts.

If possible, explore these imagery reflections with a friend's assistance. When you have become comfortable with doing this yourself, then consider using it with a person who is ready for such insight.

Have pen and paper available.

1. Begin by sitting quietly and bringing your attention to your breath. Allow yourself to just watch your breath's rhythm and flow. If you notice your mind wandering, this is perfectly natural. As soon as you notice this, choose to bring your attention back to your breath. Do this for five minutes.

2. Now bring your attention to your imagination. Imagine yourself as a child. Notice how old you are, where you are, and what you are doing. What is your mood? Take in as much information as you can and then make some notes about what you experienced.

3. Now close your eyes and center yourself in your breath again. Imagine yourself as a child in the place you grew up in. What room are you in? How does it feel to be there? Who else is in the house and what are they doing? Again, take in as much information as you can and then make some notes for yourself.

4. Now close your eyes and center yourself again. Imagine yourself as a child at school. What are you experiencing there? How do you feel in relationship to the other children and the teacher? When you are ready, make some notes for yourself.

5. Now close your eyes, center yourself, and imagine yourself as a child in a place you went to feel safe. What was it about this place that gave you this feeling? When you are ready, make some notes.

6. Now close your eyes, center yourself, and imagine yourself as a child standing in front of you right now. What do you feel toward this child, and what do you want to do?

Be open to what you experience, and make some notes when the experience is over.

### *Discussion*

The Images of Childhood Survey is filled with information. Exploring the images with a person in recovery can provide immediate insight into the sources of vulnerability as well as how it is experienced. Having the person make notes allows for a sense of control while doing this exploration. If the person prefers, he can discuss the images with you one at a time.

The first suggestion, imagine yourself as a child, is open-ended. Significant features of the image include the child's age, who the child is with, his mood, and where he is. Why did this particular childhood image come forward? There are an infinite number of other memories and images that could have presented themselves. Why this one?

The person's emotional reaction to this child is of particular significance. It is not unusual for someone in early recovery to be repulsed by the child. Some people will find the child unbearable, wanting to push him away or even kill him. This reaction is frequently linked to severe trauma in early childhood. The person is reacting negatively to reconnecting with the child's vulnerability. Allowing the adult self to open his heart to the child's pain is too threatening.

The traumatized child is fully present in the adult's experience and comes forward at every vulnerable moment. The process of recovery requires that the person develop the capacity to understand this. He needs to tolerate the child, not just withdraw or escape from the emotional experience. Cultivating insight and compassion for the child through fully understanding what he has experienced becomes the work of psychotherapy and the second recovery, the recovery from trauma.

Not all reactions to the child are negative. Some people have immediately positive and nurturing reactions to the child imagery. In some cases, people who have not cried for years will open to the child in the image and cry for him. These tears are highly positive and a great source of healing.

The second image, the child at home, offers insight into the home environment and the nature of the relationships with family members. It often vividly illustrates family dynamics. Are the people together and interacting? Are they off in different rooms, isolated from each other? Is mother asleep on the couch after dinner with the children in front of the TV? Is the client alone in his room, hoping he will not be noticed by his drunk father arriving home late from work and the bar? This part of the imagery offers information to help to enrich understanding of the child in the first image.

The third image, the child at school, gives you information about the child in the world. Is it a safe place? Does the child have friends and feel approved of by his peers? Is school a place of feeling ashamed for not being smart enough or not having the right clothes?

The person's memory of a teacher is also significant. It represents his relationship to authority figures and rules. Was the relationship hostile? Was the child rebelling? Was there a teacher who was a source of attention and affirmation that was not received at home?

The fourth image, a safe place, is often the most difficult image to connect with. The person in recovery may have no memory of safety. This can be an upsetting realization. On the other hand, images of a safe place such as cuddling with a beloved pet, spending time alone in nature, absorbed in some creative activity or reading, spending time with a friend's loving family can be the foundation for understanding what creates safety apart from drugs and alcohol.

The fifth image, bringing the child into the present moment, introduces the possibility of healing. Understanding what the child's experiences were gives the person suggestions how to care for himself in his recovery.

# Petra

Petra recalled with great pain the humiliation she felt in elementary school because the only thing she ever had for lunch were peanut butter and jelly sandwiches. The reason for this was that her alcoholic mother never got up in the morning. Petra, the oldest of four children, made lunch for herself and her sister at night before she went to bed. Peanut butter and jelly was the only thing that was ever available.

At school, she made a point of telling her friends that she hated any other kind of food.

### Observations

The memory that came back to Petra in this imagery was the day she opened her lunch bag and found that her mother had put some of her favorite cookies in it. She was afraid that her friends would notice her eating the cookies and would realize she had lied to them about not liking anything but peanut butter and jelly. So, she made believe she hated the cookies and gave them to a friend. This imagery dramatically illustrated the sense of shame that Petra experienced on a daily basis as a child, not to mention the tragedy of the neglect and deprivation.

The Images of Childhood Survey exercise demonstrates the capacity of the imagination to bring past experience into the present moment. It teaches us how the lower unconscious is a dynamic part of our present experience.

# THE MIDDLE UNCONSCIOUS

In the *middle unconscious* (number 2 in figure 11.1), time orientation is to the present, to what is happening now. Fred was experiencing his middle unconscious when he became concerned about how he appeared to people in the present moment. The middle unconscious includes any information that, though not present at the moment, is easily called into awareness. The energy of this level is largely absorbed in drives for social approval and belonging or fears of social disapproval and exclusion. This is the domain of self-consciousness, of social identity and role, and social functioning.

## EXERCISE
### The Party
Read this through and then try it for yourself.
1. Close your eyes . . . Imagine you are getting ready to go to a party.
2. What are you imagining will happen?
3. What are you concerned about?
4. How much anxiety is involved with how you look?
5. What negative social images come to mind?

**6.** If people will like you, what is it about you they will like?

**7.** What are you imagining as pleasing about yourself?

**8.** Make notes about your reflections.

### Discussion

This exploration of the middle unconscious brings into awareness the degree to which the person is controlled by social approval. Her agonizing over how people are perceiving her is fully demonstrated. This information is especially important to uncover because people in early recovery cannot remember the last time they were in a social situation without the mood-altering effects of drugs or alcohol or both. Whether it is the disinhibiting effects of alcohol, the sedating or anxiety-reducing effects of depressant drugs, or the confidence-building effect of cocaine or other stimulant substances, mood alteration was often a prerequisite to go out to a dance club, a party, or other social outings.

It may take years of recovery before a person feels ready to return to socializing freely. There will be a need for the development of stress management skills in the face of socializing without the use of drugs to modify her mood.

People in AA and other twelve-step programs often prefer to limit their socializing to other program people. It is not only because they will be in a drug-free environment. It is also because there is a feeling that they can be vulnerable and honest without being judged.

---

## THE HIGHER UNCONSCIOUS

The *higher unconscious* (number 3 in figure 11.1) holds the energy and spiritual qualities that connect to something greater than our own separate biological and social reality. The higher unconscious time orientation is to the future, to the possibilities of what will happen. As soon as Fred was able to observe himself with compassion, he was contacting energies of the higher unconscious. The love and compassion he felt became more than just personal. It included love and compassion for all the people around him. This is an expansion of consciousness beyond just personal survival or social approval.

## Spiritual Qualities

The higher unconscious is the source of intuitive and imaginative insights, illumination, creative-symbolic expression, and the drive toward meaning and purpose. It contains a sense of inner guidance, wisdom, and deep intuitive knowing. The felt impulse toward union with something greater than our own separate consciousness and the desire for mystical union are emotions originating in this realm. Near death experiences; mental, physical, and emotional healing; inspiration and joy; compassionate forms of love and altruism all emerge from this aspect of our nature. Assagioli emphasized that higher consciousness is a living reality, a fact, not a metaphor or an abstraction.

## EXERCISE

### The Higher Self

Read through this exercise and then try it for yourself. After the experience is over, make notes for yourself.

This exercise can be varied in many ways. The essential feature of it is that the person is imagining meeting some form of wisdom. In this example, we use the phrase *a wise being*. Each person has a unique way of imagining this wise being.

1. Close your eyes and center on your breathing.

2. Reflect on a question about yourself, about your choices, about your direction.

3. Now begin to imagine a road in front of you . . . Sense yourself walking on it.

4. Now imagine, in the distance, a wise being of any kind coming your way.

5. When you meet, ask your question and be open to what happens.

6. Make notes.

## Discussion

This higher self exercise demonstrates the possibility of connecting with a deeper source of wisdom within the person. The suggestions are deliberately vague to allow for any symbols that make intuitive sense to the individual. This work is a vital aspect of the recovery process because it gives the person a source of guidance for living.

---

## Healing Instinct-Impairment

Guidance for living is a key resource for many people in recovery because they grew up in homes where their perceptions of reality were never validated. Consequently, the person never learned to trust himself. This factor, combined with numerous incidences of poor judgment during the addiction, leaves him instinct-impaired. *Instinct-impaired* refers to being cut off from a basic sanity, a basic instinct and intuition about reality and how to care for oneself. The impairment is the person's loss of contact with a source of knowing. Helping to understand this process of alienation from self-knowledge and then introducing the possibility of reclaiming this may at first evoke anxiety. Once this possibility is accepted, a sense of hopefulness and then excitement is generated.

## A Science of the Higher Self

As early as the 1930s, Assagioli called for a research-based science of the higher self. Using his model and techniques, we have gathered twenty years of clinical anecdotal notes about the effects of higher self work. The following items recur consistently:

- the higher self's time orientation is to the future
- the higher self offers specific intimate wisdom about the person
- the purpose of the wisdom is the expansion of love

As noted, the higher self's time orientation is to the future. The past is treated with interest only as a source of learning, and the present is seen as the place the future begins. This orientation to the future seems to tie the higher self to a species-survival function within the brain. The purpose of learning, the expansion of love, can also be seen as a species-survival function, since love counteracts the destructive aspect of human nature and binds the person to life. Religious interpretations of this ground of love could also be applied here. For the authors, the phenomenon itself is of primary interest. Speculations regarding its origin and function are another area of research.

# THE FIELD OF CONSCIOUSNESS

The *field of consciousness* (number 4 in figure 11.1) is whatever we find ourselves presently aware of. This field is usually absorbed by the unreflective, conditioned flow of images, sensory stimuli, half-thoughts, and impulses that are in a constant state of change. This field is the aspect of our consciousness that most meditative practices seek to alter, focus, or control. An important aspect of this field is that it expands in all directions.

Looking at the diagram, you see that the field of consciousness is drawn as a circle. If the circle enlarges, if awareness expands, we become more aware of our higher, lower, and middle unconscious. In Fred's case, opening up his awareness to his lower unconscious, his fear-driven responses, and the conditioning of his childhood provoked a corresponding opening up of his higher unconscious awareness. It can be compared to the shift in viewpoint when one climbs up high enough to be able to see an entire landscape rather than just the trees directly in front of you.

## EXERCISE

### Mindfulness

Read this through and then try it for ten minutes. Do this easily; try not to work at it. You are just practicing noticing what comes into your field of consciousness. You only have to observe, to witness.

1. Close your eyes and center on your breathing for a moment.

2. Now let go of your breathing and notice what comes to you; e.g., a thought, a body sensation, a feeling, an image, a sound from outside.

3. Now notice what comes to you next.

4. Continue witnessing the flow of your experiences in an open, curious, noninterfering way.

### Discussion

This exercise derives from the Buddhist meditation practice of mindfulness or insight meditation. It asks the person to be a noninterfering witness to their field of consciousness. Much can be learned just by doing nothing but witnessing. This exercise also cultivates a calmness and begins to build a skill of quiet, calm self-observation. This is discussed in more detail in the section on the "I."

---

## THE PERSONAL SELF OR "I"

In the vignette at the beginning of this chapter, Fred was able to step back and observe his destructive inner voice. When we step back from our immediate experience, we take on the role of observation. This place of observation is a different part of us than the part that is having the experience. This observing part of us is what Assagioli called the "I" or personal self.

The *personal self* (number 5 in figure 11.1) is our center of awareness, analogous to our observing ego. It is the aspect of our psyche cultivated in meditative practices and referred to as the witness or the observer. It is the part that can watch ourthoughts, feelings, sensations, and impulses from a point of neutral observation. In Assagioli's language, it represents the "realization of oneself as living center of awareness" (1965, p. 112). It is a reflection of the universal consciousness experienced on the human, individual level.

## A Mental Health Practice

Assagioli advocated deepening this experience as an essential aspect of mental health because it brings the following health benefits:

- The person can step back from the immediate contents of awareness, notice them, and then choose whether or not to react to them.

- With practice, the person builds up a deeper skill for making contact with the center of his consciousness, with the enduring, nontransitory aspect of his mental-emotional life.

Throughout psychospiritual literature, this identification with consciousness itself has been considered a gateway to spiritual development.

## EXERCISE

## Self-Identification

This script is from *What We May Be* by Piero Ferrucci (1982, pp. 66–67). It is a classic book for inner development. In this exercise, Ferrucci offers a way to experience the reality of the self as independent of what it observes. Read it one step at a time, try it, and then go on to the next step.

1. Become aware of your body . . . of the contact of your body with the chair you are sitting on, of your feet with the ground, of your clothes with your skin . . . of your breathing . . . just notice in a neutral way all the physical sensations you can . . .

2. Become aware of your feelings. What feeling are you experiencing right now? . . . And which are the principal feelings you experience recurrently in your life? . . . Do not judge . . . Just view your usual feelings with an objective attitude . . .

3. Turn your attention to your desires . . . Adopting the same impartial attitude as before, review the main desires which take turns in motivating your

life. Often you may be identified with one or the other of these but now simply consider them, side by side . . .

**4.** Observe the world of your thoughts. As soon as a thought emerges, watch it until another one takes its place, then another one, and so on. If you think you are not having any thoughts, realize that this too is a thought. Watch your stream of consciousness as it flows by: memories, opinions, nonsense, arguments, images . . .

**5.** The observer—the one who has been watching your sensations, feelings, desires, and thoughts—is not the same as the object it observes. Who is it that has been observing all these realms? It is your self. The self is not an image or a thought; it is that essence which has been observing all these realms and yet is distinct from all of them. And you are that being. Say inwardly: "I am the self, a center of pure consciousness." Seek to realize this . . .

## Discussion

This meditation exercise can be used repeatedly with people in recovery. Making a tape of this for the person to work with on her own would also be helpful. The meditation experience may at first feel just relaxing. As the subtler levels of awareness become available to her, there may be an experience of deep peacefulness at the realization that it is not necessary to respond to every thought and feeling that passes through. The sense of watching and not needing to react is freeing. The realization that a feeling does not need to be acted on brings relief.

---

## THE TRANSPERSONAL SELF

The *transpersonal self* (number 6 in figure 11.1) is universal consciousness, the actual source of personal consciousness. It is an insight realized in mystical states throughout human history and referred to as God, Atman, the Tao, the eternal, and so on.

Assagioli was clear the transpersonal self objectively exists, because ". . . it is proven by direct experience; it is one of those primary experiences which are evidence of themselves . . . and therefore have full scientific value . . ." To address any critics who questioned the reality of the transpersonal self, Assagioli added, ". . . one has to create the conditions for having the experience and scientists up to now have not taken the trouble to do that" (cited in Hardy, 1987, pp. 31–32).

## *Transpersonal Images*

In line with Assagioli's statement that it is necessary to create the conditions conducive to experiencing the qualities of the transpersonal self, he encouraged his patients and students to practice identifying with transpersonal images. Transpersonal images can be seen cross-culturally as ways of depicting expanded states of consciousness. He chose images that depicted going from the isolated, separate self to conscious contact with the transpersonal self. He used these images to help clients have direct experiences.

Assagioli identified fifteen classes of transpersonal images and suggested that they be used for meditation practice (Assagioli, 1991, p. 89):

- introversion
- going deeper, descent
- broadening, expansion
- reawakening, revival
- light, enlightenment
- fire
- development
- empowering
- love
- a way, path, pilgrimage
- transmutation, sublimation
- liberation

- new birth, regeneration
- resurrection, return
- elevation, ascent

In line with the use of symbols, Assagioli developed a meditation on the unfolding of a rose. This was one of his favorite images. He pointed out that flowers are frequently used to represent the soul or the spiritual self in both eastern and western traditions.

## *EXERCISE*

### *The Rose*

Read the instructions through and then try the exercise for yourself.

**1.** Close your eyes and connect with your breathing.

**2.** Allow your mind to focus fully on the sensation of your breath passing through your nostrils . . . As soon as you are aware of any other thoughts or sensations, bring your attention back to your breath.

**3.** Now, in your imagination, experience a rosebush . . . Notice it in as much detail as possible.

**4.** Now become aware of a tightly closed bud on one of the branches . . . Imagine this bud growing and beginning to bloom.

**5.** Now identify with this rosebud as it emerges with its beauty and its vitality . . . Experience it blossoming in you . . . Stay with this experience and explore it in any way that feels right for you.

### *Discussion*

Assagioli's concept of the transpersonal self is based in the fact that each of us is both an individual and part of the universe. Although we experience most of our life as an individual, we also have occasional senses of our innate connection to the universe.

Identification with the life process of a flower opening is one way of making conscious contact with our transpersonal self.

Access to the transpersonal part of the self, to spiritual consciousness, can literally change our mind. Time is shifted from clock time to eternal time, values clarify around what really matters, and the right use of life seems obvious. Spiritual consciousness can be a mental revolution with resulting emotional, behavioral, and quality of life benefits.

---

*Carl Jung and the Effect of the Transpersonal Self on Recovery* An important historical note is that Carl Jung believed that personally experiencing the transpersonal self was the essential factor in recovery from addiction. It was this insight of Jung's that served as one of the primary inspirations for the founding of Alcoholics Anonymous (Jung, cited in Sparks, 1987).

Roland H., a successful American businessman who had struggled with alcoholism for many years, sought out Jung for treatment. He spent a year in Europe under Jung's care. During that time he stopped drinking and considered himself cured.

Upon arriving back in the United States, Roland H. quickly resumed his drinking and was soon drinking more than ever. When he wrote to Jung asking to resume treatment, Jung declined. Instead, he told Roland H. to seek out a spiritual awakening, as that was the best hope of cure for his alcoholism.

*The Oxford Movement and Bill Wilson* Roland then joined the Oxford Movement, an organization of spiritual seekers that emphasized meditation, prayer, and service. In these surroundings, Roland H. did experience a spiritual awakening that led to relief from his alcoholism.

Roland H.'s success in his recovery led him to reach out to other alcoholics through the Oxford Movement. Bill Wilson, one of Alcoholics Anonymous's founders, had friends who had sought help through the Oxford Movement. They introduced him to the principles and practices of this organization. Bill Wilson, following failed attempts at sobriety and in a deep state of depression, had a powerful experience that he credited with assisting in his eventual recovery. He described crying out in despair: "If there be a God, will He show Himself" (Alcoholics Anonymous, 1984).

Wilson then went on to describe "There immediately came to me an illumination of enormous impact and dimension . . ." which caused an immediate "release from the alcohol obsession . . . At once I knew I was a free man."

***The Beginning of Alcoholics Anonymous***   Inspired by his own experience, Wilson continued his study with the Oxford Movement and began a study of the world's literature on spiritual experiences. In his discussions with other alcoholics trying to become sober, Bill Wilson began to conceptualize the Oxford Movement ideas into a series of steps as a foundation for recovery. These guidelines then became the cornerstone for the founding of the Twelve Steps of Alcoholics Anonymous. In 1961, Wilson wrote to Carl Jung to tell him about the success of AA and how its formation had been influenced by Jung's work with Roland H. Jung wrote back to Wilson, reconfirming the importance of spiritual development in recovery: "His (Roland H.'s) craving for alcohol was the equivalent, on a low level, of the spiritual thirst of our being for wholeness; expressed in medieval language, the union with God . . . The only way to such an experience is that it happens to you in reality, and it can only happen . . . when you walk on a path which leads to higher understanding . . ." (Jung, cited in Sparks, 1987).

While Bill Wilson's description of his spiritual awakening was sudden, it is important to know it is not necessary for this awareness to occur in such a dramatic form. In Alcoholics Anonymous's literature, this point is clearly made:

> . . . most of our experiences are what the psychologist William James calls the "educational variety" because they develop slowly over a period of time. Quite often friends of the newcomer are aware of the difference long before he is himself. He finally realizes he has undergone a profound alteration in his reaction to life; that such a change could hardly have been brought about by himself alone . . . our members find that they have tapped an unsuspected inner

resource which they presently identify with their own conception of a power greater than themselves (Alcoholics Anonymous, 1987, 569–570).

# THE COLLECTIVE UNCONSCIOUS

The *collective unconscious* (number 7 in figure 11.1) holds our genetic memory, our myths, our cultural, racial, and ancestral influences, and the feelings and energies that come with these influences. Jung felt the collective unconscious held the essential patterns of the mind which he called the archetypes. In his view, one example of a universal archetype is the higher self or wisdom figure. This archetype is a recurring pattern in every culture, with stories, qualities, and attributes attached to it.

Archetypes relevant to addiction theory are the drunken writer, the intoxicated poet, the ecstatic musician, and the mystical artist. In each case, the person is being inspired by drug experiences. Through drugs, these figures are thought to experience breakthroughs beyond normal consciousness. Because of their artistry, they are then able to render their ecstatic, drug-based experiences into artistic forms for the rest of us to experience.

The archetype of the drunken writer is not a cliché: eighty percent of the American writers who won the Nobel Prize for Literature were active alcoholics. These writers included Fitzgerald, Hemingway, Steinbeck, Faulkner, Lewis, and O'Neil (Keehn, 1989).

## EXERCISE

### Imagery from the Collective Unconscious

Read this through and then try it for yourself.

**1.** Close your eyes and center on your breathing . . . Now begin to imagine a myth or folktale that has always spoken to you, that has always had a personal meaning for you.

**2.** Take as much time as you need to imagine yourself participating in this story . . . taking part in it.

**3.** Fully imagine being several different characters in the tale.

**4.** What feelings and what thoughts does participation in this evoke in you?

**5.** To what aspect of your present life does this story connect?

## *Discussion*

Seeing our life in larger terms or in universal terms can give us more compassion and perspective. We are not simply taking place in a separate, isolated drama. Our impulses and our desire to live our life with purpose comes from our heritage as a member of our species and our historical roots. For the person in recovery, the decision to live a sober life can be seen in such larger terms. The second step of AA states: "Came to believe that a power greater than myself can restore me to sanity."

# IMPLICATIONS OF ASSAGIOLI'S MODEL OF CONSCIOUSNESS

Note that the lines of the diagram in figure 11.1 are not solid. This is to show that the boundaries are permeable, fluid, and changing. The levels are not discrete, self-contained categories. As Fred walked down the hallway, he was experiencing contrasting feelings and thoughts from many different levels of consciousness.

One of the clinical goals of working with this psychosynthetic model is to broaden the field of consciousness to include awareness of the subtler, higher unconscious realities, thereby freeing the individual from a limited experience of who he is. With the cultivation of awareness at the personal and transpersonal level, the possibility of choosing the way we want to respond to experiences, both in our actions and in our deepest emotions and attitudes, becomes a real possibility.

This human possibility is a provocative stance to take. It challenges us to be responsible (response-able) at a very basic level. The reality of this deep level of change is demonstrated by Fred. His choice goes far beyond not using drugs: it includes choosing to change his self-destructive emotional responses and attitudes to ones that are life-affirming and loving.

## SUMMARY

The healing process in addictions must include movement into spiritual awareness. As expressed by Janet Quinn, Ph.D., R.N., a healing art can be thought of as ". . . a skillful practice which facilitates the integration, harmony, and balance of mind-body-spirit in the recipient . . . one cannot practice a healing art without attending the spiritual nature and needs of the recipient" (1985, p. 117).

To help in spiritual development, a comprehensive and clear model is needed. Psychosynthesis provides an expansive, hopeful vision that is grounded in insights about human development and human potential.

## REFLECTIONS

What is my own view of human possibility? Of my own possibilities?

Can I imagine that working with a detoxifying addict can be the beginning of her spiritual development? Can I hold such a big picture? What is the effect of thinking this way?

### References

Alcoholics Anonymous. (1984). *Pass it on.* New York: AA World Services.

Alcoholics Anonymous. (1987). *Alcoholics anonymous.* New York: AA World Services.

Assagioli, R. (1965). *Psychosynthesis.* New York: Penguin.

Assagioli, R. (1991). *Transpersonal development.* London: HarperCollins.

Coles, R. (1990). *The spiritual life of children.* Boston: Houghton Mifflin.

Ferrucci, P. (1982). *What we may be.* Los Angeles: Tarcher.

Hardy, J. (1987). *A psychology with a soul.* London: Routledge & Kegan Paul.

Keehn, D. (1989). Writers, alcohol, and creativity. *Addiction and Consciousness Journal, 4*(1), 9–14.

Quinn, J. (1985). The healing arts in modern health care. In D. Kunz (Ed.), *Spiritual aspects of the healing arts* (pp. 116–124). Wheaton, IL: Theosophical Publishing House.

Sparks, T. (1987). Transpersonal treatment of addictions. *ReVision, 10*(2), 49–64.

## Suggested Reading

Alcoholics Anonymous. (1974). *Pass it on.* New York: AA World Services.

# THE PATHS
# OF SPIRITUAL
# DEVELOPMENT

*We are traveling with tremendous speed toward a
star in the Milky Way. A great repose is visible on the
face of the Earth. My heart's a little fast. Otherwise
everything's fine.*

Bertolt Brecht

## Susan

Susan was in her seventh year of recovery. She felt frustrated because
she was not able to personalize the spiritual part of recovery: "I don't
know what's wrong with me, I just can't meditate. I've tried it and it
does nothing for me. I know that I'm a spiritual person. I know that
it is important to me. Why can't I get anywhere?"

## PERSONALIZING SPIRITUALITY

The person facing the challenge of a drug-free life must let go
of the isolation of self-absorption. She must recognize that she is
not alone in a personal tragedy. This humbling realization asks
her to recognize the humanness of her vulnerability. Witnessing
others in their struggle and acknowledging the commonality is
just the beginning.

The real challenge, if she is to develop and mature, is to find a worldview or framework that helps in understanding this vulnerability. There is a need to find a way to frame the truth of her own fears and to embrace more. Everyone has the innate desire and capacity to develop this wisdom. The possibility of this experience is real and available. It is necessary to find ways to cultivate it in order to achieve inner peace. Inner peace and compassion are the emotions of wisdom.

## The Spiritual Impulse

Each person has the ability to connect with their transcendent nature. *Transcendent nature* refers to the aspect of people that exists beyond their socially conditioned personalities. It is often referred to as spirit, soul, or essence. Each of us has had many experiences that we can identify as transcendent moments: moments that have asked us to redefine our sense of self in relation to the world. This is a given, not something that is reserved for a special few.

There is a drive within us to experience transcendence, a union with something greater than our own small, separate identity. This drive is as real as the drive to survive and as powerful as hunger for food and sexual expression.

## The Repression of the Sublime

Just as cultures and societies may demand that we deny and repress our free speech or our sexuality, modern scientific culture has encouraged us to repress the transcendent aspect of our being. Transpersonal psychiatrist Roberto Assagioli called this "the repression of the sublime" (1965). *Repression of the sublime* is denial, neglect, or negation of innate human spirituality. This results in defending against experiences, ignoring inner wisdom, and not recognizing connection with spirit or higher self.

## Individual Differences and Spirituality

The value of bringing psychological insights into our exploration of spirituality lies in the fact that we bring our personality with us on this journey. A transpersonal psychological perspective can help in broadening our definition of spiritual connection and in delineating the different ways individuals experience this connection.

We will explore eight characteristic paths through which people experience connection beyond their own separate ego identity. The eight paths of transcendence are:

- aesthetics and beauty
- service
- social action and justice
- knowledge and wisdom
- ceremony and ritual
- senses and energy
- meditation
- devotion

We each have our own personal preferences, different cognitive capacities and skills, and personal and cultural history, all of which affect our choice of path.

## THE PATHS

All the world's spiritual and wisdom traditions use some or all of these paths as part of their teaching and as a way of deepening the spiritual learning of their adherents. Let us now look more closely at each of these.

### *The Path of Aesthetics and Beauty*

*Look carefully in an animal at a spirit alive;*
*every flower is a soul opening out into nature;*
*a mystery touching love is asleep inside metal.*
*"Everything is intelligent!" And everything moves you.*

Gerard De Nerval

## CASE STUDY | *Miriam*

Miriam was a 76-year-old woman who had started drinking heavily after the death of her husband ten years ago. Up until that time, she had been a social drinker. Six months ago, she stopped drinking because she was frightened by the forgetfulness and confusion she was experiencing.

Miriam had difficulty participating in AA because she felt too different from the people there. She was older than most of them and her drinking had never interfered with her life until recently. She was also very turned off by the talk of spirituality. She said she was not at all interested in religion or spirituality. She had no use for God since God let her father and brother be killed in a concentration camp.

Miriam did a lot of traveling after her husband's death, using a large portion of her limited funds to do this. She traveled with passion and fervor. She went to France and sought out Gothic cathedrals. She adored the stained glass windows, especially the rose windows. She expressed being awed by the beauty of these places, but purely on an aesthetic level. It had nothing to do with the spirituality of the places.

Miriam traveled to India, not on a tour but on her own, because there were very particular places she wanted to visit. There were places she had seen pictures of in books, especially an island where there were caves filled with Buddhas. She arranged for a young guide to bring her there, and this too was an awesome experience.

Miriam went to Mexico to visit the pyramids. She described experiencing a sense of timelessness and also a sense of familiarity as though she belonged there. She felt embraced by the sun and delighted by the colors and scents of this ancient place.

**Observations**

You can listen to Miriam and hear the quest of a woman searching for spiritual experience. She resonated very deeply with the aesthetic path but was limited in her concept of spirituality. The path of aesthetics and beauty is the creation of or meditation on art and beauty as a way of spiritual development. Miriam's feelings of love and transcendence, timelessness and peace, were not from an intellectual appreciation of this art and beauty. Where were these feelings coming from?

**Aligning with Truth**   One way to think of artistic inspiration is that the artist is aligning with some essential insight or truth about the universe and is expressing it through the art. Leonard Bernstein wrote about his experience conducting an orchestra:

. . . it takes minutes before I know where I am—in what hall, in what country, or who I am. Suddenly, I become aware that there is clapping, that I must bow. It's very difficult. But marvelous. A sort of ecstasy that is nothing more and nothing less than a loss of ego. *You* don't exist. It's exactly the same sort of ecstasy as the trance you are in when you are composing and you are inspired. You don't know what time it is or what's going by (cited in Ferrucci, 1990, p. 17).

We can appreciate Bernstein's description of his experience because, typically, common language fails us when expressing moments of transcendence. When we are deeply moved by a work of art, it is because the artist has succeeded in communicating something nonverbal or beyond words. We are on the same wavelength. That is why, for example, Jonathan, a 37-year-old marketing specialist, can refer to the room at the Museum of Modern Art in New York City that contains Monet's *Waterlilies* as "my church."

***Aligning with the Path of Beauty***    All of us have the capacity to be moved by beauty. If we allow ourselves to be drawn deeply into the aesthetic experience, there is a loss of our sense of time and place, we merge with the beauty, and feel open to love. Think about times when this has happened to you. Perhaps you were at a concert, or watching a sunset, or rapt in the beauty of a campfire, or at the magnificence of a newborn child. You experience awe and awakening of new awareness. Perhaps the experience extends beyond the initial stimulus and you carry that sensitivity to beauty with you, feeling open to the beauty of simple things, and feeling an enlivening of your senses. Perhaps there is an opening up of your heart to feelings of love as well. For some people, this aesthetic sensitivity can be a meditation, an act that brings them fully into the present moment where love and joy are felt. Some people find this to be their natural path to transcendence.

The world's spiritual traditions certainly recognize the power of this path. The art of the world, the greatest architecture, paintings, frescoes, sculptures, music, and poetry have all been created for and inspired by worship and spiritual celebration. The following exercises will help you experience this path.

---

## *EXERCISE*

### *Reflection on Art*

**1.** Find an image that you feel attracted to; it can be a favorite painting or photograph.

**2.** Sit in a comfortable position and place the image at eye level.

3. First observe this image in as much detail as possible.

4. Notice what you are feeling as you observe this image.

5. Close your eyes and imagine the image inside you. Again, notice what feelings this evokes.

6. Now open your eyes and contemplate this image with an openness to the information it holds for you.

7. Make some notes on your experience and draw your inner image.

---

## EXERCISE

### Reflection on Natural Object

1. Find a flower, a stone, a piece of wood, something that appeals to you.

2. Now sit in a comfortable position and place it in front of you.

3. Turn your attention to your breathing.

4. When you feel centered, turn your attention to the natural object.

5. Just look at it; ignore your opinions of it or what you are thinking about it. The object itself is your meditation, your focus of contemplation.

6. After a few minutes of giving your attention to the object, close your eyes and notice your overall body and feeling state.

7. Make some notes on your experience.

### Discussion

If these practices appeal to you, then keep the images or objects in a place where you will see them often. Let them serve as a reminder to reconnect with your inner wisdom and spiritual self. This practice works well with any image or object you feel a healing connection with. A simple direct gaze at art or a natural object can bring you into centeredness and peace.

# The Path of the Senses and Energy Experiences

*Man has no Body distinct from his Soul for that called Body is a portion of Soul discerned by the five Senses, the chief inlets of Soul in this age.*

*Energy is the only life and is from the Body and Reason is the bound or outward circumference of Energy.*

*Energy is Eternal Delight.*

William Blake, 1793, from *The Marriage of Heaven and Hell*

# Melanie

Melanie described why she loved skiing so much. She had always loved the physicality of the sport, especially when she found herself on a steep, quiet slope where she could not see her path. Everything around her would appear totally white as sunlight glistened on the surface of the snow. She felt completely at one with her skis, her body supple and balanced. Speeding into timelessness, oneness with the mountain, no thoughts, no more Melanie, just the moment. It has not happened every time, but those moments are why she skis. Thinking of those moments brings tears to her eyes.

## Observations

The path of the senses and energetic experiences is a way of spiritual development that emphasizes body experience. Physical activities can create the feeling of oneness, of being part of something greater. Athletes such as Melanie know this experience. It happens in the moment when effort departs. It is an experience of flow, of effortless effort. It occurs when the basketball player cannot miss the shot.

He is described as "unconscious" or "hot" or "in the zone." The ball goes in every time. It is no longer about winning the game. It is a transcendent state. The player is no longer separate from the object of the action. It is an experience of oneness. The other players can see it when it is happening.

There are different ways to experience oneness through the body and the senses. The experience of learning to use our body in a new way, of mastering a skill to the point of not having to struggle to do it, can create this experience. It is the combination of heightened awareness and intention that allows it to occur. It can also occur when our body is failing us, when we give up fighting our physical experience and just observe it and let go into it.

# *Janine*

Janine is a 29-year-old nurse in recovery from alcoholism. As part of her spiritual exploration, she became interested in Native American healing traditions. She attended a seminar on this in the Utah canyonlands. Afterwards, she went camping with some friends.

One evening she was walking by herself and sat on a rock to watch the sunset. After sitting for a while staring at a butte, she suddenly experienced a bright light emanating from the center of the rocks in the distance. She was not frightened. She felt drawn to the light, as if being pulled into it. She began to see figures, some of whom appeared to be shamans and medicine men, some on foot and some on horseback.

As suddenly as the vision appeared, it disappeared. Janine continued to sit on the rock for a while in a state of timelessness. Eventually her friends came searching for her in the dark with flashlights. She had no words to describe her experience. She just returned to the campsite and went to sleep.

Several months later, Janine described her experience to a nurse therapist. She knew this nurse worked from a holistic perspective, and so Janine was eager to get her reaction to the experience. The nurse, after asking many questions, commented that what Janine was describing had the qualities of a spontaneous mystical experience. Janine was excited by this and said: "I'm so relieved that you don't think I'm crazy. I knew that something special had taken place. It has stayed with me and I feel peaceful whenever I reconnect with it. It helped me in my work. I'm more comfortable with my critically ill patients."

And then Janine asked: "Does this mean I have to devote my life to having more of these?" The therapist said it was important for Janine to reflect on the vision and decide what meaning it held for her. It was a vision that she could continue to integrate for the rest of her life.

### Observations

While sitting on that rock, Janine allowed herself to let go. She had spent time participating in Native American rituals that encouraged her to deepen her observation of nature and her connection to it. These rituals taught her a new way to be in nature. She opened up to the energy of the canyonlands, allowing herself to extend beyond her personal boundaries and to connect with a larger reality.

This type of energy experience, connecting with life energy, is another form of spiritual connection achieved through the body. This is the experience that is so beautifully described in the Blake quote.

In the yogic tradition, this life energy is called prana. In Taoism, it is called chi. Both systems are referring to a life force that exists within us but is at the same time connected to a universal life energy, a vitalizing force. People can have heightened experiences of connecting with this energy, either spontaneously as Janine did, or through training and practices that encourage it.

***Embodied Spirituality***   The concept of energy and experiences of energy appeals to the person who is drawn to an embodied spirituality. Some people are naturally more aware of or sensitive to sensual, kinesthetic experience. The sensorial-energetic path is for the person who feels connected to the earth, who finds peace in the garden and is connected to the cycles of nature. Traditional cultures that follow this path have identified physical places that generate energy, and consider these places sacred.

Our skin holds us in, creating a boundary between us and expanded levels of consciousness. For some people, the way to heighten awareness is through working with the body. Through imagery and body awareness practices such as biofeedback, Tai Chi, yoga, Chi Gong, Alexander Technique, stress management, and relaxation training, some people feel safe enough to let go. They are able to extend their boundaries and allow in other possibilities. Their vigilance is dropped, and a sense of expansiveness, well-being, and union takes place.

***Subtle Energy***   In Western cultures, this energy has been called magnetism and libido. Modern researchers such as Elmer Green at the Menninger Foundation are using the phrase *subtle energy.* Subtle energy is the most recent western term for life energy and its applications to healing. Practitioners of therapeutic touch and other forms of hands-on healing cultivate awareness of this energy and the ability to direct it. Researchers at the Menninger Foundation are studying therapeutic touch practitioners and other energy healers to measure changes in electromagnetic fields brought about by these practices (Green, Parks, Guyer, Fahrion, & Coyne, 1991). Preliminary results indicate that practitioners do have the ability to affect physical systems at the level of electromagnetism. This research is significant because it lends scientific validity to the concept of energy fields and the ability of people to interact with them. For some people, confirmation of this ability to interact with the electromagnetic fields that comprise an element of the universe becomes a reassuring spiritual reality.

## EXERCISE

### Connecting with Life Energy

This exercise, developed by a clinical nurse specialist (Schaub, 1995) focuses on body awareness and connecting with life energy. As with all exercises, we recommend that you explore this personally before using it with a client.

Preparation for Imagery Induction:

1. Get yourself comfortable in your chair and close your eyes.

2. Place your hands gently on your lower abdomen just below your navel, and bring all your attention to the sensations in your hands.

3. Notice the slight rise and fall of your hands as they move with the breathing.

4. Notice the tactile sensations of the surfaces of your hands and fingers . . . What are they in contact with? . . . Bring all your awareness into these tactile sensations, noticing them at subtler and subtler levels . . . (Pause)

5. Now notice the temperature of your hands . . . (Pause)

6. Notice the weight of your hands . . . (Pause)

7. Now notice any inside-the-skin sensations, perhaps you are aware of tingling or pulsing . . . (Pause)

[**Note:** This induction is used because it is a very embodied turning inward. Suggesting that the person place her hands on her lower abdomen is a way of making contact with her energy center.]

8. Bring your attention to the center and be aware of the sensations here at subtler and subtler levels.

9. Notice the movement of your chest with each breath and the passage of breath into your lungs.

10. Bring awareness to your heartbeat . . . (Pause)

11. Now bring your awareness to your nose and be aware of breath passing through your nostrils . . . Notice the slight cool sensation of the air touching the inside of your nose . . . (Pause)

[***Note:*** The client should be deeply relaxed at this point. This can be assessed by noticing slowing of breathing, relaxation of facial muscles, flushing of skin. If necessary, continue to bring awareness to other sensations until client is relaxed.]

**12.** Imagery Suggestion . . . Now move your awareness to your imagination and take a moment to reflect on all the systems that are functioning in your body/mind at this moment . . . Your heart and your circulatory system . . . Your immune system . . . Your respiratory system . . . Your senses . . . Be aware of all of these . . . (Pause) . . . Realize that you do not need to do anything to make these systems function . . . They are a part of your body's wisdom . . . And now be aware that within you is a source of life energy . . . A vital spark that has been part of you since the moment of your conception . . . It has always been a part of you . . . Guiding and energizing your body/mind . . . Use your imagination to get in touch with this source of life energy . . . Locate this source in your body . . . Feel its strength and energy . . .

## Discussion

This exercise serves as an extended meditation on the body and has the potential to create a healing shift for the person in recovery. Much of the activity associated with addiction is abusive to the body. This imagery initiates a process of befriending and appreciating the body. It also introduces the possibility of working with the body as a way of opening to spirituality. This is usually a new concept for the person in recovery.

---

## The Path of Ceremony and Ritual

> . . . *They went down to the River and Made a Sweat Lodge. As before, the Stones were Heated, and The Songs Sung. But this time they were Sung by All the People, because they All Knew them. And they Held their Braids to their Heads and Listened to their Hearts, and to those of their Brothers and Sisters, and they were Healed.*

> Hyemeyohsts Storm

# Mary

Mary entered the Twelve-Step meeting for partners of people in recovery. It was available every day at noon. Mary went as many days as she could. It provided her with a brief sanctuary from the hectic workday and gave her a place to express herself honestly without fear of judgment. The format of the meeting was the same each time. Each person spoke if they chose to. No one commented directly on what was said, but someone might comment on how they identified with the feelings. At the end of the meeting, a brief prayer was said. This ceremony has been a part of Mary's life for the past four years, ever since her husband entered AA. During his active alcoholism, she had completely lost touch with her feelings. The meeting became a ceremony of contacting and expressing feelings.

**Connecting with Mystery**   People have used ceremony to connect with the mystery of life since the dawn of human history. The path of ceremony and ritual uses communal and individual rituals and symbolic actions to deepen spiritual connection. Part of the richness of these practices comes from the powerful synergy of a like-minded group of people joining together with shared intention. This act of communion and community has the ability to draw people out beyond their separateness and into a unity with something greater. For Mary and many other people, their participation in Twelve-Step meetings serves this purpose. There is tremendous healing in knowing "I am not alone."

# Michael

On the day Michael stopped drinking, he bought himself a single red rose. He promised himself he would always have a red rose on his table to remind him of his healing journey away from alcohol.

***Formal Ceremonies***   In more formalized ceremonies, the set structure and the incorporated elements, such as special garments, candles, incense, prayers, music, and symbolic objects, create a sacred space that serves as an invitation to spirit to be present. Pageantry, theater, and dance are creative expressions that are often incorporated into ceremonies. Part of the intention is to allow the individual observers to become participants in the sacred story being told through the symbolic actions. This taps into the collective unconscious described in chapter 11.

***Personal Ceremonies***   Meaningful spiritual ceremonies and rites of passage are not prevalent in our present culture. It is also true that the religious ceremonies and practices that one has been raised with can lose the richness of their meaning because they were experienced in a mindless and rote way. This therefore speaks to the value of creating personally meaningful ceremonies for our day-to-day life.

Dossey (1995, p. 78) described the need for a special place where one can be alone and deepen ". . . understanding of being connected with self, others, and a higher self." In this space ". . . anxieties and fears are reduced; feelings of helplessness are lessened."

## The Path of Social Action and Justice

*If I am not for myself, who will be for me?*
*If I am only for myself, what am I?*
*And, if not now, when?*

Hillel

## CASE STUDY | *Annemarie*

Annemarie had grown up in a rural midwestern town. She always felt drawn to the Native American culture that existed around her. While in high school in the early 1960s, she began getting involved in the Native American rights movement. Eventually, she worked with the tribal councils on issues related to land rights.

This was a time in Annemarie's life when she felt exhilarated by the work she was doing. She experienced deep satisfaction for what she had helped to achieve politically. She felt enriched by the friendships she made within the Native American community.

Twenty-five years later, Annemarie was living in New York City and working as a social worker. In her personal life, she had begun to face the fact that she was drinking alcoholically. She knew people who had gotten free help through Alcoholics Anonymous, but she felt hostile to the whole concept of AA.

She was turned off by the religious language in the program. She had always felt suspicious of religion in general because she equated it with passivity and narrow-mindedness. She was also turned off to the very first step of AA, that you were asked to admit you were powerless over alcohol and to believe that a "power greater than yourself" could help you.

Her identity as a political activist had been with her from those early days in the Native American movement to her current job in social work. As an activist, she felt diametrically opposed to the idea of powerlessness. She finally sought help for her drinking by entering therapy with a nurse clinical specialist.

### *Observations*

In exploring Annemarie's activism, the nurse began to encourage her to wonder about the motivation and intentions in her activism. What difference did it make to Annemarie if Native Americans kept their rights to tribal lands? Why was she willing to work long hours in a New

York City battered women's shelter? Why was she so moved by these concerns and yet she would not take care of herself, except by numbing herself with alcohol? What is at the heart of the person motivated by altruism and social concerns?

Annemarie was on the path of social action and justice, the social activist and political path, in which the suffering from injustice is reduced through ethical actions, transcending self-centered fears in the process.

**The Essence of the Motivation**  In response to these questions, Annemarie used words like *justice* and *empowerment* to explain her actions. Why was justice important to her? She was not an oppressed or battered person. Like many other people, she could just look the other way and deny these realities.

The nurse was pursuing this kind of questioning to get to the essence of Annemarie's activism. What began to emerge was Annemarie's deep feelings of compassion for people. She spoke of the pain she experienced when she watched the news on television or heard of injustices or suffering. This compassion allowed her to connect to the world around her in a very deep way.

Annemarie's social work and her social activism were part of living a life of being true to her values and feelings. By being true to them, she was also experiencing herself in unity with all people. She was experiencing herself as transcending her own separateness, of feeling at one with others.

Reassessing her work in the light of these feelings, she began to see her activism as a spiritual path. This was an exciting shift for Annemarie. She had always thought spirituality would not be available to her. She had thought her outrage at suffering in the world would keep her from the promises of spirituality as peace and wisdom. Instead, she now saw that her activism was her spirituality.

***Spirituality and Courage***    Courageous leaders such as Gandhi and Martin Luther King very directly drew strength from their spiritual values. Gandhi said, "Fearlessness is the first requisite of spirituality. Cowards can never be moral."

Martin Luther King, in a sermon he gave in 1967, less than four months before his assassination, spoke of the Greek concept of agape. He described it as "the love of God operating in the human heart" (King, 1993, p. 293).

He then explained:

> . . . When you rise to love on this level, you love all men, not because you like them, not because their ways appeal to you, but you love them because God loves them. This is what Jesus meant when He said, "Love your enemies." And I'm happy that he didn't say, "Like your enemies," because there are some people that I find it pretty difficult to like . . . I can't like anybody who threatens to kill me day in and day out. But Jesus reminds us that love is greater than liking. Love is understanding, creative, redemptive good will toward all men . . . I've seen too much hate to want to hate . . . and every time I see it, I say to myself, Hate is too great a burden to bear" (p. 293).

The path of social action is the hero's path. The hero goes into the unknown and experiences the fears and makes new discoveries to help the rest of us. The social action path is about acting in the world while connected to meaning and higher purpose. These are the people throughout history and in every culture who have changed the world for the better.

# The Path of Service

*The quality of mercy is not strained,*
*It droppeth as the gentle rain from heaven*
*Upon the place beneath. It is twice blessed:*
*It blesseth him that gives and him that takes.*

Shakespeare, *The Merchant of Venice*

# Marty

Marty had been drug- and alcohol-free for four years. He was in a successful, healthy relationship for the first time in his life. He was working at a job he liked. Every Friday Marty participated in an AA meeting on the rehabilitation unit where he had first been hospitalized. He was sharing his experiences in sobriety with the patients on the unit who were just starting their own recoveries. He was giving back, or serving these patients as an act of gratitude for having recovered himself. This giving back was an integral part of his personal and spiritual healing.

Marty took the action of going to the rehab meetings even if he did not feel grateful and, suddenly, he felt grateful. In his action of giving back by sharing his experience with others, he actually received a new experience for himself—more gratitude, more inner peace, and a perspective on how far he had come from his years of addiction.

# Melody

Melody had worked as a nurse for over twenty years. For the past nine years, she had been actively involved in AA. She was a sponsor for three other women in the program. She was instrumental in starting a special meeting for people who wanted to focus on spiritual development as part of their recovery.

## Observations

Marty and Melody are using the path of service as part of their emotional and spiritual development. The path of service is characterized by an emphasis on reducing another person's suffering, transcending separation, and increasing the experience of love and interconnectedness in the process. A crucial aspect of recovery is letting go of the persistently self-absorbed, self-pitying, resentful consciousness that is common in the psychological dynamics of all people in addiction. Initially, the act of giving back is a practice of learning about gratitude and responsibility.

*Sponsorship*    An example of service in AA is the practice of sponsorship. A newcomer is advised to find a sponsor, someone who has successfully achieved sobriety and can be a source of guidance and support. The sponsor makes a commitment to be available to the newcomer at any difficult time. The sponsor should be someone who has been in AA long enough to have developed strong sobriety and has utilized the AA steps person-ally. In addition to having a strong understanding of the process, the sponsor hopefully has developed enough self-esteem to feel worthy of the sponsor role. Ideally, the person who has benefited from having a sponsor should in time become a sponsor herself for another newcomer.

*Taking Ethical and Loving Actions*    Marty and Melody are each, in their own small and meaningful way, practicing the path of service. We can point to more dramatic examples and seek inspiration from the heroes of this path, such as Mother Teresa and Florence Nightingale, but each person's act of service becomes part of the larger panorama of people throughout the world taking ethical and loving actions. The world's spiritual traditions have different names for this. In Judaism, it is called a mitzvah. In yogic philosophy, it is karma yoga. In Catholicism, there are religious orders practicing nursing and medicine.

*Service as Relationship*    Piero Ferrucci wrote: "Service is much more than mere activity; rather, it is a way of being and entering into a relationship. Of all the ways in which we can relate with others, service is the most fertile and harmonious" (1990, p. 86).

He went on to make an analogy from physics: "Entropy [the measurement of disorder] exists when a relationship detracts from an individual's independence, when it damages his or her self-image, when it decreases faith in life, and when it causes feelings of inadequacy, guilt or unworthiness—in other words, when it lowers the level of consciousness."

This is an important element to examine in considering the path of service. Much has been written about the dysfunctional family and interpersonal relationships that occur in the life of the person in addiction. If this is the chosen path, then it is especially important for the person in recovery to enter it with a commitment to self-awareness and truthfulness.

## The Path of Knowledge and Wisdom

*The sense of wonder is based on the admission that our intellect is a limited and finite instrument of information and expression, reserved for specific practical uses, but not fit to represent the completeness of our being . . . It is here that we come in direct touch with a reality which may baffle our intellect but which fills us with that sense of wonder which opens the way to the inner sanctuary of the mind, to the heart of the great mystery of life and death . . .*

Lama Govinda

## Franklin

Franklin had been a hippie. He spent his college years experimenting with hallucinogens such as LSD, mescaline, and psilocybin. After college, he lived on a commune for one year where he continued using hallucinogens and also began daily marijuana use. He continued to smoke daily for years, usually first thing in the morning to get started, and after work to relax, and before bed, to sleep better. The dazed forgetfulness of marijuana use began to seriously interfere with his work, and Franklin was threatened with loss of his job.

He had already lost several girlfriends who could never make emotional contact with him because he was usually high. The loss of girlfriends did not bother him because would simply smoke marijuana when he was bothered by anything. The threat of job loss, however, broke through his denial. He was financially barely getting by. He lived from paycheck to paycheck. If he lost his job, he had no extra money. He also was shocked by the observation of his boss that Franklin was obviously hung over a lot. Franklin thought he had been disguising the effects of his marijuana addiction. Instead, he realized everyone at work suspected drug use.

He joined a group therapy program for marijuana smokers and began to reduce his smoking. He then received acupuncture treatments to balance his system so that he could withdraw from marijuana completely. In his recovery, he began to miss some of the unusual states he used to experience with both hallucinogens and marijuana. These were heightened states of insights, of enhanced perceptions of colors and music, and at times he would feel he was looking into cosmic levels of reality by seeing the underlying structures in a leaf or a stone.

Such states were difficult to articulate to others, but he found that the mystics of all cultures also had such experiences, and some of them had effectively described these states. Franklin began to realize that his early drug experiences were marked by many of these mystical states, and that these states had been the original reason for a sense of loyalty he had developed to drug-taking.

He also saw that at one point his drug-taking had deteriorated into daily use to simply not be nervous about being in the world. This crossover to drugs as a way to reduce anxiety had begun in the commune and continued when he left the commune to live in the regular world.

In his recovery, he began to see that in the early drug experiences he felt that he was learning special information about reality.

He missed this learning, this search for new experiences, and his discovery of mystical literature began to offer him an alternative way to resume his thirst for such spiritual, transpersonal learning.

# Veronica

As part of her recovery, Veronica reads the Bible everyday. She takes a few words and meditates on them. She had lost interest in religion in adolescence, seeing churchgoers as hypocrites who did not live the principles of their religion. Now, drug-free and struggling with vulnerability, Veronica knew she needed to help herself. She went briefly to AA but did not like the way the men behaved toward her. She knew her judgment was off and knew she could pick the wrong man to get involved with. She joined a women's counseling group and was impressed by one of the group members who had returned to her religious roots.

Veronica bought a Bible and began studying on her own. Then one day she casually overheard somehow say that the Bible is really a way to study how the world works. She suddenly felt free of her resistance against her early religious experiences, and she saw the Bible as a book of knowledge. She found that some of the teaching stories would start to make her cry, as if something was opening and releasing inside her. She would then feel lighter and calmer throughout the day.

## Observations

Both Franklin and Veronica can be seen as having entered the path of knowledge and wisdom. The path of knowledge and wisdom is, in its essence, the mental search for what is true. The search can take very different forms and come from many different perspectives.

***The Search for Truth***   We may think of the scientist and the researcher as people on this path. Often, they consider themselves preeminently rational and dismiss the spiritual quest as irrational. The entire subject of consciousness is viewed as something to be reduced to measurable and mechanical terms. A current example of this is in comparing and reducing human consciousness to computer functions.

But what was the origin of the scientific method? It was Bacon trying to bring the search for truth into the world. Up until that time, the university was the province of the aristocracy and the clergy who were both from the upper classes. The purpose of the university was to study philosophy; literally, the love of wisdom. The method of this study was through rhetoric and discourse. This was believed to be the path to ultimate knowledge.

Ideally, the scientist by contrast sought truth by observing phenomena in the minutest detail, methodically, conscientiously, and objectively, free of the constraints of theology and politics. The search for truth was now available to the common man, not just the nobles and clergy.

Anyone could know the secrets of the universe by observing its component parts. What is it that drives the scientist to know more and more, to always have another question? She is on a quest. What is it that moves the mathematician and physicist? Is it a sense of awe at the complexity of things? Every answer brings new questions. Knowledge expands out farther and farther, to the infinity of the universe, and deeper and deeper down to smaller and smaller particles.

How can this not create a sense of awe and wonder? It is unfortunate for the searcher who loses touch with the original impulse to know the truth. The search for knowledge is not an attempt to manage and control the world, although science has deteriorated into this attempt. The true scientists know we are working in ignorance of the mysteries of life. The spiritual, the essential aspect of this impulse, is to enter the mystery, to be part of it, to feel awe, to be moved by amazement.

Wilder Penfield was a Canadian neurosurgeon and a pioneer in brain consciousness research. Toward the end of his career, he wrote *The Mystery of the Mind* (1975). The book was a personal account of his years of study. He beautifully articulated the path of knowledge. His lifelong search had been to understand the nature of consciousness as it related to the physical organ of the brain. He searched to understand if neuroelectric and chemical reactions could explain the existence of awareness in the human experience: ". . . the nature of the mind remains, still, a mystery that science has not solved. But it is, I believe, a mystery that science will solve someday. In that day of understanding, I predict that true prophets will rejoice, for they will discover in the scientist a long-awaited ally in the search for Truth" (p. xiii).

This search for truth is certainly exemplified in the researcher or scientist, but it can also be seen in Franklin and Veronica who made commitment to their own study of truth. The potential of such study is exemplified in the beautiful Zen phrase, "To study meditation is to study the self. To study the self is to forget the self. To forget the self is to be enlightened by the ten thousand things."

## The Path of Devotion

*I am so small I can barely be seen. How can this great love be inside me?*

Rumi

The path of devotion is characterized by surrender, adoration, and worship. It is the primary path of any religious tradition in which belief and faith are emphasized. Its premise is that we are too small to know the ultimate answers, but that we can enjoy, even love, the wonders we are part of. Far from the researcher who personally seeks out knowledge, this path asks us to give up the search for knowledge and to give in, to surrender to powers greater than us.

This power or powers is often identified as God or gods or deities or transcendent spiritual teachers who are the ultimate answer. In some cases, the spiritual teachers are considered part of God (e.g., Jesus), while in other cases (e.g., Buddha), the teacher is a human with vast spiritual knowledge. On the path of devotion, the person uses his mind and emotions to surrender to something beyond himself and to believe in the power of that greater life.

***The Concept of Surrender***   The concept of surrender and admission of powerlessness is an inherent aspect of Twelve-Step programs. It is an element that has been criticized by people advocating for women, African-Americans, and other populations that are working toward overcoming powerlessness. From this perspective, the step of surrender is seen as counterproductive.

We offer a broader understanding of this process, one which views surrender as ultimately holding the potential for deep, meaningful empowerment. We offer an extended case example of this path because it is one of the most misunderstood spiritual practices.

## CASE STUDY | *George*

By the age of six, it was obvious George was different. He did not play the way boys usually do. It had nothing to do with his mind. He was clearly highly intelligent and sensitive and loving. His father, an active alcoholic, did not like this difference in George. The father taunted George. George's brother learned to join in with the father in his taunts. He did this to try to please the father and to keep his frightening temper from turning on him. His mother did not help George either. Afraid of the father's rages, she began to beat George whenever she saw behaviors she felt were unacceptable to the father.

What could any child make of this physical and verbal abuse? The young mind has no perspective on such abuse. The child completely assumes it is his fault. To the child, it is clear there is something very wrong with him. From this history, we can assume George lived in a constant state of heightened fear, of fight/flight, of vigilance. He remembers vividly a scene from the third grade. The teacher raised her hand to adjust her glasses, and George literally jumped out of his chair: he was sure he was going to be hit.

By thirteen, George knew what was different about him. He was developing secret crushes on boys in his class. His sexuality did not have a name yet, but his classmates had started to call him a sissy. Between home and school, George had no relief from violence and humiliation. His only escape was in the Catholic church. He would go into the church and pray in front of a statue of the Virgin Mary.

George's prayers in front of the Mary statue in his church brought him some peace. He would feel that someone in the world, Mary, was caring for him. He felt devoted to her and felt she knew his suffering. When he would be in a humiliating or frightening moment at school, he would think of Mary and some calm would come to him. Feeling that no one else in the world was on his side, he felt Mary was with him.

At the same time, George was searching for anything else that would ease his emotional pain. This is a common memory for many people who become addicted: they remember actively searching for something to end the pain. George first found it in alcohol and then in tranquilizers and sedatives. He got the alcohol from his father's supply and the pills from his mother's supply. The entire family was medicating their emotional pain.

Alcohol temporarily freed him from his fear state, putting him into a dull oblivion. The pills gave him confidence he could medicate himself anywhere whenever he needed to. In addition to his mother's medicine cabinet full of pills, George also got to know the drug dealers at school for a second source of pills. He eventually developed a third source of pills: doctors. By the end of high school, he was able to convince any doctor of his need for a prescription for tranquilizers. He was using his intelligence to manipulate his way into a large supply of pills. He had three different doctors prescribing pills. He had three different pharmacies filling the prescriptions. By the time he went away to college, he knew he was gay and he sensed he could not live without drugs and alcohol.

George entered recovery at the age of 31. He had lost his second job because of extreme verbal fights with his coworkers. The rage that is the legacy of abused children had been coming out of him more and more. The drugs were no longer giving him relief. By now in his addiction, he was taking drugs to offset the feelings from taking drugs. In the cycle of addiction, he was using drugs to reduce the nervous system disturbance caused by his drug use. He was in a vicious cycle of use, disturbance, use, disturbance, and so on. The original emotional pain was now long buried inside the addiction.

When George lost his second job, he was broke and soon lost his apartment. He had no choice: go back to his family house or live on the street. His father had died two years ago. His brother was married, lived far away, and was reported to be an active alcoholic. His mother lived in the family home by herself.

George moved into the house completely despondent. He was hitting bottom. He went to a local AA meeting but felt afraid of disclosing anything personal in the town he had grown up in. He began to go to meetings in a nearby city.

George had an immediately positive reaction to the religious language of AA. He began returning to church and tried to pray to Mary again. Thinking he was by now a sophisticated and cynical adult, he thought that the praying would feel foolish and childish. Instead, he found it helpful. (See the following discussion regarding prayer in the work of Dossey in DiCarlo, 1996.)

His early recovery was marked by several panic attacks. Once a person has had a panic attack, he lives in fear that he will have another attack. So here was George, now 31, trying to stay drug-free, living in his family house, and in fear all the time. He felt like nothing had changed. His entire life seemed doomed. He thought again and again about killing himself and about drinking and drugging again. He felt too ashamed and ugly to go to counseling and too desperate not to go. Fortunately, he reached out to someone at AA and got the name of a nurse therapist. In the depths of fear, he made a life-affirming choice. He began to benefit from the therapy relationship, which in turn increased his involvement in AA. He began to move toward sanity one day at a time.

### Observations

George is now 34. He is working, has his own apartment, has not had any more panic attacks, and is active in AA. In his inner life, he communicates with Mary when he feels that no one else knows him.

What actually happens to him in this devotion? In his mind, he turns away from a fear and begins to imagine Mary's face. He thinks about who she is. He begins to feel the pain she must have felt, and he begins to sense she would understand his pain. At this point, it is clear he is utilizing Mary as an empathic mother, as a compassionate, soulful, mothering energy. He begins to feel that quality inside him. Now Mary is not just a good mother. Now she is a universal fact of life, a force of nature that he can believe in. George can believe the world is also good. This begins to restore his desire to be here. He begins to feel one of the most powerful of all human emotions, hope.

***Devotion to Mary***   To further understand this vignette, a brief discussion of Mary is necessary. Within Christianity, Mary is a figure of greater or lesser importance depending upon the denomination or sect. In most Protestant churches, Mary is a minor figure. In Catholicism, she is an object of devotion among some believers. For Catholics, she is the mother of the son of God and therefore worthy of worship. In the Catholic world, there have been many reports of Mary appearing in visions, causing healings and miracles.

Perhaps the two most well-known locations for these events are Fatima in Portugal and Lourdes in France. More recently, Mejugorje in Bosnia has developed a reputation as a place where Mary was appearing and communicating with several children. The attraction to Mary can also be understood as a symbol of all the compassionate mothers of the world who suffer when their children suffer. In other words, she represents the compassionate feminine energy in the universe and is an object of devotion.

***Prayer***   One of the main forms of practice in the devotional path is prayer. Dr. Larry Dossey has been studying and synthesizing experimental research in prayer. A physician of internal medicine, he is the former chief of staff at Humana Medical City Dallas Hospital. His thoughts on the nature of prayer are provocative and offer new possibilities for the devotional path:

> The prevailing notion that prayer is asking for something . . . is woefully incomplete. I want to get away from that common way of looking at prayer. Prayer for me is any

psychological act which brings us closer to the transcendent . . . Prayer may involve words . . . It can involve silence, nonactivity. It can even be done in the subconscious or when we sleep at night. So I prefer to use the term "prayerfulness" to capture those activities we have traditionally called prayer.

Dr. Dossey goes on to say:

Nonlocal manifestations of consciousness—among which prayer is one type—display characteristics that are not displayed by any known form of energy . . . Prayer and so on are not a function of the amount of distance a person is from their target. These activities are just as effective when done on the other side of the earth as when they are done closeup. . . . What I am saying is that the psyche has ways of manifesting far beyond anything known to materialistic science (Di Carlo, 1996, pp. 78–79).

## *The Path of Meditation*

*The Ultimate Truth is wordless,*
*the silence within the silence.*
*More than the absence of speech,*
*More than the absence of words,*
*Ultimate Truth is the seamless being-in-place*
*that comes with attending to Reality.*

Shimon ben Gamliel

# *John*

After his first heart attack, John, a 58-year-old teacher in recovery, began to look for treatment of his coronary artery disease. He decided to try the approach of cardiologist Dean Ornish. Ornish's patients have been able to reverse coronary arterial clogging, reduce or discontinue medication, reduce or end chest pain, lose weight while eating more, and feel more energetic and calm (Ornish, 1990). All of this is accomplished without surgery or medication. It is accomplished through the alternative health practices of:

- stress management (meditation, imagery, hatha yoga)

- diet

- exercise

- stopping smoking and other addictions

After trying the Ornish approach for a week, John gave up. He could not comply with all the lifestyle changes. In frustration, he called Ornish on the telephone and asked him to recommend only the single most important practice in the approach. Dr. Ornish immediately told John, "Meditate."

John was surprised . He thought surely that diet or exercise would be the priority. John asked Ornish why meditation was the key practice. In response, he was told that meditation counteracts some of the pounding the body takes from a worried mind.

**Meditation and New Consciousness**   The path of meditation is characterized by discipline and an act of will; the person deliberately sets out to expand perceptions and attention. It is utilized in every culture on earth to help the mind and to experience new states of consciousness. When Ornish advised John to meditate, he was directing him to one of the oldest self-help tools on the planet.

**Worry and Meditation**   John's worried mind is of course not his whole mind. The worried mind is a habitual pattern in the mind. This worry pattern keeps the mind on alert, vigilantly scanning for possible dangers and imagining all the bad things that could happen.

The worry pattern draws our intelligence and our imagination into its service and produces a fearful version of reality. Oddly, the worry appears to be helping us. It appears to be watching out for us. By worrying, we even get the feeling we are doing something about a situation, as if worry were somehow capable of changing reality.

In John's case, meditation will begin to move him from his worried mind to his whole mind. This deliberate act, plus the need to meditate in a consistent way over time, is what characterizes meditation as a way of discipline.

***Retraining the Mind*** Physical benefits of meditation are well documented (Murphy, 1993). Mental and emotional benefits are subtler and are therefore more difficult to measure. Stress reduction is the most researched variable of meditation because it can be operationalized and quantified through biofeedback technology. Kabat-Zinn (1990) calls his hospital-based meditation training program a stress reduction clinic.

Stress reduction, however, does not answer the larger issues in recovery. A person in recovery will not benefit sufficiently from meditation by becoming calmer. As psychologist and spiritual teacher Karlfried Durckheim (1992) saw it, "superficial harmony" becomes progressively harder to maintain (p. 9).

The path of meditation goes deeper: it offers a way to retrain his mind. If the mind can move from fear to meditation, new perceptions, including innate inner wisdom, can start to become available.

## *Types of Meditation*

In general, meditation techniques can be classified as concentrative, receptive, and creative. All meditative traditions have all three types of meditation, but tend to emphasize one technique over another, especially to beginning students.

***Concentrative Meditation*** Concentrative techniques emphasize a single-minded focus on one object—the breath, a phrase, a thought, an image, a repeated movement. In such techniques, the goal is to ignore all other experiences and to keep returning attention to the single meditative object. This concentrated focus on one object has great potential: it can lead to states of blissful ease. Such experiences can give the person in recovery an ability to change her state from fear to peace and thus give a new sense of self-control. Examples of concentrative techniques include:

- the focus on breath in the early phases of Zen and mindfulness training

- focus on mantra in transcendental meditation

- focus on a single word linked with the breath cycle (the relaxation response technique) developed by cardiologist Herbert Benson

Focus on breath is particularly effective for the person in recovery. This is true because moments of vulnerability produce holding of breath or shortening of breath, resulting in at least mild hyperventilating. Hyperventilating in turn produces more excitation, more anxiety. Focus on the breath restores a more normal breathing cycle, and the change in respiration rate calms the entire physical sense of self. Having developed a concentrative meditative practice, several clients can now travel and be in places that were previously sources of phobic fear.

***Limitations of Concentrative Meditation***    There is a limitation to concentration techniques. By turning attention over and over again to one object, all other experiences are ignored. In the extreme, other experiences may even be repressed, kept out of awareness. Concentrative meditation can bring temporary peace to the body/mind, but its avoidance of thoughts and feelings does not assist in new learning and development.

***Receptive Meditation***    Receptive techniques begin with a concentration technique such as focus on breathing. They then gradually let awareness open to the stream of experiences:

- body sensations
- thoughts
- feelings
- moods

- sounds

- energy shifts

This receptive behavior is sometimes called witness consciousness, or being the observer, or engaging the observing ego (Assagioli, 1965). One brief case study gives a sense of the possibilities of receptive meditation.

---

## CASE STUDY | *Glen*

Glen, a 35-year-old with a diagnosis of HIV positive and in recovery from heroin addiction, was referred for meditation training by a physician because of episodes of extreme fear and anger. Glen had refused medication for his episodes, rightly asserting he was having extreme feelings because of the extreme situation he was in. He said he did not want to learn any mental tricks or simple relaxation techniques or be hypnotized out of his fear and anger. Quite clearly, he knew he needed some new way to work with his states of mind.

He was first trained to follow his breathing and to say out loud any experiences he was having moment to moment. After several training periods, he was instructed to verbalize internally whatever he was noticing. The technique was then shortened to (1) following his breathing, (2) noting internally with a single word whatever he was experiencing, (3) then returning to his breathing. He was taught to (1) consider his breath as his center, (2) be interested in whatever thought or image or feeling or sensation pulled him away from his breath, away from his center, (3) keep his attention long enough on the off-center experience to know what it was, e.g., worrying, (4) mentally note, "Worry," (5) then return his attention to his breath, to his center. This inner movement from center to off-center and back to center was taught as the normal flow of the meditation period. No attempt was made, as it is in concentrative meditation, to stay fixedly focused on the center. Rather, the receptive technique is to be able to receive whatever is being experienced, and then to be able to center oneself again. In this way, he was establishing a base of relaxation in his breathing and at the same time not denying whatever experiences were present.

Within two weeks of daily practice, Glen began to realize he was having a wide variety of internal experiences, of which fear and anger were only two. When the fear or anger did come, they were like big waves, taking him over. But then they would pass. He began to realize fear and anger were present along with questioning, sensitivity, religious searching, self-hatred, self-compassion, practical thinking, remembering, and so on. His fear and anger were not blunted or denied. They were instead simply experienced in a receptive way within a larger array of experience. This technique has been successfully taught to many medical patients in extreme situations (Kabat-Zinn, 1990).

### Observations

Receptive meditation, or mindfulness, is particularly suited for anyone with learned self-hatred. The very technique asks the person to be receptive to himself. It asks him to notice the full range of his inner and outer experiences. Glen noticed, in meditation, an array of experiences, some pleasant, some unpleasant, some new, some depressingly familiar, all coming and going, coming and going. Inherent in receptive meditation is the insight that what the person hates most about himself is, at one level, just another passing thought. He can cither attach to it or let it go. Letting thoughts go does not magically change self-hatred, but it does take some of the energy out of it. In time, the person learns meditatively he can attach to the thought or just notice it and let it go. Choice becomes involved in thoughts, feelings, and urges that previously seemed to be beyond his control.

Mindfulness meditation teacher, Shinzen Young, works with people in recovery. He indicates an important moment takes place in meditation when the person in recovery realizes he can let go of thoughts or urges that previously caused him to act self-destructively (1988).

***Creative Meditation*** Creative meditation can be added to concentrative and receptive techniques. Creative meditation brings the vast resource of the imagination into meditative practice. The absence of the imagination in meditative practice is an unnecessary deprivation. The imagination is a dominant force in human nature and deserves to be utilized in our clients' service. Two religious traditions that greatly utilize the imagination in the path of meditation are Roman Catholicism and Tibetan Buddhism. They both utilize art and images extensively to awaken spiritual experiences.

The imagination is a key concept in the psychospiritual meditation practices of European psychiatrists Carl Jung and Roberto Assagioli. Creative meditation is the most active form of meditation because of the interaction between the conscious mind, imagination, feeling states, and periods of emptiness and silence.

# *Frances*

Frances, 50 years old, was in recovery from alcoholism and was terminally ill with lung cancer. She presented the belief that she had somehow caused herself to have this fatal disease. The author did not accept such a theory, but also had to respect Frances's way of understanding her suffering. She asked for help in understanding how or why she had done this.

She was taught to follow her breathing (concentrative), then to open to her stream of experiences (receptive), and then to imagine a wisdom figure with whom she could dialogue in her mind (creative). She was instructed to ask the wisdom figure about the illness. In her imagination, she met a spiritual teacher who brought her to a scene from early childhood: Frances was locked out of her house and desperately had to urinate. She urinated in her pants and then hid in the backyard in humiliation.

At the conscious level, this disturbing memory seemed to her to have nothing to do with her question about her illness. She returned to her creative meditative technique and asked the imagined spiritual teacher for more information: she was led to another disturbing childhood memory. Frances began to realize these images were all telling her how many times she wanted to die from humiliation. She then felt compassion for the little girl in the memories and cried with relief at feeling such kindness toward herself. Her self-hatred softened as she continued her meditation practice.

Other forms of creative meditation include:
- reflecting on a philosophical principle
- contemplating a spiritual image
- imagining light or energy moving in the body
- identifying with the life force (Schaub, 1995)

## Cautions with Meditation

Of all the forms of meditation, creative meditation is the most active and can rather quickly bring up thoughts and feelings and images from all levels of consciousness. It therefore needs to be practiced and understood by the nurse before it is introduced to a patient. In general, teaching meditation without an integrating framework of psychological and spiritual development is shortsighted (Shapiro, 1994). It may produce calmness but will not produce the kinds of spiritual developments that are possible. In western psychology, Roberto Assagioli's psychosynthesis, Carl Jung's individuation process, and Ken Wilber's spectrum of consciousness (Wilber, Engler, & Brown, 1986) offer psychospiritual frameworks for development through meditation.

The path of meditation is also recommended as an adjunct to any of the other paths. It attunes the whole mind for fuller participation in all forms of spiritual development.

## SUMMARY

The core reason for vulnerability is the separate, survival-based experience of the small self in the world. The movement from this fearful, unnatural separateness to a communal and spiritual sense of self is enhanced by actively entering a path of spiritual development. These paths are ancient and time-tested ways to open to a larger sense of reality and heal the intense vulnerability at the core of addiction.

## REFLECTIONS

What paths of spiritual developments have I tried in my life?

Am I aware of my current path?

Is there a path that is natural to my way of being?

## References

Assagioli, R. (1965). *Psychosynthesis.* New York: Penguin Books.

DiCarlo, R. (1996, Winter). Interview with Larry Dossey. *Quest*, 78–79.

Dossey, B., Keegan, L., Guzzetta, C., & Kolkmeier, L. (1995). *Holistic nursing: A handbook for practice.* Gaithersburg, MD: Aspen Publishers.

Dossey, L. (1993). *Healing words.* New York: HarperCollins.

Durckheim, K. (1992). *Absolute living.* New York: Penguin.

Ferrucci, P. (1990). *Inevitable grace.* Los Angeles: Tarcher.

Green, E., Parks, P., Guyer, P., Fahrion, S., & Coyne, L. (1991). Anomalous electrostatic phenomena in exceptional subjects. *Subtle Energies, 2*(3), 69–94.

Kabat-Zinn, J. (1990). *Full catastrophe living.* New York: Delta.

King, M. L. (1993). A Christmas sermon on peace. In D. Wells (Ed.), *We have a dream* (pp. 288–295). New York: Carroll & Graf.

Murphy, M. (1993). *The future of the body.* Los Angeles: Tarcher.

Ornish, D. (1990). *Dr. Dean Ornish's program for reversing heart disease.* New York: Ballantine Books.

Penfield, W. (1975). *The mystery of the mind.* Princeton, NJ: Princeton University Press.

Schaub, B. (1995). Imagery in health care: Connecting with life energy. *Alternative Health Practitioner, 1*(2), 45–47.

Shapiro, D. (1994). Examining the content and context of meditation. *Journal of Humanistic Psychology, 34*(4), 101–135.

Wilber, K., Engler, J., & Brown, D. (1986). *Transformations of consciousness.* Boston: New Science Library.

Young, S. (1988). *Overcoming compulsive behavior.* Oakland, CA: Thinking Allowed Productions.

## Suggested Reading

Ferrucci, P. (1990). *Inevitable grace.* Los Angeles: Tarcher.

# 13 | OBSTACLES TO SPIRITUAL DEVELOPMENT

*Spiritual growth is demanding and imposes
responsibilities from which the selfish, self-centered
"I" wants to escape.*

Roberto Assagioli

## *Reggie*

Reggie has been in recovery from alcoholism for five years. He goes
to AA three times a week. He wants to experience spiritual progress.
For him, this would mean he is more at peace in the world.

Reggie experiences instability, generalized fear, and lack of
confidence off and on throughout every day. Any event without these
feelings is a good one. Any event with these feelings is a bad one
because these feelings ruin everything; they undermine his sense of
self. They undermine his belief in himself. In terms of recovery, these
feelings undermine his belief that he has gotten somewhere. When
these feelings come, he feels that his recovery is a lie, that he has not
changed at all. It is these moments that bring the thought to drink
again. If he is not getting away from the feelings that made him
drink, why not drink again? Is drinking really so bad? Perhaps this
time he can handle the drinking better.

In Alcoholics Anonymous, they call this stinking thinking, or B.U.D.—building up to a drink. It is the logic of the addiction. You feel bad, use something, you deserve it, you can handle it.

Reggie says no to the addict logic in his mind and prays to God to remove these negative thoughts and feelings from him. If the feelings go away, Reggie feels more belief in God. If the feelings do not go away, Reggie sees God as ineffective. This is the state of his spiritual development five years in recovery.

## Jean

Jean was praying. She suddenly felt a peace and a lightness of being come over her. She began to cry with gratitude. She knew this was an important moment. Looking around her room, she saw everything as inherently beautiful and all living things as of equal value and poignancy. She felt moved by creation and felt in the right perspective toward her own personal struggles. She went into her kitchen and began to eat. She was not hungry but she kept eating. Then she felt bloated and almost sick.

## THE IMPORTANCE OF STUDYING OBSTACLES ON THE SPIRITUAL PATH

As was stated at the start of this book, we choose to stay entirely practical. Just as you do, we face people every day who are suffering. We do not have time for abstractions or nice ideas. If something works, we use it and encourage it. If it does not work, we let it go. Spiritual development has proven itself clinically.

Spiritual development is a very practical matter. There is a vast difference between a person in recovery who has contact with spiritual consciousness and one who does not. The opportunity of the spiritual aspect of recovery is to live less in vulnerability and more in wisdom and compassion. The founders of AA discovered this for themselves and passed it on to others.

The fact that someone chooses the journey toward spiritual consciousness does not mean quick success. This journey is difficult. The study of obstacles to spiritual development becomes important and can make the journey more effective. *Obstacles to spiritual development* are mental and emotional attitudes and fears that block the opening of the personality to spiritual consciousness.

Reggie, for example, could only take a few steps on the journey before he became discouraged by his demand for a responsive God. Reggie's obstacle is his rigid belief in what God is for. God is for helping you. If God does not come to help you, God does not exist. If God does help you, God at least temporarily exists.

Jean's obstacle is very different. She is open to spiritual consciousness. She wants to experience a sense of contact with something greater than herself. In the vignette, she received that contact. It was initially highly positive. She was moved to tears of gratitude. Then she became frightened by the new feelings it brought her and began to feel the need to get rid of the feelings. The psychiatrist Roberto Assagioli refers to this as one of the crises of self-realization; to actually have a spiritual experience and not be able to tolerate it. Jean resorted to compulsive eating, an old defense she used against vulnerability.

## OBSTACLES TO SPIRITUAL DEVELOPMENT AND THE STAGES OF ACCEPTANCE

This section describes the classic and clinically observable obstacles to spiritual development. You can use this to assess if your clients' spiritual development is blocked by a particular obstacle.

Also included is a model for the stages of acceptance of spiritual development. The *stages of acceptance*, developed by the authors in collaboration with transpersonal theorist Michael Follman, describe the process the personality goes through in accepting or rejecting spiritual experiences. With guidelines to the obstacles and stages of acceptance, you have assessment tools for working with the spiritual development of your clients and yourself.

You may also want to research other models of spiritual development. One excellent example is the work of Ken Wilber (1977, 1980, 1995). Wilber's work falls within the category of transpersonal psychology. *Transpersonal psychology* is a movement within western psychology to study the aspects of consciousness explored within the world's religious and wisdom traditions for their relevance to psychological development. The roots of the movement are in the works of the European doctors Carl Jung, Roberto Assagioli, and Karlfried Durckheim, and the American psychologist, William James.

The religious traditions of course offer the most thorough study of spiritual development, but we have an obstacle in recommending such works: the works are all religion-specific. As nurses, our work brings us in contact with people from many religious traditions. We cannot function professionally with one religion's view. We encounter

- people with varying degrees of interest in their tradition

- people who have been raised without any formal tradition

- people whose religious tradition is very foreign and incomprehensible to us

- people who have actively rejected their tradition

With such diversity in our patient populations, we simply cannot utilize a religion-specific idea of spiritual development. We need assessment guidelines that are comprehensive but outside of any religion-specific model.

## *Entering a Path*

This chapter assumes the person in recovery has decided to enter a path of spiritual development. *Entering a path* means making a deliberate decision to cultivate spiritual attitudes and behaviors. If the person has not entered a path, he may of course still be having spontaneous spiritual experiences. Spiritual experiences are a part of our nature and can happen at any time. Entering a path simply tends to increase such experiences and makes the development more dynamic.

Entering a path also means being both open and discerning. Rigid mental concepts or naive, unquestioning acceptance of any path is not entering it. Entering means engaging in it, bringing your full self to it. If you choose the path of meditation, for example, it means receiving training and guidance in meditation and practicing it on a disciplined basis. Meditation works best for those who actually practice it.

***Acceptance of Experience*** As was discussed in chapter 12, all paths have the same potential, moving oneself from an isolated sense of self to conscious contact with one's transpersonal nature. The choice of path is dependent on your personality style, your previous experiences, and many other subjective factors. Once you have made a choice of path, knowledge of the obstacles becomes relevant.

There is a crucial difference between entering a path and actually receiving the benefits of the path. The difference is the degree to which you accept spiritual experiences into your personality and allow your personality to be changed by the experiences. The reasons for the nonacceptance of experiences are varied but tend to fall within one of the classic obstacles to spiritual development.

***Personality Issues and Obstacles*** Spiritual development is an aspect of human development. Therefore, the person encounters all of the personality issues that are activated at any time of transition and change. The nurse's training and knowledge in personality and human development becomes relevant to spiritual development as well (Smith, 1986).

## THE FIRST ASSESSMENT TOOL: OBSTACLES TO SPIRITUAL DEVELOPMENT

The five clinical issues that are obstacles to spiritual development are:

- childhood experiences with religion
- traumas that destroyed trust

- social fears
- ego fears
- irrational and ignorant thinking

## Obstacles Originating in Childhood Experiences with Religion

Childhood experiences with religion that form obstacles to spiritual development include:

- childhood training leading to immature spirituality
- negative experiences with organized religion
- negative feelings toward God as a male father figure
- no experiences with religion

***Childhood Training Leading to Immature Spirituality***   This first obstacle is rooted in childhood religious training about God as the father in the sky looking down on the earth. For children with this training, it is natural to pray directly to God for help. The child does not always see an outcome to the prayer. Praying that his parents would not get divorced; the parents get divorced anyway. Praying that the dead pet would be revived back to life; the pet is buried and gone forever. Praying that the other children at school will stop taunting him; the taunts go on.

The child's mind has not yet developed the capacity to tolerate ambiguity. The child's thinking is black or white, always or never, yes or no. The child prays for something specific, and the seeming absence of any response from God disappoints the child deeply. The child may also wonder why God does not care. Reggie, 48 years old and five years in recovery, is still praying with that same childhood disappointment intact. His spiritual understanding has not matured at all.

Another example of this was seen in a woman who had just gone to her first AA meeting. She was immediately turned off by the "God talk." When she was asked what bothered her about it, she looked with disbelief at the author and said, "There's no guy in the sky looking out for me; that's all lies." Her young disappointment was very present in her 55-year-old face.

The nurse can find out about this obstacle through direct questioning. Adapted from *Mental Health Psychiatric Nursing* by Beck, Rawlins, and Williams (1984, pp. 215–216), your questions can include:

- Do you engage in any spiritual or religious practices? Describe them.
- Are they the same practices you grew up with? Does this pose any conflict for you?
- Do you believe in any power greater than yourself? Describe your belief.
- If so, what is your relationship to the greater power?
- Do you think your spiritual beliefs provide you with support?
- Do they cause you any conflict?

Beck et al. (1984) suggested that you assess the person's beliefs according to three possible effects:

- inspiring beliefs
- ineffectual beliefs
- deleterious beliefs

Inspiring beliefs lead to growth, peace of mind, and strong inner force. Ineffectual beliefs are colorless; they do not hamper or support the person. Deleterious beliefs cause stress because they are associated with fear, anger, guilt, shame, anxiety, or physical and interpersonal disturbances.

Beck et al. went on to advise: "Through the spiritual assessment, the nurse needs to distinguish beliefs that act to sustain the client from those which are a source of conflict. In this way, both the power and the problems can be clarified as a basis for nursing intervention" (p. 216).

What would be your assessment of Reggie's beliefs?

In *Classification of Nursing Diagnoses* (1984, p. 507), Kim, McFarland, and McLane would assess Reggie's beliefs as "Childlike, immature love of God, dependent type of love (expectations of God to magically take care of problems)." For Kim et al., Reggie's relationship to God is characterized by "distance/separation/absence," which they see as a cause of distress in the areas of forgiveness, love, hope, trust, and meaning and purpose (pp. 506–508).

***Negative Experiences with Organized Religion***    Negative experiences can include:

- seeing hypocrisy in adult religious leaders
- feeling insulted or humiliated at religious meetings
- being frightened by religious dogmas of punishment
- witnessing family conflict over religion

The result of these experiences is that the person is always in conflict trying to reconcile the negative versus the positive aspects of her religious education.

The negative experiences can also be far more traumatic. Direct physical and sexual abuse by religious workers destroys a child's ability to ever find peacefulness or comfort from her religion. In fact, it often creates a lifelong mistrust of any formal religious structure.

***Negative Feelings toward God as a Male Father Figure***
The clear male model of God in the western religions can be troubling if the child's own father was frightening. This can be compounded, as referred to earlier, if the male God does not intervene on the child's behalf against the real abusive father.

God as male has contributed to the exclusion of women from full participation in many religious systems. Some traditions have prayers or rituals that clearly express valuing sons in preference to daughters.

Reaction against God as male has resulted in growing interest in Goddess traditions, nature-focused practices, or neutral (e.g., the universe) religious terminology. These explorations are motivated by the desire to go beyond cultural-bound descriptions of God as male.

***No Experiences with Religion***    Some children are never exposed to a model of spirituality or philosophical thought. Others are raised in an environment of overt hostility to religion and spirituality. Unless an interest develops later, the child can become a man who simply accepts society's reality as absolute.

Society's goals become his goals, and he focuses only on the problems society presents to him.

To summarize, the four childhood experiences with religion that form obstacles to spiritual development are:

- childhood training leading to immature spirituality and magical thinking

- negative experiences with organized religion

- negative associations to God as male father figure

- no experiences

What obstacles would you add to this list? What are your own experiences and the experiences of your colleagues and friends? Where do your own beliefs fall in Beck et al.'s three question assessment?

## Obstacles Originating in Traumas that Destroyed Trust

Trauma is a severe negative experience. It destroys the person's trust in the world as a place of any safety. It tears away the belief of any order in the world. We make basic assumptions about the world. Trauma reorganizes our assumptions around fear. The need for healing from such trauma can continue throughout the lifespan.

As we have shown, the person in addiction probably never felt safe in the world. The vulnerability was too great. Living was trauma enough. Incidents of greater trauma may have occurred that are additional factors in her addiction history. Examples of trauma include:

- physical violence

- rape

- incest

- sexual molestation

- emotional abuse

- death of a parent or close family member or friend

- abandonment

- serious illnesses

- hospitalizations and surgical procedures

- harassment and terror

The person's underlying experience of life becomes one of stress and distrust. Unless this trauma can move toward healing, spirituality will have little effect. The return of traumatic memories or symptoms can erase any spiritual ideas or values. The person can be continually thrown back into basic instincts of survival and the resulting fight/flight mechanisms.

***The Second Recovery***   We have referred to the need for a second recovery. It is the need to recover from trauma as well as from addiction. Second recovery is typically not dealt with by alcohol and drug treatment centers. It is not mentioned in Alcoholics Anonymous, even though many AA members could be helped by it.

If the nurse learns of trauma in the person's history, it is important to distinguish it from the problems of addiction itself. It is a great relief to the person in recovery to have this distinction made for him. This provides him with a better understanding of his struggles and a perspective on why his treatment program is not resulting in him feeling more at ease in the world.

We wonder if the need for second recovery is a reason for such a low rate of success in drug treatment. We wonder how often the pain in addiction can actually be placed on addiction itself. In how many cases is addiction really a person self-prescribing medication for traumatized feelings?

Second recovery requires intervention by professionals with specific understanding of trauma and post-traumatic stress disorders. Any nurse working in the addictions field should have knowledge of and training in the treatment issues involved in trauma.

## *Obstacles Originating in Social Fears*

### *Larry*

Larry has been sober from alcohol for eight years. He feels grateful that his life is now sane and directed. His spiritual development has helped him greatly from the first day of recovery to the present.

He does not talk at work about his recovery because he is afraid of being thought of as an alcoholic. One day, though, he did mention his interest in spirituality. The other men looked at him without saying a word. Larry experienced it as if he had brought up the most embarrassing subject possible.

---

***Social Disapproval*** Spirituality, though a totally natural part of human nature, is not an easy and open subject. People speak hesitatingly, guardedly, about their spirituality, almost as if they were discussing a taboo in public. Larry's experience is very familiar.

The social obstacle to spiritual development is fear of disapproval. *Disapproval* is a general term to refer to a range of similar fears, including fears of

- criticism

- embarrassment

- exclusion

- ridicule

- exile

- not belonging

- not fitting in

- being seen as odd

- being seen as an outsider

- being judged

Roberto Assagioli referred to this embarrassment around spirituality as "repression of the sublime" (1965). *Repression of the sublime* is denial, neglect, or negation of innate human spirituality. Assagioli compared the twentieth century repression of spirituality to the nineteenth century repression of sexuality that Freud confronted in his theories of human behavior.

Now sexuality seems completely in the open. Children can turn on their television set and watch sexually explicit material. This does not, however, mean that sexuality is unrepressed: it simply means it is openly for sale.

It is probably true that sexuality is now easier to talk about than spirituality. How many of us would be willing to talk about our spiritual longings at a social affair? We can guess that we might receive a lot of silent disapproval, as Larry did.

***The Nurse as Role Model***    Despite this social fear, it is vitally important that the person in recovery be able to talk openly and often about her spirituality. The nurse is in an ideal position to assist in this opening of a socially difficult subject.

As nurses, your entire tradition is rooted in spirituality, and nursing philosophy has always included spirituality as a core need of the patient. The very founder of modern western nursing, Florence Nightingale, was a deeply spiritual person. Nurses of course have a much deeper tradition than that. Nursing reaches back to the healers of every culture on earth, with current nurses being the direct descendants of the European tradition of nursing-nuns in the Middle Ages (Keegan, 1994). From this viewpoint, nurses can be role models for intelligent, grounded, open spirituality.

## Ego Fears

Social disapproval, as powerful a force as it is, does not constitute the major social obstacle to spirituality. There are more interior fears about our spirituality. These are ego fears. The ego, organized around survival and social functioning, is threatened by any spiritual experience that might change the person's identity and ability to function. The ego fears about spiritual experiences are often expressed in the following ways:

- fear of "going out there" and never coming back
- fear of going crazy
- fear of getting high through spirituality and returning to drug use
- fear of becoming dysfunctional
- fear of being changed in some unknown way

- fear of becoming indifferent to everyday life
- fear of becoming God-like and grandiose

The resolution of these ego fears is discussed in the Stages of Acceptance model that follows this section on obstacles. The four stages of acceptance are:

- denial
- relationship
- testing
- the open personality

The Stages of Acceptance model offers the nurse a method to (1) assess the person's acceptance or rejection of his spiritual nature, and (2) assist the person in moving through the stages.

## Obstacles Originating in Irrational and Ignorant Thinking

Predictable irrational and ignorant thoughts regarding spirituality include:

- it is escapism and fantasy
- it has nothing to do with this world
- it is childish and regressive
- it is not scientific
- it is strange to be interested in such things
- it could be dangerous
- it shows an unwillingness to deal with reality
- only special people know about it
- it is wishful thinking and magical thinking
- if you are spiritual, you never get angry
- if you are spiritual, nothing bothers you
- you become indifferent to the world
- it is illogical and irrational

It is important to find out if the person is thinking in these irrational and ignorant ways. Each of these thoughts can block spiritual development by keeping the mind afraid of such development. The fact is that spirituality is as natural as our hand, as important as our rationality, and deserves accurate and intelligent attention. It represents one of the key developments awaiting each person in the course of his life. Carl Jung concluded at the end of his career that the essential emotional problem in the adults he had seen was their failure to have developed a spiritual viewpoint of life. Irrational and ignorant thinking, which of course cause fears in many areas of life, can keep this key development from happening.

The nurse as a health care professional is not exempt from these fears. At a case conference or clinical rounds, the nurse may hesitate to introduce the subject of the patient's spirituality for fear of appearing irrational and being judged by colleagues. No professional wants to be viewed as strange or escapist or nonscientific. It is therefore important for us to examine our own thinking about spirituality.

## THE SECOND ASSESSMENT TOOL: THE STAGES OF ACCEPTANCE

The four stages of acceptance (Schaub & Follman, in press), denial, relationship, testing, and the open personality, provide an assessment tool for the nurse in discerning the patient's spiritual development. These stages are observable in all people, but each person moves through the stages at an individual pace. Some of the factors that influence moving through the stages are:

- the degree of defensiveness activated by spiritual experiences

- the capacity the person has to tolerate ambiguity

- the frequency and persuasiveness of new spiritual experiences

- the availability of proper guidance

# The Implications of Spiritual Experiences

In chapter 10, we offered lists of spiritual experiences cited by Gifford-May and Thompson (1994, pp. 124–129). To highlight some of the items, their list included:

- becoming a field of energy

- merging with objects

- becoming conscious of being conscious

- expanding in all directions

- becoming a field of awareness that is cosmic

- experiencing great love

- experiencing serenity and contentment

- experiencing joy quietly pervading all things

Gifford-May and Thompson's list was gathered from a group of ten meditators who either practiced repeating a phrase (mantra), imagining a picture in the mind (visualization), or paying attention to their breathing. Our culture's version of human nature offers no model that can explain how repeating a phrase, imagining an image, or paying attention to breathing can lead to such a range of experiences. Such experiences confront the socially defined ideas of who we are.

As one example from Gifford-May and Thompson's list, the meditator reported "you are a field of awareness that is cosmic" (1994, p. 124). Mainstream medical and psychological thought would be compelled to diagnose such an experience, reducing it to pathology. We are then confronted with the question: Are such meditative experiences pathological or are they pointing to something of fundamental importance in human nature?

As helping professionals, we must be willing to investigate such phenomena. Unfortunately, what happens more often is that the experience is denied. We consider the first stage of acceptance to be this denial, this refusal to investigate spiritual phenomena. This stage reflects that a struggle in development is underway.

## First Stage of Acceptance: Denial

### Anita

Anita felt in conflict every day about what to do with her life. She had made a decision to stop using cocaine, but she felt no other sense of direction or purpose. She read about visualization and decided to use one of the book's techniques—to meditate on an image of a wise being. In her imagination, she asked the wise being to give her direction. The imagined wise being told her to expand love. Anita felt moved and began to cry. She then switched to anger and told herself the imagined experience was "crap."

The ego is an organizing process oriented toward biological survival and social approval. When the ego is confronted with an unexplainable experience from the spiritual level of human nature, its initial reaction is often to deprive the experience of any attention. As in Anita's case, the experience is labeled as strange, is not thought about in depth, is not talked about with others, and soon becomes a dim memory, a vague dream fragment. The experience is exiled, not allowed into the person's sense of self. The stages of acceptance, therefore, are first characterized by the protective ego denying the reality of the experience. The ego is attempting to protect its survival.

***Attempts to Minimize Anxiety***   Through this denial, the ego minimizes anxiety. Denial of unexplainable experiences retains the illusion that everything is known and under control. This illusion of control has an important developmental function. It allows adults to risk the many uncertainties of life without being stopped by too much anxiety or too much depression. How many situations could we tolerate if we realized how little control we have? Without our illusion, could we tolerate the fact we are traveling together on a spinning planet moving through infinite space?

***Extreme Circumstances*** Under extreme circumstances, the ego cannot retain the illusion of control. Such circumstances include:

- impending violence
- destructive and manipulative relationships
- a betrayal of trust
- severe economic fear
- late stage drug addiction
- physical entrapment
- natural disasters

The illusion of personal control collapses, and the result can be a massive surge of anxiety (a panic attack). In many cases, a second panic attack is never experienced, but the one episode of loss of control can have a haunting effect for years. The ego, therefore, has very good reasons for suppressing any experience outside of its control.

***The Ego and Spiritual Consciousness*** Our ego, with its organizing processes and its need to maintain balance and control, therefore has an inherent problem with our spirituality. Our spiritual consciousness is largely unknown and unfamiliar to us and consequently is not in our ego's control.

Many meditative and spiritual traditions recognize the problem of the ego's control needs. Many of the spiritual writers unfortunately conclude that the ego is an interference to spiritual development and needs to be dissolved. Some of the traditions even suggest the ego is an enemy.

This is an unnatural and harmful view. The ego exists for developmental purposes and is not the enemy of spiritual development. As Assagioli put it, "The ego is a personal reflection of higher organizing processes in nature, and so the idea of getting rid of the ego is silly" (undated notes). Epstein (1995) offered a framework for the coordination of egoic processes and spiritual experiences. The engagement of the ego in spiritual development enhances the process and reduces obstacles along the way.

### *Spontaneous Spiritual Experiences that Challenge Denial*

Spiritual feelings and understandings happen every day to everyone. These experiences are by nature subtle and are therefore easily ignored or suppressed.

Certain experiences, however, are too real to be denied. These experiences

- are often a surprise

- have an energetic or emotional impact

- carry an intuitive value

The religious writer C.S. Lewis (1984) indicates that such experiences are distinctly different than imagination. He describes that he had a very rich imaginative life, and yet his early spiritual experiences were of an entirely different quality.

## *Stan*

Stan was lying in the recovery room after back surgery. In his groggy state, he suddenly experienced a clear, highly complex inner dialogue with several beings who said they were his past lives. He found the inner dialogue fascinating and intimate, and it produced a great sense of physical peace and a new clarity about his life direction. When the nurse came in to check on him, he smiled broadly at her. Stan had had no previous experiences of this kind, had absolutely no interest in past lives, and was not a meditator.

## *Joan*

Joan was walking down a city street when she felt a wave of joy. Everything in the street scene was pervaded with this quiet joy, and she sensed she was seeing into the nature of reality that lies just below the surface of daily life. Thirty seconds later, the experience was gone, and she was feeling fear as she saw an angry argument between two cab drivers. This happened to her years ago, and she can still relive those thirty seconds of joy in intricate detail.

---

Cited in chapter 10, Ferrucci (1982) categorized a list of spontaneous spiritual experiences shared with him by his psychotherapy patients. Some highlights from Ferrucci's list include:

- the apprehension of some truth concerning the nature of the universe
- a sense of unity with all beings
- an extraordinary inner silence
- liberation
- cosmic humor
- a deep feeling of gratefulness
- an exhilarating sense of dance
- resonating with the essence of beings
- loving all persons in one person
- feeling oneself to be the channel for a stronger force to flow through
- ecstasy
- an intimation of profound mystery and wonder
- the delight of beauty
- creative inspiration
- a sense of boundless compassion
- a transcendence of time and space

There are countless examples of such unexplainable experiences. They are often seen as important because they seem to come into consciousness on their own. They seem to have a life of their own. Recovering from surgery and anesthesia, Stan felt dull and uncomfortable and certainly not in a mood to enter into a complex, strange, life-changing inner dialogue.

The occurrence of a profound, spontaneous, nonordinary experience starts a process of wondering about it. A relationship with the experience begins to form. The experience is quietly insistent and outlasts efforts to get rid of it, to deny it. Denial is not possible, and the second stage of acceptance has begun.

## Second Stage of Acceptance: Relationship

When a profound spiritual experience occurs, a shift takes place in the person's mind. The shift is characterized by the following feelings and intuitions:

- something new has happened
- something of fundamental importance has happened
- there are no memories to which to compare this experience
- the experience is its own immediate memory
- the experience means more than can be presently understood
- there is a desire to be true to the experience, to affirm it, to somehow protect it
- there is a reticence about telling anyone who might question and criticize the experience
- there is a fear that the experience is insubstantial and could be easily dismissed

**The Longing**    The conflict between affirming and questioning is a mental one. Emotionally, a very different inner event is taking place: longing. (In chapter 2, we discussed the Transpersonal Intoxication Model and the Transpersonal Existential Model as two explanations for addiction. In both models, the human longing for union with something greater is at the heart of the theories.)

The person now longs to have the experience again and longs to know the source of the experience. He does not know it yet, but this longing has now become part of his emotional life. Longing is the first emotion of spiritual consciousness.

In time, the spiritual experience that created the longing will go through a process of testing. For now, though, the longing itself feels like proof of something important. This longing proves to have great resiliency. It can be ignored for years and yet never leave. As in Joan's vignette, people with past spiritual experiences often live the rest of their lives with this longing even if they never have another experience. They often misunderstand and mislabel this longing, thinking it is another feeling with a similar tinge; e.g., sadness, dissatisfaction, frustration, emptiness.

The longing, however, is distinctly different. Religious traditions interpret this longing as the search for God. The works of the German mystical poet, Rilke, and the Indian mystical poet, Kabir, are filled with descriptions of longing. Psychiatrist Gerald May, in his book *Addiction and Grace* (1988), saw the longing as God's grace.

C.S. Lewis, in his book *Surprised by Joy* (1984), described the longing this way:

> . . . As I stood beside a flowering current bush on a summer day, there suddenly arose in me without warning, and as if from a depth not of years but of centuries, the memory of . . . when my brother had brought his toy garden into the nursery. It is difficult to find words strong enough for the sensation which came over me; Milton's enormous bliss of Eden comes somewhere near it. It was a sensation . . . a desire, but desire for what? . . . And before I knew what I desired, the desire itself was gone, the whole glimpse withdrawn, the world turned commonplace again, or only stirred by a longing for the longing that had just ceased. It had taken only a moment of time; and in a certain sense everything else that had ever happened to me was insignificant in comparison (pp. 15–16).

Lewis then described two other spontaneous spiritual experiences. He indicated that the experiences made longing "the central story" of his life. His discussion of the effects of these experiences is very relevant to spirituality and addiction:

> . . . I will only underline the quality common to the experiences; it is that of an unsatisfied desire which is itself more desirable than any other satisfaction . . . It is a particular kind of unhappiness or grief . . . It is a kind we

want . . . I doubt whether anyone who has tasted it would
ever . . . exchange it for all the powers in the world . . . I
call it joy . . . Joy . . . has indeed one characteristic . . . the
fact that anyone who has experienced it will want it again
(pp. 15–16).

In reading Lewis, we sense the struggle involved in
articulating ineffable spiritual experiences. Yet, at the same
time, they hold power to change forever someone's relationship
with the world. This fact is the very reason AA has spirituality in
its program of recovery. The founders of AA were motivated to
sobriety through such spiritual experiences. (See the discussion in
chapter 11, regarding Bill Wilson's spiritual awakening and his
subsequent correspondence with psychiatrist Carl Jung as one
example of recovery from addiction through spiritual experience.)

***The Dynamics of Longing***    The spiritual experience and the
longing to repeat it shifts the person into a new consciousness
and a new viewpoint of being in the world. Transpersonal theorist Michael Follman (personal communication, January 12, 1996)
indicated there are at least nine interacting dynamics in longing:

- The longing feels like a search for a long lost memory
  or for something you already know.

- The many different paths are there to help you reach
  this lost memory or preknowing.

- This memory feels as if it is not of this lifetime; it is
  greater than your lifetime.

- The ego is not searching, but it can cooperate with
  the search.

- There is the sense that part of you is already connected;
  the search is for more awareness of the connection.

- This awareness is not based in the senses, it is an
  overall feeling.

- Perhaps the longing cannot enter full awareness until
  there is no more concern about controlling what it will do
  to you. On this point, Follman indicated that unmet needs
  from the person's emotional development make her feel

she must control events until her needs are satisfied. This suggests that emotional healing through counseling must precede a further opening to the longing.

- The longing feels like it is for home; not the household home but a deeper "being home."

- The longing for home feels completely true; you just need a way to find it. This gives a sense of destiny to the longing; the person knows she is supposed to be acting on this feeling.

In view of Follman's characteristics of longing, the longing seems a highly purposeful dynamic inside the person. It keeps the person "homesick," keeps the person desiring to reproduce the spiritual experiences. Trying to reproduce spiritual experiences is a way of experimenting with consciousness in order to know more. Is the purpose of longing to attract us into deeper and deeper knowing? If so, it seems to serve a developmental or even evolutionary purpose.

Regardless of speculation, longing has sweetness, pleasure, resilience, and a timeless patience to it; it is certainly an emotion worthy of further understanding.

***Longing and Addiction***  As described in chapter 11, Jung (cited in Sparks, 1987) saw spiritual longing as the very essence of addiction. Jung saw addiction as thirst for something more. In this view, drug use turns out to be a mistaken attempt to satisfy a deep inner feeling of missing something, a deep inner thirst.

We appreciate this view. We see that some of our clients could clearly describe their addictions as a thirst, a spiritual longing. For most people, however, longing to end vulnerability is the actual emotional experience that leads to addiction. We have chosen to emphasize vulnerability in order to align our model of recovery with the actual experiences of our clients' emotional life.

***Moving from the Relationship Stage to the Testing Stage***  At the relationship stage of acceptance, the longing is having its influence on the person's spiritual development. The spiritual experiences, however, can not yet be assimilated into her personality. They must satisfy the following instinctual needs:

- the biologically driven need to know if they threaten survival

- the socially driven need to know if they threaten approval

In short, are the experiences safe and are they functional? Often unconsciously, the person begins to test the experiences against these two important needs.

## *Third Stage of Acceptance: Testing*

At the testing stage, the ego's capacities to observe, analyze, compare, organize, and integrate are brought into the service of accepting or rejecting a spiritual experience. The ego is now in the service of changing consciousness.

This testing of the spiritual experience can be seen in three searches:

- searching for a meaning, such as a religious equivalent, for the experience

- searching for a method that can reproduce the experience

- searching for others who can confirm the external reality of the experience

***Searching for the Meaning of the Experience***    Religious ideas and symbols are useful at this point. They reduce some of the anxiety the ego feels about being alone with the ambiguity of the experience. Organized religions, however, usually offer little personalized information. By nature, organized religions are codified and hierarchical, far removed from the personal experiences and mystical insights of their founders.

As an alternative, the esoteric branches of religions tend to offer the searcher more specific information. The Christian mystics, the Zen aspect of Buddhism, the Sufi aspect of Islam are examples of groups whose literature emphasizes and describes personal spiritual experiences. Bad translations, varied historical and cultural contexts, and unfamiliar terms, however, can make their descriptions difficult to compare to one's own experience. Recently, one of the world's religious leaders, the Dalai Lama, called for the emergence of a new lay spirituality that would assist spiritual and moral development (Dalai Lama, 1995).

## Brian

Several years into recovery, Brian had begun eleventh step work in AA. Eleventh step work refers to seeking "conscious contact with God as we understand Him." Through prayer and meditation, he began to have many experiences of consciousness expansion. The experiences motivated him to read the Bible to look for descriptions of similar experiences. He also began to buy books on eastern philosophy and esoteric western mysticism. He was doing his own comparisons of what each source was saying and always felt a breakthrough of joy when he found commonalities. By finding commonalities in different traditions, he felt he could trust his own experiences more.

Ideally, the person finds an exact description of his own experience in a credible religious text. This provides the experience with a traditional confirmation of its reality.

However, a too literal religious conception of the experience at this time may prevent further development. Religions have emotional, cultural, and political biases and may assert certain experiences over other experiences and may even discredit essential realities of human nature. As one example, the authors previously referred to traditions that suggest getting rid of, dissolving, or even killing the ego. Such suggestions increase suffering. Yet, at the same time, these traditions contain highly detailed information about spiritual experiences. The person must draw upon that profound guide, common sense, for resolving these discrepancies.

The recent development of transpersonal psychology now offers another source of information about such experiences.

Transpersonal psychology integrates spiritual knowledge with psychological knowledge. In time, transpersonal study may influence even traditional religious practice.

In seeking meaning for their experience, some people return to their own original religion with new insights. Others adopt a foreign tradition that seems to have information about these experiences. Still others glean information from traditions and teachers but continue in the ambiguity of not committing the experience to a system. The ego's desire for meaning, however, does not rest in this state of ambiguity. As part of its comparing and organizing functions, the ego begins to create its own word and image memories for the experience. This is an important step in personalizing and accepting the experience.

***Searching for a Method to Reproduce the Experience***   As discussed earlier, the longing makes the person want more spiritual experiences in order to satisfy the longing. The ego wants more spiritual experiences in order to test out their reality and reliability. As a result, the ego actively joins the longing in a search for spiritual methods. In effect, the ego is serving the longing. The ego is now willing to expose itself to methods that may change its very identity. This willingness lowers defenses, which in turn leads to the likelihood of more experiences. The act of meditating and opening to spiritual experience is now being enhanced by the ego's cooperation.

Inherent in searching for methods is a form of acknowledgment. The ego has acknowledged the importance of the experience. Denial is no longer involved.

***Searching for Confirmation from Others***   With more experiences, the person's acceptance of a new sense of reality increases. At the very least, the new reality is that reality is a far more complex and mysterious place than was felt before.

A fear develops, however, that this new reality is only private and is perhaps distorted by ignorance and wishful thinking. Is it really possible that one individual can glimpse aspects of transcendent reality? The person is appropriately fearing grandiosity. This fear serves a useful function. It keeps her in balance, not making too much of any experience. At the same time, spiritual maturity also means she should not make too little of the experience (Durckheim, 1990). Ironically, it is the nongrandiose person who fears grandiosity, while the grandiose person does not fear it at all. The result of grandiosity is exaggerated claims, manipulation, and disappointment. Kornfield (1993, pp. 309–321), in his chapter on "Spiritual Maturity," offers an excellent discussion of the realistic expectations of meditation and spiritual development. His general theme is that after all the experiences, spirituality always returns to the challenge of living with acceptance, wisdom, and compassion in daily life.

To resolve the private doubts, the person begins to search for others who can verify, modify, or redirect the testing of the person's experiences. The false or grandiose form of this search would be to seek out approval and confirmation of one's own conclusions. The true form of the search would be in the egoic spirit of learning more, analyzing, comparing, organizing, integrating and, ultimately, developing.

***Seeking Confirmation in Twelve-Step Programs*** The person in Alcoholics Anonymous or another spiritually based Twelve-Step program has many fellow searchers to talk to about his experiences. However, it should not be assumed that he will receive helpful guidance. People in AA are no clearer about spiritual development than anyone else. They are more interested and more motivated, but this does not necessarily bring clarity to helping someone else. Usually, within AA, it is the members who are the most serene who have the best spiritual guidance. They are not simply talking about spirituality. For them, the spiritual life is not a theory. They are living it: they "walk their talk."

***The Nurse as Source of Guidance*** The nurse can play a significant role for the person in the testing stage. The nurse represents extensive training and experience in human development and health, coupled with a bio-psycho-social-spiritual view of the person, and can listen with discernment and openness to the person's spiritual questioning. (In chapter 10, we identified a nursing assessment tool adapted from Dossey et al. (1995) to bring spiritual questions into more focus.) The nurse also serves as an important testing source because she is not motivated to direct the person to any particular teacher, group, method, or school of thought. Instead, she is motivated by the ethics of her profession to be guided by the needs of the person.

Increasingly, psychospiritually oriented health professionals are offering models of meaning and spiritual development. Their appeal as guides is that they combine spirituality with the clinical knowledge of human personality patterns and dynamics. As one example, psychiatrist M. Scott Peck's book, *The Road Less Traveled* (1978), combines psychiatry with Christian theology and has been a bestseller for many years.

## Fourth Stage of Acceptance: The Open Personality

This stage has been reached through the conscious cooperation of the ego and the longing. The spiritual experiences are now considered familiar. They are accepted as a normal part of the self. Spiritual consciousness is now as factual to the person as biological and social consciousness. Any acts of meditation or other spiritual practices, while invaluable throughout the life span, are now secondary to a generalized openness to spiritual consciousness.

***Energy, Presence, and Knowing***   With this openness, two distinct types of experiences become more frequent. One type involves energy shifts in the body/mind. For example, a single spiritual thought can cause chills and a sense of release throughout the body. The second type involves contact with deeper presence and deeper knowing. Experiences of presence and knowing evoke love in the forms of compassion, gratitude, and joy. Clearly, the mental and emotional health implications for reaching this stage are profound.

***Presence***   The experience of presence is the "being" aspect of a human being (Durckheim, 1990), an experience of consciousness without content (Assagioli, 1965). In the Twelve Steps of Alcoholics Anonymous, the eleventh step refers to presence as "conscious contact with God as we understand Him"

(AA World Services, 1987). Hartnett (1986, p. 46) called presence "an awareness that includes me." The authors have heard many people use the terms "my true home," or "at one," or "whole," or "my deepest self" to try to convey the quality of the experience. Follman (personal communication, January 12, 1996) also used "home" as descriptive of the goal of the longing.

***Deeper Knowing*** The deeper knowing experience is one in which highly organized wisdom is seen in inner images, or felt in the body, or heard in the mind. The wisdom does not feel memory-driven. It does not feel like information the person would have made up. Rather, it has a sense of spontaneous truth, of rightness. The knowing, even if experienced as a metaphor, has a quiet power and an immediate understanding to it. Such knowing is often the source of creative and scientific breakthroughs and spiritual realizations (Ferrucci, 1990). This knowing experience can be understood in many ways. Wilber (1977, 1980, 1995), for example, places wisdom development within a spectrum of consciousness.

In the Vulnerability Model of Recovery, the knowing experience indicates the person has gained access to the higher self. The higher self phenomenon was discussed in chapter 9. The higher self is a neutral term referring to a higher organizing process of the brain/mind which yields wisdom, guidance, and compassion. Access to the higher self is a developmental marker remarkably unknown to mainstream psychology, but well-known to the world's spiritual traditions (Dossey et al., 1995).

# *SUMMARY*

The nurse needs to be aware of obstacles to the spiritual development of the person in recovery. These obstacles are predictable and identifiable through careful assessment. In some cases, the obstacles can be removed simply by recognizing them as false fears. With other obstacles, however, additional emotional healing will be necessary before the person can truly benefit from the innate spiritual part of his nature.

# REFLECTIONS

What are the attitudes toward spirituality you were raised with?

Have these attitudes remained a part of your belief system?

What are the obstacles to your own spiritual development?

## References

AA World Services. (1987). *Alcoholics anonymous.* New York: AA World Services.

Assagioli, R. (undated notes). Assagioli Archives, Institute of Psychosynthesis, Florence, Italy.

Assagioli, R. (1965). *Psychosynthesis.* New York: Penguin Books.

Assagioli, R. (1991). *Transpersonal development.* London: HarperCollins.

Beck, C., Rawlins, R., & Williams, S. (1984). *Mental health-psychiatric nursing.* St. Louis: C.V. Mosby.

Dalai Lama. (1995, Fall). Interview. *Tricycle, 5*(1), 34.

Dossey, B., Keegan, L., Guzzetta, C., & Kolkmeier, L. (1995). *Holistic nursing: A handbook for practice* (2nd ed.). Gaithersburg, MD: Aspen Publishers.

Durckheim, K. (1990). *The way of transformation.* London: Unwin Hyman.

Epstein, M. (1995). *Thoughts without a thinker.* New York: Basic Books.

Ferrucci, P. (1982). *What we may be.* Los Angeles: Tarcher.

Ferrucci, P. (1990). *Inevitable grace.* Los Angeles: Tarcher.

Gifford-May, D., & Thompson, N. (1994). Deep states of meditation. *Journal of Transpersonal Psychology, 26*(2), 117–128.

Hartnett, R. (1986). *The presence at the center.* Center City, MN: Hazelden.

Keegan, L. (1994). *The nurse as healer.* Albany, NY: Delmar Publishers.

Kim, M., McFarland, G., & McLane, A. (1984). *Classification of nursing diagnoses.* St. Louis: C.V. Mosby.

Kornfield, J. (1993). *A path with heart.* New York: Bantam.

Lewis, C. S. (1984). *Surprised by joy.* San Diego: Harcourt Brace.

May, G. (1988). *Addiction and grace.* San Francisco: HarperCollins.

Peck, M. (1978). *The road less traveled.* New York: Simon and
Schuster.

Schaub, R., & Follman, M. (in press). Meditation, adult development
and health: Part three. *Alternative Health Practitioner.*

Smith, J. (1986). *Meditation: A sensible guide to a timeless discipline.*
Champaign, IL: Research Press.

Sparks, T. (1987). Transpersonal treatment of addictions. *ReVision,*
*10*(2), 49–64.

Wilber, K. (1977). *The spectrum of consciousness.* Wheaton, IL: Quest.

Wilber, K. (1980). *The atman project.* Wheaton, IL: Quest.

Wilber, K. (1995). *Sex, ecology, and spirituality.* Boston: Shambhala.

## Suggested Reading

Assagioli, R. (1991). *Transpersonal development.* London: HarperCollins.

# APPENDICES

**Appendix 1:** Nursing Process: Assessment

**Appendix 2:** Nursing Diagnoses Applicable
to Addictions

**Appendix 3:** CAGEAID Questionnaire

**Appendix 4:** The Vulnerability Model of Recovery

**Appendix 5:** The Twelve Steps of
Alcoholics Anonymous

# 1 NURSING PROCESS: ASSESSMENT

The nurse assesses the following parameters:

1. restlessness, impulsiveness, anxiety
2. selfishness, self-centeredness, lack of consideration
3. stubbornness, irritability, anger, rage, ill humor
4. physical cruelty, brawling, child/spouse abuse
5. depression, isolation, self-destructiveness
6. aggressive sexuality, often accompanied by infidelity, which may give way to sexual disinterest or impotence
7. arrogance that may lead to aggression, coldness, or withdrawal
8. low self-esteem, shame, guilt, remorse, loneliness
9. reduced mental and physical function; eventual blackouts
10. susceptibility to other diseases
11. lying, deceit, broken promises
12. denial that there is a problem
13. projection of blame onto people, places, and things

---

Adapted from *Holistic Nursing: A Handbook for Practice* (2nd ed.), by B. Dossey, L. Keegan, C. Guzzetta, and L. Kolkmeier, 1995, Gaithersburg, MD: Aspen Publishers. Copyright 1995 by Aspen Publishers. Adapted with permission.

# 2 | NURSING DIAGNOSES APPLICABLE TO ADDICTIONS

The following nursing diagnoses are based on the Unitary Person framework as explicated by the North American Nursing Diagnosis Association (NANDA).

| | |
|---|---|
| **Exchanging:** | Altered nutrition (more or less than body requirements) |
| **Communicating:** | Impaired verbal communication |
| **Relating:** | Altered social interaction |
| | Altered family processes |
| | Altered sexuality patterns |
| **Valuing:** | Spiritual distress |
| **Choosing:** | Ineffective individual or family coping |
| | Altered judgment |
| **Moving:** | Impaired physical mobility |
| | Decreased physical mobility |
| | Sleep pattern disturbance |
| | Self-care deficit |
| **Perceiving:** | Altered self-concept |
| | Self-esteem disturbance |
| | Chronic low self-esteem |
| | Personal identity disturbance |
| | Altered sensory/perception |
| | Hopelessness |
| | Powerlessness |

| | |
|---|---|
| **Knowing:** | Knowledge deficit |
| | Altered thought processes |
| **Feeling:** | High risk for violence: self-directed or directed at others |
| | Anxiety |
| | Fear |

---

Adapted from *Holistic Nursing: A Handbook for Practice* (2nd ed.), by B. Dossey, L. Keegan, C. Guzzetta, and L. Kolkmeier, 1995, Gaithersburg, MD: Aspen Publishers. Copyright 1995 by Aspen Publishers. Adapted with permission.

# 3 | CAGEAID QUESTIONNAIRE

## *CAGE Questions Adapted to Include Drugs (CAGEAID)*

Have you felt you ought to cut down on your drinking (or drug use)?

_____ Yes        _____ No

Have people annoyed you by criticizing your drinking (or drug use)?

_____ Yes        _____ No

Have you felt bad or guilty about your drinking (or drug use)?

_____ Yes        _____ No

Have you ever had a drink (or used drugs) first thing in the morning to steady your nerves or get rid of a hangover (or to get the day started)?

_____ Yes        _____ No

In a general population, two or more positive answers indicate a need for more in-depth assessment.

From *Addictive Disorders*, by M.F. Fleming and K.L. Barry, 1992, St. Louis: C.V. Mosby. Reprinted with permission.

# 4 THE VULNERABILITY MODEL OF RECOVERY

The Vulnerability Model of Recovery is a theory that seeks to unify all models of addiction. It honors biological, emotional, social, familial, neurochemical, and spiritual explanations of addiction, and identifies the essential theme embedded in all of the explanations. The basic points of the Vulnerability Model are:

1. Addiction is a repetitive, maladaptive, avoidant, substitutive process of getting rid of vulnerability.

2. This addictive process is triggered by an experience of vulnerability that is believed to be intolerable.

3. Vulnerability is anxiety ultimately rooted in the human condition of being conscious, separate, and mortal. As such, this vulnerability is a normal emotion, an elemental aspect of our actual human situation.

4. People who have a greater degree of vulnerability (explanations for which range from genetic to biochemical to characterlogical to familial to cultural to spiritual) have a greater degree of need to get rid of it.

5. Getting rid of vulnerability is accomplished by trying to feel powerful or by trying to feel numb. Trying to feel powerful is an act of willfulness. Trying to feel numb is an act of will-lessness. Drugs are selected to help produce these results. Trying to feel powerful or numb are both choices. Made repeatedly, they

become addictive, producing predictable but brief
episodes of relief from vulnerability.

6. People in recovery from addiction begin to heal
their feelings by recognizing and respecting their
vulnerability.

7. Continued recovery is based on developing new,
nonavoidant responses to vulnerability.

8. This vulnerability, however, cannot be effectively
responded to on a long-term basis by the separate,
ego-level, temporary sense of self, since it is that sense
of self which is at the very root of the vulnerability.

9. Advanced recovery therefore requires the development of an expanded sense of self that is communal
and spiritual in awareness. Such spiritual development
is a normal aspect of adult development, despite the
fact that it is ignored by most western psychology.

10. Communal awareness is provided by Alcoholics
Anonymous and other Twelve-Step programs through
fellowship and service to others in recovery. Spiritual
awareness requires development that has been
studied by the world's wisdom traditions and,
more recently, by transpersonal psychology.

11. Many people in recovery do not experience spiritual
awareness because this aspect of human nature has
been neglected and poorly understood in modern
culture. Assagioli referred to this issue as repression
of the sublime.

12. Transpersonal approaches offer insights and practices
that can: (a) lift repression of the sublime, (b) energize
spiritual awareness and increase inner peace, and
(c) work at the deepest root of the addictive process.

---

Groups and education in the Vulnerability Model can be arranged through contact with
Dr. Richard Schaub, (516) 673-0293.

*Appendix*

# 5 THE TWELVE STEPS OF ALCOHOLICS ANONYMOUS

1. We admitted we were powerless over alcohol—that our lives had become unmanageable.

2. Came to believe that a power greater than ourselves could restore us to sanity.

3. Made a decision to turn our will and our lives over to the care of God as we understood Him.

4. Made a searching and fearless moral inventory of ourselves.

5. Admitted to God, to ourselves, and to another human being the exact nature of our wrongs.

6. Were entirely ready to have God remove all these defects of character.

7. Humbly asked Him to remove our shortcomings.

8. Made a list of all persons we had harmed, and became willing to make amends to them all.

9. Made direct amends to such people whenever possible, except when to do so would injure them or others.

10. Continued to take personal inventory and when we were wrong promptly admitted it.

11. Sought through prayer and meditation to improve our conscious contact with God as we understood Him, praying only for knowledge of His will for us and the power to carry that out.

12. Having had a spiritual awakening as the result of these Steps, we tried to carry this message to others, and to practice these principles in all our affairs.

# *G L O S S A R Y*

**A.A.A.** The three actions that lead to living with willingness: *attention*, noticing what is *actually* happening, choosing a life-*affirming* response.

**Acupuncture** Deriving from Chinese medicine, focuses on correcting imbalances and blocks in the human energy system.

**Acute abstinence syndrome** Occurs when the blood alcohol level drops far below the level the alcoholic's body needs, resulting in tremors, hallucinations, deliriums and/or convulsions.

**Body armoring** The conscious and unconscious control of the body as a major coping style, resulting in rejection of the body as a source of pleasure or contact.

**Centering** The conscious act of quieting and focusing the mind and body.

**Choice** In regard to addiction, the freeing of the person's consciousness from mental obsessions and physical compulsions.

**Collective unconscious** Holds our genetic memory, our myths, our cultural, racial, and ancestral influences, and the feelings and energies that come with these influences.

**Compulsions**   Demanding, repetitive actions.

**Consciousness expansion**   Experiencing the self beyond the limits of ordinary personality awareness; includes mystical, spiritual, meditative, and religious states of awareness.

**Coping skills**   Healthy responses that help you through difficult situations.

**Detoxification**   The physical process of withdrawing from chemical use.

**Drivenness**   The desperate need for constant activity and busyness, done with a sense of time urgency (sometimes referred to as hurry sickness), clearly seen in workaholism.

**Dry drunk**   An alcoholic who is not drinking (is therefore "dry") but has retained all the mental characteristics of active addiction.

**Emotional education**   A step-by-step process of deepening recovery through (1) realizing the need for recovery from trauma, (2) realizing that feelings are not facts, (3) realizing the normalcy of shifting feelings, and (4) recovering access to intuition.

**Emptiness**   An emotional experience marked by absence, longing, varying degrees of numbness, feeling that something essential is missing.

**Entering a path**   Making a deliberate decision to cultivate spiritual attitudes and behaviors.

**Field of consciousness**   Consists of whatever we find ourselves presently aware of and is usually absorbed by the unreflective, conditioned flow of images, sensory stimuli, half-thoughts, and impulses which are in a constant state of change.

**H.A.L.T.**   Refers to *H*ungry, *A*ngry, *L*onely, *T*ired, an acronym used in AA to remind the person in recovery of the typical situations that reactivate the desire to use drugs.

**Higher self**  The inner source of wisdom and guidance for living which becomes more available as the person develops deeper levels of self-awareness.

**Higher unconscious**  Holds the energy and spiritual qualities that connect us to something greater than our own separate biological and social reality with a time orientation to the future.

**Hitting bottom**  The point at which the person in addiction cannot tolerate the addiction anymore.

**Holistic approach**  A bio-psycho-social-spiritual view of the person, consistent with traditional nursing philosophy.

**Human condition**  Refers to the actual facts of human existence.

**Imagery**  The conscious use of the power of the imagination.

**Inner tyrant**  A self-attacking, destructive mental pattern in the addicted person's thinking process.

**Instinct-impaired**  Being cut off from a basic sanity, a basic instinct and intuition about how to care for oneself.

**Intervention**  A planned confrontation of the addicted person by important people in her life, with the intention of getting her into treatment.

**Learned self-hatred**  Self-hatred originating in messages of disapproval from others that becomes internalized. Self-hatred is not an innate human condition, it is a learned feeling.

**Lie technique**  A nonjudgmental way of studying lies for the sake of new learning.

**Lower unconscious**  This represents the sum total of our past biological and psychological conditioning, as well as genetic and parental influences.

**Magical thinking**  A child-like belief in having immediate, wish-fulfilling and simplistic answers to the complex situations of life.

**Meditation**  A conscious choice to focus attention, which leads in turn to a state of dynamic stillness.

**Middle unconscious**  Time orientation is to the present, to what is happening now and includes any information which, though not present at the moment, is easily called into awareness.

**Mood swings**  Rapid shifts in emotional states.

**New consciousness**  An AA concept that refers to a reorienting of life away from addictive thinking and toward an understanding of life's purpose or God's will.

**Obsessions**  Demanding, repetitive thoughts and urges.

**Obstacles to spiritual development**  Emotional attitudes and fears that block the opening of the personality to spiritual consciousness.

**Path of aesthetics and beauty**  Creation of, or meditation on, art and beauty as a way of spiritual development.

**Path of ceremony and ritual**  Uses communal and individual rituals and symbolic actions to deepen spiritual connection.

**Path of devotion**  Characterized by surrender, adoration, and worship, it is the primary path of any religious tradition in which belief and faith are emphasized.

**Path of knowledge and wisdom**  In its essence, this is the mental search for what is true.

**Path of meditation**  Characterized by discipline and an act of will, the person deliberately sets out to expand perceptions and attention.

**Path of the senses and energetic experiences** A way of spiritual development that emphasizes body experience.

**Path of service** Characterized by an emphasis on reducing another person's suffering, transcending separation and increasing the experience of love and interconnectedness in the process.

**Path of social action and justice** The social activist and political path, in which the suffering from injustice is reduced through ethical actions, transcending self-centered fears in the process.

**Performance of feelings** An insincere, false, contrived, and seductive emotional style used by the person to manipulate and control others.

**Personal self** Our center of awareness, analogous to our observing ego.

**Projection** Disowning unacceptable feelings, then attributing those feelings to someone else.

**Psychosynthesis** A school of psychology developed by Roberto Assagioli, M.D., that recognizes and studies the spiritual dimension of human experience.

**Rationalization** Twisting rational thought in order to lie to oneself or others.

**Recovery** The mental, physical, and spiritual actions that lead to living a conscious, sane life.

**Relapse** The breaking of abstinence and the return to drinking and drugging, even if on one occasion.

**Relatedness to God** A feeling of living with a deeper presence in the self and in the world.

**Repression**   A total numbing of awareness to certain information.

**Repression of the sublime**   Denial, neglect, or negation of innate human spirituality.

**Second recovery**   The need to recover from childhood trauma as well as from addiction.

**Self-hypnosis**   The conscious choice of entering a relaxed state and suggesting new thoughts to the mind.

**Shame reaction**   The state of feeling bad about yourself even though you did nothing wrong.

**Spiritual awakening**   A phrase used in AA to refer to a realization that the isolated individual is in fact participating in a universe of divine intention and order.

**Spirituality**   The innate impulse in each person to know about the universe he is born into.

**Stages of acceptance**   The process the personality goes through in accepting or rejecting spiritual experiences.

**Subtle energy**   The most recent western term for universal energies, life energy, and human energy fields, and their application to healing.

**Sober**   A balanced attitude toward living without resorting to chemicals to alter difficult feelings.

**Suppression**   The active attempt to keep information out of awareness.

**Transcendent nature**   The aspect of people that exists beyond their socially conditioned personality, often referred to as spirit, soul, or essence.

**Transpersonal images**   Can be seen cross-culturally as ways of depicting expanded states of consciousness.

**Transpersonal psychology**   A movement within western psychology to study the aspects of consciousness explored within the world's religious and wisdom traditions and their relevance to psychological development.

**Transpersonal self**   Universal consciousness, the actual source of personal consciousness, an experience realized in mystical states throughout human history and referred to as God, Atman, the Tao, the eternal, and so on.

**Victimized thinking**   A mental pattern pervaded by self-reference, self-absorption, and self-pity.

**Willfulness**   A forceful use of bio-psycho-social-spiritual energies.

**Willingness**   A balanced use of bio-psycho-social-spiritual energies.

**Will-lessness**   A complete withdrawal of bio-psycho-social-spiritual energies.

# B I B L I O G R A P H Y

Alcoholics Anonymous. (1984). *Pass it on.* New York: AA World Services.

Alcoholics Anonymous. (1976). *Alcoholics anonymous* ("The Big Book"). New York: AA World Services.

American Psychiatric Association. (1994). *Diagnostic and statistical manual of mental disorders* (4th ed.). Washington, DC: Author.

Assagioli, R. (undated notes). Assagioli Archives, Institute of Psychosynthesis, Florence, Italy.

Assagioli, R. (1965). *Psychosynthesis.* New York: Penguin Books.

Assagioli, R. (1974). *Act of will.* New York: Viking.

Assagioli, R. (1991). *Transpersonal development.* London: HarperCollins.

Beck, A., & Emery, G. (1985). *Anxiety disorders and phobias: A cognitive perspective.* New York: Basic Books.

Beck, C., Rawlins, R., & Williams, S. (1984). *Mental health-psychiatric nursing.* St. Louis: C.V. Mosby.

Becker, E. (1973). *Denial of death.* New York: Free Press.

Bly, R. (1977). *The Kabir book.* Boston: Beacon.

Buxton, M., Smith, D., & Seymour, R. (1987). Spirituality and other points of resistance to the 12-Step recovery process. *Journal of Psychoactive Drugs, 19*(3), 275–286.

Coles, R. (1990). *The spiritual life of children.* Boston: Houghton Mifflin.

Dalai Lama. (1995, Fall). Interview. *Tricycle, 5*(1), 34.

DiCarlo, R. (1996, Winter). Interview with Larry Dossey. *Quest,* 78–79.

Dossey, B., Keegan, L., Guzzetta, C., & Kolkmeier, L. (1995). *Holistic nursing: A handbook for practice* (2nd ed.). Gaithersburg, MD: Aspen Publishers.

Dossey, L. (1989). *Recovering the soul.* New York: Bantam.

Dossey, L. (1993). *Healing words.* New York: HarperCollins.

Durckheim, K. (1990). *The way of transformation.* London: Unwin Hyman.

Durckheim, K. (1992). *Absolute living.* New York: Penguin.

Epstein, M. (1995). *Thoughts without a thinker.* New York: Basic Books.

Ferrucci, P. (1982). *What we may be.* Los Angeles: Tarcher.

Ferrucci, P. (1990). *Inevitable grace.* Los Angeles: Tarcher.

Freud, S. (1964). *The future of an illusion.* Garden City, NY: Doubleday Anchor Books.

Gifford-May, D., & Thompson, N. (1994). Deep states of meditation. *Journal of Transpersonal Psychology. 26*(2), 117–128.

Good people go bad in Iowa, and a drug is blamed. (1996, February 22). *New York Times.*

Gorski, T., & Miller, M. (1982). *Counseling for relapse prevention.* Independence, MO: Independence Press.

Govinda, L. (1990). *Creative meditation and multi-dimensional consciousness.* Wheaton, IL: The Theosophical Publishing House.

Green, A., & Green, E. (1977). *Beyond biofeedback.* Fort Wayne, IN: Knoll Publishing.

Green, E., Parks, P., Guyer, P., Fahrion, S., & Coyne, L. (1991). Anomalous electrostatic phenomena in exceptional subjects. *Subtle Energies, 2*(3), 69–94.

Hardy, J. (1987). *A psychology with a soul.* London: Routledge & Kegan Paul.

Hartnett, R. (1986). *The presence at the center.* Center City, MN: Hazelden.

Hartnett, R. (1994). *The three inner voices: Uncovering the spiritual roots of addiction and recovery.* New York: Serenity Publications.

Hazelden Foundation. (1987). *The twelve steps of alcoholics anonymous.* New York: Harper/Hazelden.

Helms, J. M. (1995). *Acupuncture energetics: A clinical approach for physicians.* Berkeley, CA: Medical Acupuncture Publishers.

Kabat-Zinn, J. (1991). *Full catastrophe living.* New York: Delta.

Keegan, L. (1994). *The nurse as healer.* Albany, NY: Delmar.

Keehn, D. (1989). Writers, alcohol, and creativity. *Addiction and Consciousness Journal,* 4(1), 9–15.

Kim, M., McFarland, G., & McLane, A. (1984). *Classification of nursing diagnoses.* St. Louis: C.V. Mosby.

King, M. L. (1993). A Christmas sermon on peace. In D. Wells (Ed.), *We have a dream* (pp. 288–295). New York: Carroll & Graf.

Kornfield, J. (1993). *A path with heart.* New York: Bantam.

Landrum, P., Beck, C., Rawlins, R., Williams, S., & Culpan, F. (1984). The person as a client. In C. Beck, R. Rawlins, & S. Williams (Eds.), *Mental health psychiatric nursing: A holistic life-cycle approach* (pp. 286–331). St. Louis: C.V. Mosby.

Levey, J. (1987). *The fine arts of relaxation, concentration and meditation.* London: Wisdom Publications.

Lewis, C. S. (1984). *Surprised by joy.* San Diego: Harcourt Brace.

Mason, L. J. (1985). *Guide to stress reduction.* Berkeley, CA: Celestial Arts.

Masterson, J. (1988). *The search for the real self.* New York: Macmillan.

May, G. (1991). *Addiction and grace.* San Francisco: Harper.

McCoy, A. (1991). *The politics of heroin.* Brooklyn, NY: Lawrence Hill Books.

McCrady, B., & Irvine, S. (1989). Self-help groups. In R. Hester & W. Miller (Eds.), *Handbook of alcoholism treatment approaches* (pp. 153–170). New York: Pergamon.

McPeake, J. D., Kennedy, B. P., & Gordon, S. M. (1991). Altered states of consciousness therapy. *Journal of Substance Abuse Treatment, 8,* pp. 75–82.

Milam, J. R., & Ketcham, K. (1988). *Under the influence.* New York: Bantam Books.

Murphy, M. (1993). *The future of the body.* Los Angeles: Tarcher.

Nebelkopf, E. (1981). Drug abuse treatment. *Journal of Holistic Health, 6,* 95–102.

Ornish, D. (1990). *Dr. Dean Ornish's program for reversing heart disease.* New York: Ballantine Books.

Peck, M. (1978). *The road less traveled.* New York: Simon and Schuster.

Penebaker, J. (1990). *Opening up.* New York: Avon Books.

Penfield, W. (1975). *The mystery of the mind.* Princeton, NJ: Princeton University Press.

Quinn, J. (1985). The healing arts in modern health care. In D. Kunz (Ed.), *Spiritual aspects of the healing arts* (pp. 116–124). Wheaton, IL: Theosophical Publishing House.

Salewski, R. (1993). Meeting holistic health needs through a religious organization. *Journal of Holistic Nursing, 11,* 183–196.

Schaub, B. (1995). Imagery in health care: Connecting with life energy. *Alternative Health Practitioner, 1*(2), 45–47.

Schaub, B., Anselmo, J., & Luck, S. (1991). Clinical imagery: Holistic nursing perspectives. In R. Kunzendorf (Ed.), *Mental imagery* (pp. 207–213). New York: Plenum Press.

Schaub, R. (1995a). Alternative health and spiritual practices. *Alternative Health Practitioner, 1*(1), 35–38.

Schaub, R. (1995b). Meditation, adult development and health. *Alternative Health Practitioner, 1*(3), 205–209.

Schaub, R. (1996). Meditation, adult development and health: Part two. *Alternative Health Practitioner*, *2*(1), 61–68.

Schaub, R., & Follman, M. (in press). Meditation, adult development and health: Part three. *Alternative Health Practitioner.*

Schroeder-Sheker, T. (1994). Music for the dying. *Journal of Holistic Nursing*, *12*, 83–99.

Shannon, C., Wahl, P., Reha, M., & Dyehouse, J. (1984). The nursing process. In C. Beck, R. Rawlins, & S. Williams (Eds.), *Mental health psychiatric nursing: A holistic life-cycle approach* (pp. 198–236). St. Louis: C.V. Mosby.

Shapiro, D. (1994). Examining the content and context of meditation. *Journal of Humanistic Psychology*, *34*(4), 101–135.

Smith, J. (1986). *Meditation: A sensible guide to a timeless discipline.* Champaign, IL: Research Press.

Sparks, T. (1987). Transpersonal treatment of addictions. *ReVision*, *10*(2), 49–64.

Sullivan, E. (1995). *Nursing care of clients with substance abuse.* St. Louis: C.V. Mosby.

Welwood, J. (1982). Vulnerability and power in the therapeutic process. *Journal of Transpersonal Psychology*, *14*(2), 125–139.

Whitfield, C. (1985). *Alcoholism, attachments and spirituality.* East Rutherford, NJ: Thomas Perrin, Inc.

Wilber, K. (1977). *The spectrum of consciousness.* Wheaton, IL: Quest.

Wilber, K. (1980). *The atman project.* Wheaton, IL: Quest.

Wilber, K. (1995). *Sex, ecology, and spirituality.* Boston: Shambhala.

Wilber, K., Engler, J., & Brown, D. (1986). *Transformations of consciousness*. Boston: New Science Library.

Wing, D. M., & Hammer-Higgins, P. (1993). Determinants of denial: A study of alcoholics. *Journal of Psychosocial Nursing, 31*(2), 13–17.

Winn, M. (1977). *The plug-in drug*. New York: Penguin.

Yoder, B. (1990). *The recovery resource book*. New York: Simon & Schuster.

Young, S. (1988). *Overcoming compulsive behavior*. Oakland, CA: Thinking Allowed Productions.

# I N D E X

Note: Page references in **bold type** reference non-text material

## A

AA (Alcoholics Anonymous)
  addiction defined by, 68
  beginnings of, 190–91
  challenges to, 49
  character defect addiction model, 24–25
  detoxification units and, 48–49
  spirituality and, 149–51
  twelve step program, seeking confirmation
    in, 261
Acceptance, unthinking, 103
Actions, taking, 122
Actually, 120
  defined, 119
Acute abstinence syndrome, 37–38
Addiction
  addressing, 12–13
  Alcoholics Anonymous character defect
    model of, 24–25
  as avoidance, 63–64
  cultural model of, 24
  cycle of, 3–15
    case study, 3–4
    early stage of, 5–7
    late stage of, 11–12
    middle stage of, 8–10
  defined, 68
  dysfunctional family system model, 22–23
  ego psychology model of, 24
  general disease model of, 21–22
  longing and, 256
  medical model of, 20–21
  not a choice, 68–69
  prevention, value of education in, 47
  progression of, 10, 64

  psychoanalytic psychosexual model of, 23
  reflection on,
    beliefs/attitudes about, 19
    middle stage addiction, 9–10
  self-medication model of, 22
  theories about, 20–26
  trance model, 25
  transpersonal-existential model of, 26
  transpersonal-intoxication model of, 25
  turning toward, 7–8
  vulnerability and, 60–63
Adolescence, middle stage addiction and, 10
Aesthetics, spiritual development and,
    197–201
Affirming
  defined, 119
  response, 120
Alcoholics Anonymous (AA)
  addiction defined by, 68
  beginnings of, 190–91
  challenges to, 49
  character defect addiction model, 24–25
  detoxification units and, 48–49
  spirituality and, 149–51
  twelve step program, seeking confirmation
    in, 261
Anxiety, attempts to minimize, 250
Approval, perceived threats to, 162–64
Assagioli, Roberto
  consciousness model by, 172–74
  implications of, 192–93
Attention
  defined, 119
  turning outside self, 119–20
Avoidance, addiction as, 63–64

**B**
Beauty, spiritual development and, 197–201
Becker, Ernest, **Denial of Death**, 61
Body armoring, described, 90

**C**
Centering
  defined, 92
  for sleep difficulties, 126–27
  for stress reduction and, 125
Ceremony
  formal/personal, 209
  spiritual development and, 207–9
Character defect addiction model, 24–25
Chemicals
  nervous system disturbance and, 7
  physical healing and, 56
  unsafe feelings and, 6–7
Childhood, spiritual obstacles occurring in,
    240–43
Choice
  addiction is not a, 68–69
  liberation of, 68
  recovery of, 67–68
  spectrum of, 76–79
Collective unconscious, 191–92
Community, power of, 53
Compulsion, defined, 68
Concentrative meditation, 227–28
  limitations of, 228
Confidence, lack of, 111
Consciousness
  field of, 183–84
  holistic model of, 173–74
  model of, 171–94
    Assagioli's, 172–74
    personal self, 184–86
    spiritual, ego and, 251
    transpersonal self, 186–91
    unconscious,
      higher and, 180–83
      lower and, 175–79
      middle and, 179–80
Constricted affect, emotional willfulness and,
    87
Control, fear of loss of, 128–29
Coping skills, defined, 7
**Counseling for Relapse Prevention**, 54
Courage, spirituality and, 212
Creative meditation, 231–32
Creativity, mental rigidity and, 86
Cultural addiction model, 24

**D**
Death anxiety, 61–62
Decision making, chronic refusal in, 102–3
Denial, 29–41
  definitions of, 31–32
  experiencing, 30–31
  forms of, 33–34
  power of, 34–39
  reality and, 32–33
  spiritual recovery and, 250–54
**Denial of Death**, 61
Depression, 105
Detoxification
  defined, 47–48
  units,
    Alcoholics Anonymous (AA) and, 48–49
    Narcotics Anonymous (NA) and, 48–49
Devotion, spiritual development and, 219–25
Diet, stress and, 129–30
Dossey, Larry, study of prayer, 224–25
Drivenness, 90–91
Drugs, willful, 90
Dry drunk, described, 86
Dynamic balance, 117
Dysfunctional family system addiction model,
    22–23

**E**
Education
  emotional, 131–37
    case study, 131–33
    facilitating, 133–37
    vulnerable moment, 133
  value of, 47
Ego
  fears, 246–47
  going beyond the, 166–67
  good, 164–66
  limitations on, 165–66
  psychology addiction model, 24
  spiritual consciousness and, 251
Embodied spirituality, 205
Emotional
  education, 131–37
    case study, 131–33
    facilitating, 133–37
    vulnerable moment, 133
  skill-building, 53
  willfulness, 86–88
    spectrum of, **85**
  will-lessness, 104–5
Emptiness, feeling of, 111–12

Energy experiences, spiritual development and, 202–7
Ethical actions, taking, 214
Exercise
  consciousness,
    higher self, 181–82
    images of childhood survey, 175–76
    the party, 179–80
    the rose, 188–89
  imagery from the collective unconscious, 191–92
  lie technique, 66–67
  middle stage addiction, 9–10
  mindfulness, 183–84
  reflection on addiction, 19
  self-identification, 185–86
  spiritual development,
    connecting with life energy, 206–7
    reflection on natural object, 201
  stress management,
    centering for sleep difficulties, 126–27
    centering on stress reduction, 125
    imaging for stress reduction, 125–26
    progressive muscle relaxation, 127–28
  willfulness/will-lessness, 79–80
  willingness, 121

**F**
Facts, versus feelings, 134–35
Fear reactions, threats to approval and, 163–64
Fears, ego, 246–47
Feelings
  emptiness, 111–12
  performance of, emotional willfulness and, 87
  shifting, normalcy of, 136–37
  unsafe,
    addiction and, 5–6
    desire to get rid of, 6
    mental focus on, 6
  versus facts, 134–35
Fight reactions
  survival threats and, 161
  threats to approval and, 163
Flight reactions, survival threats and, 162
Ford, Betty, addiction and, **39**
Formal ceremonies, 209

**G**
General disease model, addiction, 21–22
God
  negative feelings toward, 242
  relatedness to, 112

Good ego, 164–66
Grandiosity, emotional willfulness and, 88
Group support, recovery and, 48–49
Guidance, nurses as source of, 261–62
Guilt, 105

**H**
H.A.L.T. (Hungry, Angry, Lonely, Tired), 69
Healing
  instinct-impaired, 132
  physical, 56
  vulnerability and, 62–64
Health practices, spiritual practices and, 157–58
Healthy self, described, 73
Higher, power, relatedness to, 112
Higher-self, 181–82
  science of, 182–83
  spirituality and, 147–49
Hitting bottom, recovery and, 46–47
Human
  condition, described, 61
  nature, spiritual aspect of, 144–47
Hungry, Angry, Lonely, Tired (H.A.L.T.), 69

**I**
Imagery
  defined, 53
  stress reduction and, 125–26
Immature spirituality, 340–42
Inner-tyrant
  case study, 73–75
  described, 73
Insomnia, addiction and, 53
Instincts, need to trust, 102
Intervention, defined, **36**
Intuition
  need to trust, 102
  recovery of, 135–36
Irritability, addiction and, 53

**J**
Justice, spiritual development and, 209–12

**K**
Knowledge, spiritual development and, 215–19

**L**
Lewis, C.S., **Surprised By Joy**, 255–56
Lie technique, 66
  exercise on, 66–67
Longing
  addiction and, 256

described, 254–56
dynamics of, 256–57
Love, vulnerability and, 62–63
Loving actions, taking, 214
Lower unconscious, 175–79

**M**

Magical thinking, 110
Mary, devotion to, 224
MAST (Michigan Alcoholism Screening Test), 12
Medical model, addiction, 20–21
Medication, stress and, 130–31
Meditation
  cautions with, 233
  concentrative, 227–28
  creative, 231–32
  defined, 53
  receptive, 228–29
  spiritual development and, 225–33
  types of, 227–32
Mental
  rigidity, 84–86
  willfulness, 83–86
    spectrum of, **85**
  will-lessness, 97–104
**Mental Health Psychiatric Nursing: A
  Holistic Life Cycle Approach**, 144
Michigan Alcoholism Screening Test (MAST), 12
  comments on, 13
Middle
  period,
    addiction, 8–10
    recovery, 56–57
  unconscious, 179–80
Mind
  disconnecting from, 101
  retraining the, 227
Mood swings, 78
Motivation, essence of, 211
Muscle relaxation, progressive, 127–28
**The Mystery of the Mind**, 218

**N**

Narcotics Anonymous (NA), detoxification units
  and, 48–49
Nervous system disturbance
  chemicals and, 7
  late stage addiction and, 11
New consciousness, meditation and, 226
Numbing behaviors, 107–8
Nurse-healer, characteristics, 14
Nutritional depletion, 130

**O**

Obsession
  defined, 68
  mental rigidity and, 86
Open personality, 262–63
Oxford Movement, Bill Wilson and, 185–90

**P**

Peace, moving to from vulnerability, 144
Penfield, Wilder, **The Mystery of the Mind**,
  218
Performance of feelings, emotional willfulness
  and, 87
Personal ceremonies, 209
Personality, open, 262–63
Personalizing spirituality, 195–97
Personal self, 184–86
Physical
  healing, 56
  willfulness, 88–91
    physical symptoms of, 89
    spectrum of, **85**
  will-lessness, 106–8
Physically willful acts, 89–90
Prayer, 224–25
Projection, defined, 34
Psychoanalytic psychosexual addiction model,
  23
Psychology, spirituality neglected by, 172–73

**R**

Rage, emotional willfulness and, 87
Rationalization, defined, 33
Reality, denial and, 32–33
Receptive meditation, 228–29
Recovery, 40–41
  abstinence and, 47–49
  case study,
  of choice, 67–68
  cycle of, 43–57
  detoxification and, 47–49
  early stage of, 47–49
  group support, 48–49
  hitting bottom and, 46–47
  initial steps toward, 50–51
  middle period, 56–57
  questioning/planning, 49–51
  relapse, 54–55
  second, 75
  spirituality and, 141–67
    nursing practice and, 141
  step-by-step, 55

transpersonal, self and, 189
vulnerability model of, 59–70
withdrawal, medical managing, 48
Relapse, 54–55
Relationship, service as, 214–15
Religion
    experiences,
        negative with, 242
        no, 242–43
Repression
    defined, 34
    of sublime, 196, 245
Rigidity, mental, 84–86
Ritual, spiritual development and, 207–9

**S**
Second recovery, need for, 75
Self
    care skills, 92–93, 123–37
        emotional education, 131–37
        making contact, 123–24
        stress management, 124–31
    hatred, learned, 164
    healthy, 73
    higher, 181–83
        spirituality and, 147–49
    hypnosis, defined, 53
    medication addiction model, 22
    personal, 184–86
    sense of, attaching to another for, 105
    transpersonal, 186–91
    turning outside, 119–20
Senses, spiritual development and, 202–7
Sense of self, attaching to another for, 105
Service, spiritual development and, 212–15
Shame, 105
    reaction, 92
Short Michigan Alcoholism Screening Test
    (SMAST), **12**, 13
Sleep difficulties, centering for, 126–27
SMAST (Short Michigan Alcoholism Screening
    Test), **12**, 13
    comments on, 13
Sober, defined, 8
Social
    action, spiritual development and, 209–12
    disapproval, 245–46
    fears, spiritual development and, 244–47
Spiritual
    assessment, 158–64
        tools, 159–60
    development,

obstacles to, 112–13
path of aesthetics and beauty, 192–201
path of ceremony and ritual, 207–9
path of devotion, 219–25
path of knowledge and wisdom, 215–19
path of meditation, 225–33
path of senses and energy experiences,
    202–7
path of service, 212–15
path of social action and justice, 209–12
practicality of, 143–44
experiences, 145–47
    implications of, 249
    spontaneous, 252–54
impulse, 196
obstacles to recover of, 235–65
    first assessment tool, 239–48
    importance of studying, 236–37
    originating in childhood, 240–43
    originating in irrational/ignorant thinking,
        247–48
    originating in social fears, 244–47
    originating in trust destroying traumas,
        243–44
    stages of acceptance and, 237–39, 248–63
practices,
    health practices and, 157–58
    nurses and, 151–57
qualities, higher-self, 181–83
searching for,
    confirmation from others, 260–61
    meaning in, 254–56
    a method to reproduce, 260
well-lessness, 108–12
willfulness, 91–95
    self-care skills, 92–93
    shame reaction, 92
    spectrum of, **85**
Spirituality
    Alcoholics Anonymous (AA) and, 149–51
    courage and, 212
    embodied, 205
    good ego and, 164–66
    higher self and, 147–49
    human nature and, 144–47
    immature, 340–42
    individual differences and, 196–97
    negation of, 95
    personalizing, 195–97
    psychology's neglect of, 172–73
    recovery and, 141–67
        acceptance and, 258–62

denial and, 250–54
open personality and, 262–63
relationship and, 254–58
suffering and, 158–64
Sponsorship, 214
Spontaneous spiritual experiences, denial and, 252–54
Stress management, 124–31
diet and, 129–30
exercise,
centering for sleep difficulties, 126–27
centering on stress reduction, 125
imaging for stress reduction, 125–26
progressive muscle relaxation, 127–28
focusing on breath, 124
loss of control, fear of, 128–29
medications and, 130–32
muscle relaxation and, 127–28
nutrition and, 130
Sublime, repression of, 196, 245
Suffering, spirituality and, 158–64
Suppression, defined, 34
**Surprised By Joy**, 255–56
Surrender, concept of, 220
Survival, perceived threats to, 163

**T**
Taking actions, 122
Thinking
irrational/ignorant, 247–48
magical, 110
victimized, 103
Trance addiction model, 25
Transcendent nature, defined, 196
Transpersonal
existential addiction model, 26
intoxication addiction model, 25
self, 186–91
Trust, destroying traumas, spiritual development and, 243–44
Truth, search for, 218–19

**U**
Unconscious
collective, 191–92
lower, 175–79
middle, 179–80
Unsafe feelings
addiction and, 5–6
desire to get rid of, 6
chemicals use and, 6–7
mental focus on, 6

**V**
Victimized thinking, 103
Vulnerability, 59–70
addiction and, 60–63
case study,
Justina, 65
Tony, 59–60
choice and, 64–66
death anxiety and, 61–62
healing potential of, 62–64
love and, 62–63
moving to peace from, 144
recovery and, 60–62

**W**
Well-lessness, spiritual, 108–12
Willful
acts, physically, 89–90
drugs, 90
Willfulness
body armoring, 90
defined, 77
drivenness, 90–91
emotional, 86–88
exercise, 79–80
mental, 83–86
physical, 88–91
symptoms of, 89
spectrum of, **85**
spiritual, 91–95
universality of, 79
Willing, experience of, 117
Willingness, 115–38
as a choice, 116–17
exercise, 121
spectrum, 118
taking actions, 122
three actions of, 119–20
Will-lessness, 77–78, 97–114
case study, Wayne, 99–101
defined, 77
described, 78
emotional, 104–5
exercise, 79–80
mental, 97–104
physical, 106–8
spectrum of, **98**
universality of, 79
Wilson, Bill, Oxford Movement and, 185–90
Wisdom, spiritual development and, 215–19
Withdrawal, medically managing, 48
Worry, meditation and, 226–27